Praise for *The Digital Pivot*

"Transitioning offline marketing to the digital world can be confusing and frustrating. That is, unless you read Eric's insanely practical guide. *The Digital Pivot* makes digital marketing simple, accessible and practical for all."

Brian Dean, *Backlinko*

"The role of digital marketing is more important in a post-pandemic economy than before. The journey to your customer starts with understanding, then living and breathing their path to discovery and influence. Eric Schwartzman is a long-time friend and has been on the front lines since day one of the digital revolution. This book will help you pivot."

**Brian Solis, digital anthropologist and bestselling author of
*Lifescale: How to Live a More Creative, Productive,
and Happy Life***

"Buy two, because you'll never want to loan your copy. This is the driver's manual you need for online marketing success: it's practical, tactical, and up-to-date!"

**Jay Baer, *New York Times* bestselling author, founder of Convince
& Convert, and coauthor of *Talk Triggers***

"Instead of paying for expensive advertising, any business can grow by creating content on the Web for free, building fans, and pointing people directly to somewhere they can buy. Eric teaches proven strategies to be effective in this new world and he shares fascinating stories of success to learn from."

David Meerman Scott, marketing strategist and _Wall Street Journal_ bestselling author of _The New Rules of Marketing and PR_

"Digital content creation is such a large opportunity for companies it's hard to even grasp. The winners are going to win big... really big. There will also be countless losers. But don't worry, this book will help you navigate through the content clutter and come out gleaming on the other side."

Joe Pulizzi, bestselling author of _Content Inc._ and The Tilt founder

"In a churning and fractured media landscape, _The Digital Pivot_ provides an indispensable roadmap to not only navigate change, but to accelerate demand, leads, and growth of your brand."

Simon Mainwaring, CEO and _New York Times_ author of _We First_

"Eric Schwartzman guides aspiring digital marketers through a simple, step-by-step process for optimizing your owned, shared, earned, and paid media. _The Digital Pivot_ is a great read that makes digital marketing accessible to everyone."

Bill Imada, chairman, IW Group

"Eric lives and breathes digital marketing. If you need to know and understand what is important, look no further than his insights. Bookmark everything this man does!"

Jonny Bentwood, global head of data & analytics, Golin

"Once again, Eric Schwartzman has demystified the complexities of digital marketing. A digital mindset is no longer an option; it's a requirement. The pace and easy to comprehend style of *The Digital Pivot* makes it an effortless and enjoyable read."

Cheryl Procter-Rogers, APR, past president, Public Relations Society of America

"Eric's four-step digital pivot framework puts first things first so you can earn more and work less."

Gini Dietrich, founder and author of *Spin Sucks*

"If I need to vet a digital sales and marketing strategy, Eric Schwartzman is the first person I call. If you're looking to pivot your business or career to digital, make this the first book you read."

Marshall Burak, provost and chief academic officer at Lincoln University and dean emeritus, College of Business at San Jose State University

"The pivot as a pirouette described by Eric is so graceful that it alone shifts your perspective. The lucid and clear explanations of first order principles in the first four chapters will alter our approach to digital marketing. Calling it digital marketing seems too small. A profoundly useful book, well written and engaging."

Matt Church, founder of Thought Leaders and The Leadership Landscape, and author of *Rise Up: An Evolution in Leadership*

"Paid, owned, and earned media are the bedrock of B2B marketing, and no one understands them better than Eric

Schwartzman. This is a practical guide to digital marketing in an attention-challenged age."

Paul Gillin, bestselling author of five books on digital marketing and founding editor-in-chief of *TechTarget*

"The savvy insights from Eric's online courses and webinars come to life for digital marketers in this must-read book. At Talkwalker, we know how important it is for businesses to protect, measure, and promote their brand. *The Digital Pivot* shares the how-tos with relevant examples for today's digital landscape.

Todd Grossman, CEO, Americas at Talkwalker, Inc.

"Eric Schwartzman goes beyond the digital transformation buzzwords to break down the secrets and strategies he's learned into a highly practical guide on what it takes to build, market, and grow a successful digital business."

Gregory Galant, CEO, Muck Rack

"Eric has created a masterpiece based upon his years of practical application. He has found a way to artfully demystify the darkness around making the transition from offline marketing to digital marketing. *The Digital Pivot* is your step-by-step blueprint to digital marketing success."

Roderick Jefferson, sales enablement thought leader and author of *Sales Enablement 3.0: The Blueprint to Sales Enablement Excellence*

"If you're looking for one book that gives you an overview of everything you need to do to successfully pivot to digital marketing, this is it. Eric has consistently been at the forefront of online marketing for the last twenty years."

Adam Taylor, president, APM Music

"Eric Schwartzman is a master of the digital landscape. In *The Digital Pivot*, he expertly guides the reader from entry point to digital success, showing what is necessary for the journey. Wise counsel for any person or organization trying to adapt to rapid technological innovation."

Scott Thomsen, public affairs director, Ventura County Fire Department and president, National Association of Government Communicators

"A crash course in online marketing written by a seasoned industry veteran. Eric leaves out all of the bull and lays out a clear blueprint through compelling stories and experiences. Get this book before your competitors do!"

Tim Ash, keynote speaker, marketing advisor, and bestselling author of *Unleash Your Primal Brain*

"Online marketing is an unimaginably vast subject. A nutshell is very, very small. Eric manages to fit the pivot to digital in a nutshell. If you know offline marketing, then this book will be your best friend for the pivot you know you'll need to make sooner or later. Start now. Start here."

Jason Barnard, Brand SERP Guy

"We live in the Age of Pivot. Everything that was once topsy is now turvy. This makes marketing a daunting and dizzying challenge. Thankfully, Eric Schwartzman has written the one and only guidebook for changing with agility and wisdom."

Shel Israel, bestselling author of *Twitterville* and *Naked Conversations* with Robert Scoble

"Eric puts a human face on the digital marketing process. Whether you're looking to refresh your arsenal of techniques to meet today's digital demands or to validate your arguments for that transition, *The Digital Pivot* covers all the bases clearly, concisely, and comprehensively. It belongs on the desk of every marketer in every market.

Kirk Hazlett, APR, fellow of the Public Relations Society of America and adjunct professor of communication at the University of Tampa

THE
DIGITAL
PIVOT

THE

DIGITAL

PIVOT

SECRETS

OF

ONLINE

MARKETING

ERIC SCHWARTZMAN

For guiding me through times of uncertainty, this book is dedicated to my father Leonard and my stepmother Anita.

Contents

Foreword

I f this whole digital marketing thing is new to you, don't feel bad. You're not alone.

In 2012, I gave a talk to a bunch of executives from a $13 billion corporation. Afterward, I asked the organizer if I could email the global CEO to thank her for the hospitality. "Oh, no," was the reply. "She's not on email yet."

This wasn't 1850. This was *2012*.

The point is, the world moves fast; the tools and rules for marketing change even faster. If you've had your head down trying to make your business successful, you can be forgiven for feeling a little left behind.

Not very long ago, what were your options for reaching potential customers? Buying TV, radio, and print ads? Today, though, you have to make sure that people can find your business with their Google searches; ensure that your website immediately gives them what they want to know; send email newsletters that aren't a waste of everybody's time; and cleverly harness tools like blogs, podcasts, online ads, and PR firms.

The payoff isn't just reaching many more people. It's also that you can reach the *kinds* of people who might be interested in whatever you sell—and you can find out exactly who's responding to your ads and how much time they're spending learning about you. Don't try *that* with a TV ad.

But unless digital marketing is your full-time job, how would you learn about all this stuff?

Oh, sure, you could read digital-marketing blogs and watch some YouTube talks. But you'll quickly discover that they're like:

"Unless your CX is best-of-breed, your long-tail keywords won't land you high on the SERP. In fact, your KPI won't be any more successful than your inbound lead generation. Get actionable analytics, develop your marketing funnel, and set up your urchin tracking modules—otherwise, how do you expect to build your psychographics and perfect your attribution model?"

I was a little worried that Eric Schwartzman, author of this book, would write like that; after all, he's spent decades doing, teaching, and influencing the world of digital marketing. Boeing, Johnson & Johnson, and Britney Spears have been his clients. (Presumably, Eric used different approaches for each one.)

Fortunately, he's managed to assume that his readers are human beings—intelligent, good at what they do, but without a background in this whole digital-marketing thing. He writes like this:

- "Your email marketing campaigns live or die based on the subject line."
- "If you're offering a free demo or trial, don't ask for credit card information up front."
- "The longer your pages take to load, the greater the likelihood a visitor will abandon your site."
- "More often than not, content that goes viral is naturally occurring, not masterminded by marketers."

- "Podcasts draw a more educated, affluent, and influential audience than radio."

That's as clear and plain-spoken as it gets. No jargon slips by without a definition; no principle is presented without a case history to back it up.

This is the Beatles, publishing all of their sheet music in one book. This is David Copperfield, revealing his own tricks. This is Warren Buffet, posting his internal rules for investing.

The term "Digital Pivot" refers to making the jump into online marketing—as Eric writes, "a journey from the old to the new way of doing business." These days, you *have* to make that pivot, or you won't survive. "The only real alternative to pivoting," he writes, "is obsolescence."

He's right. Start reading. Streamline your website. Choose your Google keywords. Study the analytics.

And for heaven's sake, get on email.

—David Pogue
Author and CBS Sunday Morning *correspondent*

Introduction

Digital business is the California Gold Rush of the modern ages—and search engine optimization (SEO) is its mantra. (SEO is the art and science of making web content discoverable through Google.) Of the 100,000 prospectors who set out to stake their claim, very few found gold. But a guy named Sam Brennan made the equivalent of $4 million a month selling picks and shovels.

Today, there are more bloggers, podcasters, and SEO gurus out there selling online courses and services then there are small and midsize businesses making money. But there are some that have found a way to generate revenue online. This book is about how to become one of them.

Those new to digital marketing can fall prey to an online influencer promoting a get-rich-quick course or costly but ineffective subscription service. Or they rush out onto social media before they have a way to convert leads or otherwise generate revenue.

The truth is, before you're ready to pivot to digital marketing, you need a big picture understanding of what it takes to build and operate a digital business. A website, social media, and search engine optimization are all just pieces of a much larger puzzle. This book explains how they fit together.

A lot of people don't want to hear this. They assume it's too complicated for them to grasp, and they shut down. They want simple answers, a get-rich-quick scheme. So they squander precious time panning for gold downstream instead of mining at the source. Meanwhile, competition online gets stiffer every day.

It's not that difficult to understand digital business or digital marketing. I wrote this book to make that knowledge accessible to anyone interested. New ways of doing business like driving demand, generating leads, and transacting e-commerce shouldn't be a mystery. I organized this book to introduce you to the steps you need to take, in order of importance.

The first four chapters lay out the foundational knowledge you need to see the forest through the trees. This is what the get-rich-quick courses conveniently ignore and why most digital pivots fail. You can't build a stable business without a strong foundation. The remaining eight chapters build on that foundation, covering each of the digital marketing specialties, from SEO to social media marketing.

In my own professional life, digital business has been a wild ride that's taken me from the Grammy Awards pressroom to the Olympics, and from the US Dept. of State to The Pentagon. To keep things lively, I use my experiences at these organizations as real world examples of what it takes to lead a digital pivot.

This is a practical book with actionable guidance. So let's get you ready to pivot.

CHAPTER 1

Art of the Pivot

Megan Fairchild, a principal dancer with New York City Ballet, can pivot precisely on the point of her toe like a music box fairy. To the layman, she makes it look effortless as she twirls delicately around on a pinpoint, flourishing her arms and hands gracefully.

But in fact, a pivot turn, or pirouette, as ballet masters call them, is a series of steps so fluidly performed as to appear as a single, elegant motion. Fairchild starts in fourth position, making sure that she's balanced and stable. She bends her knees in a plié, pushes off, turns in an arabesque position and finishes elegantly like a butterfly landing on a leaf. Fairchild makes it look easy, but she didn't become a prima ballerina through wishful thinking. She got there through hard work.

Fairchild is a role model to generations of ballet dancers striving for an apprenticeship with the New York City Ballet. As you can imagine, such a sought after opportunity takes focus, dedication, and persistence to achieve. The world is full of starry-eyed young dancers who dream of someday performing on stage. But before they go on pointe, they must learn the fundamentals—and build up the necessary strength to bear their weight on a fully extended vertical foot—or they come tumbling down.

Digital marketing, or migrating an existing business to digital marketing infrastructure, is like a pirouette. The companies that get it right appear to twirl effortlessly, disrupting their market-place, dethroning incumbents, and becoming principals in their industry. Unlike ballet, in business there are more starring roles. And you're about to learn how to land one of them. I'm going to tell you the secrets of the digital pivot. And when you're done with this book, you will understand the steps you need to take to set up, push off, and spin from the old to new way of generating demand, leads, and revenue.

No one would take a ballet teacher seriously who promised students they'd be prima ballerinas at the NYCB in a four-hour work week because it's understood that mastery of this centu-ries-old art form comes through well-defined stages of training. It takes years to achieve. Digital business, on the other hand, is in its infancy so there's a ton of confusion about what it is and how to do it well. Many fall prey to digital self-help gurus who promise overnight success with SEO, YouTube, and Facebook ads. But these approaches all fail for the same reason: they apply the steps out of sequence. The fact is, you need to learn to walk before you can run.

These gurus will tell you all you need is traffic or visitors to your website, but it's a false promise. You don't just need traffic.

You need the *right* traffic. And you need to know what to do with that traffic after it arrives. Traffic is like a pair of toe shoes. You still need the choreography to execute a pivot turn.

The four stages of a digital marketing pivot are like the four steps of a pirouette. In this book, you'll learn why some companies succeed and others fail to make a market and generate revenue for their products and services online. Just as the pivot turn is a series of individual steps, so is the digital pivot.

Like a young dancer who rushes onto stage prematurely eager to spin in her very first pair of toe shoes only to fall, most businesses pull back the curtain on their new website before they're ready to perform. I'm going to explain the elegance of a sequential approach to the pivot in a way that brings the owned, shared, earned, and paid media together into a thing of beauty that is greater than the sum of its parts. Let's break down the footwork.

MEDIA TYPE	DEFINITION
Owned Media	Your website and/or custom mobile app
Shared Media	Your social media accounts
Earned Media	Content about you with a link on someone else's website
Paid Media	Online advertising

Of the four media types, owned media is the most misunderstood and overlooked. But it is also the most important because it sets up the digital pivot. Owned media is digital media you own, which means you control the actual layout of the web page and format of the content. Your website is the core of your digital marketing strategy. Unlike on social media, on your own website, no one is displaying their ads against your content, siphoning your traffic away, or collecting commissions on your sales. Before you push off and spin, your owned media presence must be stable and balanced. Without a strong foundation, you can't find your axis. Getting ready to convert visitors to your website to customers is the first step of the digital pivot.

If you rely primarily on social networks or Amazon to connect with your customers, you'll never be a principal dancer. You're performing on a rented stage. You're twirling before you're ready. And your future is wholly dependent on a third party who can boot you off their platform without notice, like former President Trump when his Twitter and Facebook accounts were shuttered.

Before you head off to Facebook or Twitter to invite the world over to watch your pirouette, you need to study the moves first. Owned media strategies are informed by concrete research that reveals why people come to you, where they come from, and what they want.

To get prepared, you have to anticipate the questions that your buyers will ask when they're considering doing business with you. In person, that's easy. You just answer whatever questions they ask. But you can only answer one question at a time, because you can only talk to so many people in a day. Owned media lets you answer questions at scale. It's more challenging to educate people online because you have to give them the specific answers they want without overwhelming them. And it has to be easy for them to get answers on a self-service basis.

How many times have you considered purchasing something on Amazon but never clicked the "Buy" button? If a product page on Amazon doesn't convert—doesn't provoke you to click—it's usually because of either price or a question that's not answered or can't be found in the web copy. In e-commerce, if you fail to anticipate what buyers want to know, like the color of the case, which cables they will need to plug in the device, or if there is a version for left handers, you lose the sale to whoever does answer those questions.

When considering higher-priced purchases, buyers decide whether or not to contact you based on things like how long it takes to get what you're selling, what kind of volume discounts you offer, or in the case of services, how soon you can get started on their project.

A good website is a collection of webpages that make it easy for a customer to find what they're looking for in as few clicks as possible. A ballet performance has three acts, and a good website provides access to whatever it is you're looking for in three clicks. (One common fallacy in our minds is that people always enter through your home page and proceed from there. The reality is that search engines guide people quite granularly to a specific page on your site.)

On a website, products or services are organized in parent-child page relationships, and the child pages are further broken down by variation. Moving through the hierarchy is often referred to as moving through the sales funnel. But it's nonlinear because the customer journey is a continuum, so there's no way to know in what order they're going to watch your performance.

Let's say you're a public relations agency selling client services. Your homepage or parent page is about public relations services. You have a menu with links to child pages about the different types of PR services you offer, such as reputation management, crisis management, and media relations. And your child pages all link to a "contact us" page at the bottom of your conversion funnel. Like a set of Russian nesting dolls, the outer shell is the parent page. Inside that is the child page. And inside that is the conversion page. The arrangement is designed to convert awareness into purchase consideration.

Unlike creative writing or journalism, web copy does not just have to be informational; it needs to be memorable, persuasive, and compelling as well. If you don't have a website that's easy to use, well thought out, and answers the right questions to drive revenue, what is the point of investing time and energy engaging prospects on LinkedIn or Instagram? Why spend time on social media outreach if you're not prepared to convert that engagement into purchase consideration or transactions on your website?

Engaging and building community on social media is no substitute for a bad website, and there are more lousy websites out there than there are good social media marketers. Social media has its time and place. But until your website is ready for business, you're not ready to pivot because your website is where you convert leads to revenue.

So let's dive into what it takes to put owned, shared, earned, and paid media outreach into a cohesive strategy so you can pivot elegantly from the old to the new way of doing business. The road to revenue starts with owned media because that's where you generate actual transactions. There's still no shopping cart in a Facebook post or tweet. And even if someday there is, expect to pay a commission on that sale.

With the exception of soliciting user ratings or online recommendations, unless your social media marketing or digital PR drives commercial activity, why invest limited resources in awareness-building activities? (Remember, shared is social media, and earned is media about you on someone else's website.) Optimize the path to purchase first. And you can only do that on your own website.

Awareness by itself is useful for major brands with global distribution. But for small or midsize companies, generating awareness without a conversion funnel is like going on pointe without setting up first, to revert to our ballet analogy. The customer journey may end with a transaction. But when you're engaged in a digital pivot, building an effective conversion funnel is where that journey begins.

You can sell more Girl Scout cookies in front of a cannabis dispensary then a gluten-free restaurant. And you can generate more transactions if your website is optimized to help people searching for answers to the kinds of problems you can solve. You acquire leads when you focus on the right customer, in the right place, at the right time. Selectively inviting people to your website starts by understanding the digital journey your potential customers take when they're looking for solutions to problems you can solve.

4-Step Digital Pivot Framework

The fastest way to generate returns is by putting these four steps together, in this order.

Step 1 · The Set-Up: Owned Media

Whoever controls the layout controls the payout. If you don't control the user experience, you can't control the customer experience. The proximity of your content to the transactions you seek to make directly impacts the probability of conversion. In Chapter 11 on lead generation, I'll break this down in detail, but for now, close proximity means on the same web page, rather than one click away. If you can't experiment with the layout of the page, you can't optimize for conversions. And you can't change the layout of the page on Amazon, Yelp, or LinkedIn. That's why in a digital pivot, web pages precede social media posts.

The owned media set-up also involves making it easy for people to convert. The next three chapters are all about getting set up for your pivot. But for now, just be aware that you use your website visitor tracking counts to measure how people consume your content and whether or not they find what they're looking for. For considered purchases, which are products and services you need more time to decide on, a visitor's engagement activity on your website signals when prospects are ready to engage. Reach out too quickly and you'll scare them away.

You can even use web analytics to forecast revenue as long as you know the percentage of visitors that convert to sales. The next chapter is about reading the digital tea leaves so I won't go deeper here. But you can measure owned media much better than shared or earned media, and armed with those insights you're in a better position to improve performance.

There's an entire marketplace of vendors out there with software you can use to score prospects based on how engaged they are with your content, and we'll cover some of my favorites in this book. These web analytics software packages let you tally up everything from how many times a prospect opened your email campaigns to what pages they visited and how long they stayed, and you can use that engagement to separate warm from cold leads.

Unless you have a healthy advertising budget, it's much easier to generate conversions on your own website than it is on someone else's, because on your own website you control the layout of the page. You can match lead conversion magnets with content offerings by topic, problem, or need. If you're selling LED lighting for sports arenas, you might use a set of sports lighting design guides for different types of sports fields as a lead magnet to get visitors to give you their email address. If they download a sports lighting design guide for a baseball field, there's a good chance they're in the market for sports lighting. The idea is to calibrate your content to get found by the right people at the right time.

But obviously, you can't calibrate content without a website because that's where you convert leads and drive revenue. On your own website, you can insert forms to collect lead information or transact e-commerce. You can't do that on someone else's website. At least not without sharing your profits. Owned media is where you build and optimize your conversion funnels. Without that, there's nothing to optimize. Your owned media presence is the foundation of your digital pivot.

Step 2 · Pushing Off: Shared or Social Media

Social media is media you share on someone else's website. You can't build conversion funnels on Facebook, Twitter, and LinkedIn because you don't own them. But you can share content with a vibrant community in hopes of luring them to your website. The media you share could be text, images, audio, and video you create, but you share it with others on a social network, rather than on your own website. You use social media to connect with a community that's actively discussing the problems you solve.

Instead of solicitations, however, the objective here is to start conversations with influential subject matter experts and grow a community of followers. When you have conversations on social networks with online influencers, you do so in front of *their* followers, which widens your reach. The important thing to understand is that on social media, reach is a factor of engagement. Unless people like, comment, and share what you have to say, no one sees it.

So pushing off is about figuring out where your customers are most active online and who they trust so you can find your axis. To find customer-rich environments, you have to listen to the conversation for evidence of purchase-making decisions by conducting an audit with a social media monitoring platform.

Facebook, Twitter, and YouTube offer their own, albeit limited, usage stats. There are premium tools as well for monitoring broader social media usage. Search "social media monitoring" for a complete list of current providers or download my *Media Monitoring Buyer's Guide*,[1] a software agnostic guide to setting up media monitoring programs which includes reviews of the top ten platforms and features a comparison chart with user ratings. By listening for hot pockets of activity that are relevant to your business, you can identify which social networks are important for you to be active on, and who the influencers are in your space who have the greatest potential to amplify your message.

Through constructive, public interactions, you have the chance to establish your profile and build your own community of followers in stride. And the absolute fastest way to build an online following is by winning the respect of the existing influencers in your space.

A vibrant community of followers proves your legitimacy to potential clients, other subject matter experts, conference organizers, and the news media. This evidence, or *social proof*, adds to your credibility and helps advance prospective customers who might be interested in what you're selling.

---

1   https://www.ericschwartzman.com/media-monitoring-buyers-guide/

But keep in mind that traffic to your website from social networks is usually not as good as traffic to your website from Google search. Unless you're selling a low-cost, impulse purchase like a phone case or T-shirt, visitors coming from social networks are more fickle, leave your site more quickly, and have lower commercial intent to finalize a purchase.

Facebook and LinkedIn are designed to generate conversions for their advertisers. The product they sell is your attention, so the longer people stay on their platforms, the more attention they have to sell. Social networks have their own funnels, and they're optimized for their advertisers. The deal on social networks is you get to post your content for free, but they get to make it difficult for people to leave, and they get to display ads to the highest bidder, in close proximity to your posts. Social networks siphon away the traffic you generate to benefit their advertisers.

There's a Silicon Valley saying that goes like this: On the internet, if something is free, you're not the customer, *you're the product*.

Since Facebook sells your attention to advertisers, you're the product. You get to use Facebook for free, and they get to build a dossier of your hopes, dreams, and fears that they can sell to their advertisers so they can develop marketing campaigns that appeal to your psychology. That's not to say pushing off into social media can't be lucrative. The US has embassies in many hostile nations, primarily because of economic interests in their resources. You might consider building embassies on social networks whose policies you disagree with for the same reason. But on your own website, you control the user experience, so owned media is always going to be a much more powerful lead generation channel. That's why it comes first.

Social media is where you demonstrate community endorsement. If online influencers are among those endorsements, all the better.

Step 3 · Spinning: Earned Media

The spin is the most glorious part of the pivot. It's where you puff out your chest, raise up your arms, and earn the admiration of your customers and industry. Remember, earned media is content by or about you that's hosted on an influential third-party website, blog, or podcast. The harder the website is to get published on, the more glorious the admiration. Earned media includes writing and submitting bylined articles, pitching story ideas to online influencers and the news media, speaking opportunities, and entering to win industry awards.

Once your owned media is set up and you've made the push into social media and built a modest following, you're ready to twirl. Earned media takes its direction from an audit, which identifies the news media outlets that are most influential with your potential customers. You can do a basic media audit by searching your key competitors on Google News and seeing what comes up. I also cover earned media monitoring extensively in my *Media Monitoring Buyer's Guide*. The objective of earned media outreach is to get found by new audiences *to and through* relevant online influencers and news media outlets.

When I ran promotions at a global public relations agency, we sent press kits to reporters and followed up by pitching story ideas via phone. That was before I launched iPRSoftware and websites killed the press kit. Now, every company worth its weight has a website, and a website is digital media. So *every company is a media company*. The news media no longer has a lock on distribution. The internet democratized information distribution because it gave anyone with a website a way to distribute digital media worldwide.

But the internet also frustrates segmentation. Unlike in the old days, when only the media you selected got your press kit, everyone gets everything online. You can't give one message to one audience, and another message to another audience without some overlap. On the internet, you're pitching the media, customers, prospects and new hires all at once, often on the same page.

Your website is your media center, online newsroom, store, and where you find employees at the same time. And it's the primary tool third parties use to assess you for possible coverage. So it needs to be relevant for reporters, prospects, customers, and job candidates alike. Because when you pitch, they google you. And if the results they find don't reinforce your message, there's a disconnect between what you say and what they see. And it damages your credibility.

If you're pitching an editor to publish a guest contribution on their website and you can't provide links to sample articles you've written on your own website, why should they believe you're a good writer? If you can't demonstrate your ability to articulate ideas and construct cogent arguments on your own website, why should they believe you can do so on a much larger stage? That's one of the many reasons companies maintain blogs on their websites. They want to show the world that they can advance ideas of interest with a new twist. Rather than regurgitate what everyone else is saying, the idea is to take a thought leadership position on timely, important ideas. The news media and popular blogs exist to publish new ways of thinking. So it's always easier for thought leaders to earn media coverage. The objective is to establish yourself as a *thought leader*, rather than a *thought repeater*.

Earned media is about getting visibility, credibility, and links from high profile websites that lead back to your website. You start by submitting guest posts to relevant blogs in your industry. If they get published, you are rewarded with a link back to your own website. We'll get into the nitty gritty of how Google determines search ranking in Chapter 4, but backlinks from high profile websites lift your search rankings.

By getting links to your website from respected publications and blogs, you also build your credibility. When another site links to yours, it's considered an implied endorsement from a neutral third party. That reinforces your influence with people who don't know you. Because if a credible website is linking to you, it underscores your legitimacy even more than a large following on social media does because journalists are considered to be experts in whatever they cover so if they write about you, you must be important. Similarly, if a high profile media outlet publishes your article, they're essentially endorsing your point of view.

Earned media has the greatest potential to grow your reach. Because we are tribal species, we tend to trust messengers from people in our tribe more than messages from other tribes. Guest posts also underscore your credibility with reporters and journalists so contributing to respected media outlets is good way to get the attention of reporters.

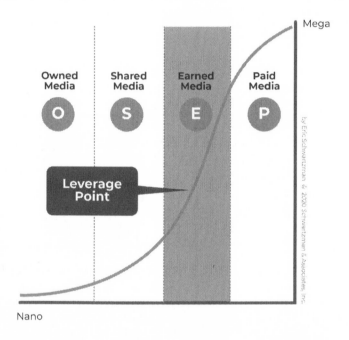

Figure 1.1 This graph charts the course from nano to mega influencer by moving through the owned, shared, earned, and paid media channels in sequence. Of all the media channels, earned media provides the greatest opportunity for growth.

The path from nano to mega influencer online illustrated in fig. 1.1 moves through each of the four media marketing channels in this order. Owned media is the set-up, shared media is pushing off, earned media is the turn on pointe, and paid media is the landing.

Of all four steps, earned media offers the greatest leverage.

Step 4 - The Landing: Paid Media

Now that your owned, shared, and earned media programs are operational, and you're driving revenue organically, you're ready to land into advertising. You've figured out how to attract and convert customers online, and you've optimized the path to purchase.

Depending on your line of business, the last stage of a pivot is the landing. By now, you've proven your ability to generate leads and commerce. You know what percentage of visitors convert into leads, what percentage of leads becomes customers, and how much the average customer spends. Now, as long as you can generate more revenue than it costs to acquire a customer, you're ready to scale through advertising. You forecast revenues by multiplying your conversion rate by your traffic counts. If you know that half of all leads request a proposal, and a quarter of all proposals result in a sale, you can figure out how much traffic you need to hit your numbers.

Online advertising isn't for everyone. If your content is desirable enough, you can drive growth entirely through owned, shared, and earned media. When there's a glut of useful information online about the problems you solve, you can fill that vacuum with worthwhile content, and come out of your pivot without having to buy any advertising. But paid media is the last step of the digital pivot because you don't want to drive traffic until you're prepared to profit from it.

There is, however, one exception. Dancers practice pirouettes without actually turning. They just balance for two counts and rehearse coming down gently as a sort of exercise. If you've secured funding, and you don't have the time to build traffic organically, you can use paid media to help you practice too. Paid media accelerates the testing process by sending you bursts of traffic fast so you can collect statistically relevant feedback on your page layouts, content, and conversion funnels. Without a large enough control group, you can't see what's working, and building organic traffic takes time. Paid media solves that problem.

One common way marketers use paid media in the set-up phase is to test product names, promotional language, and marketing copy. For example, let's say you're on the fence about what words to use to describe a new product or promotion. You can set up Google Ads and run a quick test and see which ones convert best. That way, you save yourself the time of having to attract enough visitors organically to your own website to draw a conclusion. Google Search has tons of traffic so they can give you statistically relevant numbers quickly.

We take advertising messages with a grain of salt, particularly in B2B, because we know advertisers say good things about themselves to sell their products. Their bias is conspicuous but typically overcome through creativity. Anyone can buy traffic through paid media. But when you run out of money, your traffic stops.

In his book *Content Chemistry*, Andy Crestodina likens sources of traffic to boating. Social media and email marketing are the oars. The harder you row, the more traffic you get. Stop rowing and you stop moving. Paid media is the motor. As long as you have money for gas, you can advance. But run out of gas, and you're dead in the water. Search engine optimization is like the wind. It's less predictable and you can't just switch it on. But if you can harness its power, you can relax and sail the seas for free.

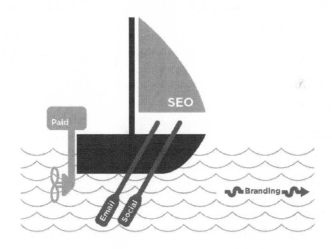

Figure 1.2 Paid media is fast but temporary. SEO is slow but durable. Email is predictable. Social media requires ongoing effort and is the least predictable media channel. Source: *Content Chemistry* by Andy Crestodina.

I've search engine optimized many websites that rank on page one for high commercial intent keywords. And I haven't touched some of them for years. Particularly in niche B2B industries, it's still possible to launch a site and get on page one in a matter of months and stay there indefinitely without much additional work. But even if you're flush with cash and need immediate results and opt to drive traffic with paid media sooner, you still need to get your owned media set up first so there's an easy to find and follow path to purchase.

Depending on the length of your sales cycle, combining advertising with content marketing can be a good way to stay in front of past visitors to your website through a process known as retargeting. Figure 1.3 is a good example.

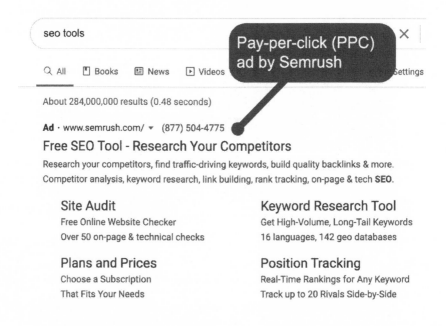

Figure 1.3 If you search the phrase "seo tools" on Google, the top result is an advertisement, which is paid media.

Semrush, a provider of SEO research and analytics tools, uses paid media to drive traffic from Google to a landing page designed to convert visitors into leads. In this case, they're using a pay-per-click ad on Google to get found by people who search the phrase "SEO tools." It's called pay-per-click because Semrush only pays

Google if someone actually clicks on their ad. If they do, Semrush directs them to a landing page designed to convert them into a free trial user of their service. Figure 1.4 shows the conversion page their Google pay-per-click ad links to.

Figure 1.4 Screenshot of the landing page Semrush links to from their Google pay-per-click ad. There is no header or footer navigation to lead the visitors astray. The only option is to sign up for a free trail.

Semrush puts a "cookie," a little snippet of code, on the visitor's device. That way, they can follow them to other websites like Facebook and Amazon to show them more ads. This is called retargeting. They use text search ads to drive awareness and identify prospective customers and retargeting to stay in front of the people who click their Google ads.

Semrush sells access to their SEO research service as a monthly subscription. Since subscriptions are an ongoing commitment, they are treated by digital marketers as considered purchases. On average, it takes Semrush around fifteen impressions to convert a prospect into a trial user, according to Anna Lebedeva, who heads growth marketing at the company. Note that the trial user still hasn't paid them a cent, so they're doing all this just to collect leads.

In addition to paid media, Semrush drives traffic through the other channels as well. In figure 1.5, which was created with a competitive web analytics tool called SimilarWeb, you can see (1) which channels drive the most traffic, (2) how each channel performs against the industry average, and (3) which channels deliver visitors who stay the longest.

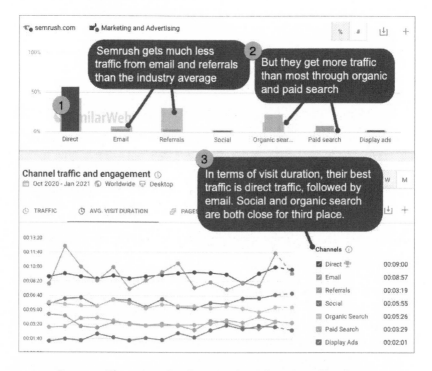

Figure 1.5 This screenshot from SimilarWeb, a digital marketing intelligence platform, benchmarks Semrush.com against broader industry averages. Source: SimilarWeb

We'll go deeper into all this later, but for now, check out the sources of traffic to Semrush.com and how long visitors from each of those channels stay on their site.

Seems like a lot of work, doesn't it? It is. But so is cold calling. And considering the direction that all business is heading, do you really have any choice?

Why do you have to learn to do it yourself? Why not just hire someone to do the footwork for you? It's a fair question that deserves a good answer. So let's stop for a minute and talk about why learning to pivot has become so integral in business today.

Minding Your Own Business

Before the outbreak of coronavirus, there were plenty of small and midsize businesses that got along just fine with a static website. These guys published an online brochure and sat the digital revolution out. They dazzled prospective customers with amazing sales pitches, charisma, and charm. Instead of maintaining a dynamic website and SEO, they took prospects out to lunch, sporting events, and a round of golf.

Some relied on foot traffic at retail operations. Others spoke at conferences and exhibited at trade shows. And still others used aggressive outbound channels like telemarketing, unsolicited email, and cold pitches via direct message on social networks to spray and pray.

But after the global pandemic shut down the travel and hospitality industries which made conventions and trade shows possible, engaging customers in person was no longer an option. In a world where customers had already started screening their emails and calls, the lockdown meant outbound sales all but collapsed overnight.

(Remember, outbound marketing is cold calling, sending unsolicited email, and direct messaging on social networks. Inbound marketing getting is found through Google organic search, conversations on social media, and links from coverage on third-party websites. So inbound marketing is owned, shared, and earned media.)

During the Spanish Flu pandemic in 1918, restaurants removed spittoons from their establishments because aerosolized saliva spread the disease. But even after a vaccine was discovered and the global population was inoculated, those spittoons were never replaced. The Spanish Flu pandemic had an enduring impact on behavior. Expect many of the things we took for granted, like face-to-face sales meetings, conventions, and on-site training to be forever changed by the coronavirus as well.

The physical restrictions imposed by the global pandemic were a wake-up call to everyone. It accelerated the shift from the old to the new way of doing business, especially for small and midsize companies that had never learned to pivot. With trade events gone, many had no choice. Not only had $101 billion in travel spending fueled by trade shows and conferences evaporated overnight, but the business deals that would have been formed at those industry gatherings sputtered too, tightening markets. Digital was the only engagement channel left standing. And those that couldn't adapt went out of business.

But amid all the carnage, technology providers and early adopters that had already pivoted to digital saw staggering growth. It wasn't just big tech players like Amazon that got richer. Up-and-comers like Zoom, Peloton, and Slack saw share prices soar. And demand for talent skilled in the art and science of all facets of digital business grew stronger, despite record unemployment.

Those with a static online brochure for a website were suddenly laid bare. They could no longer generate leads or transactions with their analog wine-and-dine workarounds. Many missed out entirely. Unlike outbound sales which focuses on relationships you already have and introducing yourself out of the blue to people who don't know you, inbound marketing is about getting discovered by people who've never heard of you but who self-identify online with a problem you can solve. If you can't press the flesh, you must reassess.

This is an exponentially larger market than the number of people you can approach, pitch, and close one by one. Rather than distracting people with cold calls and cold emails, you attract people with problem–solution oriented content designed to be found by those in need. In outbound marketing, you search for customers. With inbound marketing, they search for you.

Minding your own business is minding your ability to win purchase consideration online from people who've never heard of you. It's about minding how you're getting found and who's finding you. And it's about automating the lead generation process through organic inbound channels such as owned, shared, and earned media. You still have to have to close the deal, but demand generation happens organically. Customers self-identify. And opportunities come to you so you're no longer investing energy manually qualifying leads one by one. Since you've automated the lead generation piece of the puzzle, you can focus your sales efforts on converting qualified leads.

Increasingly, if you can't be found by prospective customers online, you can't compete. And if you can't compete, you're on your way out. Maybe fast, maybe slow. But ultimately, you're on your way to obsolescence. The US Small Business Administration reports that 40 to 60 percent of small businesses never reopen after a disaster or public health crisis. That's not all. "More than 40 percent of the nation's 30 million small businesses could close permanently ... because of the coronavirus pandemic, according to a poll by the US Chamber of Commerce."[2]

Digital Monkey Business

Unfortunately, there are bad actors out there giving lead generation a bad name. Let me shine a light on these monkeys so you can recognize them and steer clear.

Spammers

They sell email lists of addresses that are scraped and harvested off the internet. Unwitting clients buy such lists, upload them to their email marketing platforms, and carpet bomb the world.

[2]   https://www.nytimes.com/article/small-business-bankruptcy-coronavirus.html

Few recipients open their emails if the spam even gets through. And those that do make it into the inbox only serve to annoy the recipient. If enough people mark your email as spam (which it is because they never signed up to get email from you), your entire web domain could get blacklisted, and all your email could get blocked. We'll dive deeper into email marketing in Chapter 6. But don't take the bait and buy lists from these tricksters.

Link Farmers

They call themselves SEO consultants, but they actually sell inbound links from link farms, which are essentially worthless websites no one visits that publish links back to their clueless customers' websites. Google sees through this scam. And they may even regard those backlinks as *toxic*. Sites with too many toxic backlinks can get punished and manually demoted in organic search rankings by Google. Don't buy inbound links. Google's artificial intelligence is getting better at debunking this cheat every day.

Social Media Gurus

These are high-energy, motivational types who prey on folks who are new to digital marketing with advice that's so generic and basic, it's essentially useless. Some are actually top-rated bloggers and podcasters with legions of followers. Many have made a business selling the equivalent of picks and shovels to prospectors mining for digital gold. You might think you're too clever to fall for one of these swindlers. But clients spend millions of dollars on this kind of monkey business annually.

In a world where we screen out the messages we don't want to hear, the only way to break through is with content that's so good people actually elect to pull it through their filters. The difference between monkeys and mavens are their methods and their media.

The Illusion of Self-Control

While no two customer journeys are exactly alike, most paths to purchase begin on Google. We think we're avoiding pushy sales people by getting educated about how to solve our problem by ourselves online. But the truth is, we're consuming content marketing materials that were created to get found and pulled into a marketing funnel. We may be avoiding the pushy salesperson, but we're still being sold.

When I built the online newsroom for Toyota, my goal was to make it easy for people to learn anything they might want to know about their cars online. That way, when buyers walked into the showroom, they'd be ready to buy.

Prospects who use the content on your website to learn about you are self-qualifying as potential buyers. The more time they spend getting educated, the more qualified they become. By learning about you, potential buyers decide if you can satisfy their needs. If they can find the information they need to decide whether or not they want to do business with you, you don't have to waste time searching blindly for prospects to ask if they have a need.

The more you engage with qualified buyers, the more deals you get done. Why waste your time with tire kickers if you could be talking to qualified buyers instead? More qualified leads in, more sales out. It's simple math.

You still have to sell. But you don't have to prospect. The digital pivot is essentially reallocating the resources you used to invest in outbound marketing into inbound marketing. Once you're learned the basics of inbound marketing, you can compete online and leverage the power of automation to grow your business.

You don't have to be Toyota to use the web to generate leads. With the right guidance and skills, anyone can do it. And increasingly, for those still in business, everyone must do it. Outperforming competitors online requires an owned media presence that can be found by prospects so they can qualify you as a contender.

There are plenty of monkeys out there who promise shortcuts. But there are none. You need to diversify and modernize your skills. The good news is you don't need to be a specialist. But you do need general knowledge of how it all fits together, and that's what you're going to get in this book: a practical framework for executing a digital pivot.

Remember the legend of the hammer-swinging American folk hero John Henry whose physical strength was tested in a race against a steam-powered rock drilling machine? He won the race—only to die, hammer in hand.

He was small-minded. His resistance to innovation is the same kind of short-range thinking that put major brands like Blockbuster, Kodak, and Radio Shack and countless small and midsize companies out of business. Instead of learning the digital pivot, they resisted and stumbled to their ultimate demise.

Digital business is only getting more competitive. Technology doesn't wait. It keeps advancing. Resistance is futile. So let's get you on your feet so you can learn to pivot. Each of the chapters in this book will build your skills and grow your confidence, walking you through the steps of a digital pivot to a brighter, more profitable, and more effortless tomorrow.

CHAPTER 2

Data-Driven Marketing

Blair Silverberg loves numbers. At age six, while his friends were building forts and climbing trees, he was engaged in Beanie Baby arbitrage. By the time he was ten, he'd already read *The Theory of Investment Value*. While his friends were playing with Legos, Silverberg was hanging out in the investor relations section of public company websites. And before he was old enough to vote, Silverberg had turned $5,000 of bar mitzvah money into $100,000 investing in the stock market.

Today, Silverberg is CEO of Capital, which uses an analytics technology platform they built to pick startups to invest in. The platform also helps founders analyze their performance. As long as you have the right analytical tools, Silverberg says accessing institutional capital should be as easy as it looks on the TV show *Shark Tank*.

The numbers don't lie. But a handsome, Ivy League–educated founder can compensate for weak numbers with inspirational "change the world" charisma and charm. Before Silverberg even agrees to hear a pitch, he wants numbers. For him, a good pitch is nothing like what we see on *Shark Tank*. A good pitch explains how one dollar spent makes three in return. He's looking for founders who can articulate the data. And as technology continues to infiltrate all aspects of business, number crunching is no longer the domain of just investors and CEOs.

Marketing and PR used to attract people who didn't want to deal with numbers. When you pivot to digital, that's no longer the case. Today, effective marketing and PR are also based on the numbers. You don't need to be an actuary, but you do need to be comfortable analyzing data because digital businesses *are* data driven. So you need to know how to research, manipulate, and analyze data.

In this chapter, you're going to learn about website usage, search visibility, and customer experience data. Website usage data shows you how people get to your website, what pages they visit, and how long they stay. Search visibility data shows you what words people search for on Google that relate to your business. And customer experience data shows you if they're finding what they need on your website. I'm going to explain each of these more in the chapter and show you what they can teach you. But first, let's talk about why they matter.

Playing with Numbers

The byproduct of digital business is data. Mountains and mountains of data. More data than anyone could possibly analyze manually. Just as the weather maps presented on the evening news are created by visualization software that analyzes reams of atmospheric data from satellites and weather stations, there are similar tools to help you visualize website performance. Analytics software gives you meaningful insights from your data.

Paul DePodesta, the *Moneyball* baseball manager who depended heavily on the analysis of performance data (instead of more traditional methods like scouting and observation) to select players and make game-day decisions, uses these four principles to make decisions based on data. You should too.

First, Ignore Best Practices - Question the old way of doing things. Don't assume historical metrics are meaningful because when it comes to technology, best practices are always evolving. "A long habit of not thinking a thing wrong gives it a superficial appearance of being right," wrote *Common Sense* author Thomas Paine. Applying that to the world of digital business means instead of overvaluing inconsequential numbers like website visitors per month and duration per visit, look at more meaningful metrics like lead conversions and sales figures. It's the percentage of unique visitors that convert that really matters. You can't deposit website visitors at the bank.

Second, Your Ego is Not Your Amigo - To keep his ego in check, DePodesta maintains a decision-making diary that lists all the considered and external factors that come into play when he makes important decisions. That way, he can learn from his failures and improve his human decision-making algorithm moving forward. Keeping score cultivates open-mindedness. Don't fall into the trap of thinking you can outsmart the data. In digital business, analytics are how you keep score.

Third, Leave Your Gut Out of It - Put empirical analysis before gut instinct. Using player statistics, DePodesta traded his big-name, all-star players who were good at everything for average-salary baseball players who could do one or two things really well—despite the fact that everyone else was focused on drafting all-stars.

Fourth, Don't Judge a Book by Its Cover - Confirmation bias, the tendency to interpret new evidence as confirmation of one's existing beliefs, is a data-driven decision maker's worst enemy. Only 3 percent of men are six foot two or taller, but 30 percent of CEOs are six foot two or taller. DePodesta always bases his decisions on performance rather than appearance, gut instinct, or forecasts.

Analytics are foundational to performance optimization. Digital analytics platforms like Google Analytics, Google Search Console, Hotjar, Talkwalker, and SimilarWeb give you data to make smart decisions. "If there's data, let's look at the data. If it's opinion, I like my opinion," says Chris Cabrera, CEO of sales analytics platform Xactly, who expects the average tenure of a VP of sales to drop as business leaders start getting better performance data. Cabrera also says the data on diversification shows women-led sales organizations perform better and hire more diversely. When I was in basic training in the Israeli army, we had an attractive female drill sergeant. I later learned that this was a deliberate tactic the army used to drive peak performance in heterosexual men.

You can't improve what you can't measure. The hard data you get from measuring and evaluating you digital performance is the critique that informs how you set up for your pivot.

Mapping the Customer Journey

Just as you wouldn't try to drive somewhere you've never been before without directions, a digital pivot requires a roadmap too. The reason so many organizations get lost is lack of direction. But instead of roads and highways, in the digital landscape, you map out traffic sources and content funnels. Data on how people use your website, the terms they search on Google to find it, and what they read and click after they arrive are the digital bread crumbs that show you how customers find their way to and through your digital marketing conversion funnel.

In his best-selling book *AI Superpowers*, former Google China president Kai Fu-Lee writes about a Chinese financial services company called Smart Finance that uses artificial intelligence to decide who to lend money to. "[Their] deep learning algorithms don't just work on obvious metrics, like how much money is in your WeChat wallet. Instead, it derives predictive power from data points that would seem irrelevant to a human loan officer. For instance, it considers the speed at which you typed your date of birth, how much battery power is left on your phone, and thousands of other parameters," writes Fu-Lee.

The amount of available data points has grown so exponentially that mapping out the customer journey (the path people take online to becoming a customer) manually has become impossible. When you consider all the digital pathways that might result in a sale, it's just too much information to appreciate on a spreadsheet. The data keeps coming, and coming. And we're only just beginning to integrate the Internet of Things—devices like Google Home, Amazon Alexa, Ring doorbells and Bird scooters—that are geographically tethered to the web with GPS tracking technology. The availability of location data will add a whole new dimension to how we map out customer journeys. Geolocation data from the Internet of Things and check-ins on mobile apps could inform real estate developers, company expansions, and who knows what else. "It would take you months or years to dig through the same data that a good analytics platform could churn through in a matter of seconds," says John Wall, partner at Trust Insights, a sort of digital sherpa firm that helps companies build customer journey maps and make smart decisions based on data.

Validating the accuracy of your customer journey maps is of critical importance because bad data means you'll make bad decisions. So before you set out to pivot, hire a website developer who knows how to get software applications from different companies talking to each other. Developers who are good at this have experience working with APIs, which are the application programming interfaces used to connect different applications together. Software applications without APIs are like roach motels. You data gets in, but you can't get it out. Or you can hire someone like John Wall to make sure you're measuring everything you can about how people engage with you online. At a minimum, make sure you're accurately measuring your website traffic, your search rankings, and your conversion rates.

Digital analytics is a crowded industry with tons of platforms to choose from; Google Analytics is the most popular platform for website usage. Because it's a very full-featured platform, it's easy to get lost in. So let me save you some time and point out which stats are the most important.

Getting Actionable Insights about How People Use Your Website

Google Analytics measures who is using your website and how. But there are other website usage platforms out there as well. So I'll keep this discussion general enough to be useful regardless of the platform. Start with simple demographics like age and gender. Check out how the age ranges of your visitors break down. Then, tailor the sophistication level of your content to the age distribution of your site's visitors. If the majority of your traffic is younger, create more beginner-oriented content. If your average visitor skews older, create more advanced content. If you've got more women than men, make content marketing choices with that in mind. There are always exceptions, but know who you're talking to.

If you're a B2B, you want most of your traffic during business hours. When I was doing marketing and public relations for Britney Spears, I put up an online newsroom where journalists who were writing about her could download publicity stills to run with their coverage. I got a notification from my web host saying my traffic had exceeded my plan, and they threatened to shut down my site. When I checked the stats, I saw most of my visitors were downloading the images in the wee hours of the morning. And since reporters don't file lifestyle stories at 3 a.m., it was obvious these weren't reporters at all—they were fans. There aren't enough reporters in the world to generate the traffic spike we saw. I was catering to the wrong audience.

So start by looking at the demographics, day of week, and time of day of your traffic to get a bead on who your potential online customers are and whether you're attracting the right audience. Next, look at where they come from, which is the source of your traffic.

Traffic Sources

Las Vegas hospitality marketers aren't looking for customers in Las Vegas. They go to feeder markets, like Los Angeles, San Diego, and Phoenix. That's where their customers come from, so that's where they focus their marketing efforts. And they adapt their pitch to appeal to the customers in each of those markets. If you know how someone gets to your website, you can adapt your pitch to work from them. Here are the five sources of online traffic.

Search Engines

Website traffic sources are like your feeder markets, because they're where your visitors originate from. When it comes to traffic from search, it can be paid and unpaid. Paid traffic comes from Google Ads. Unpaid traffic comes from Google's search results. Visitors from Google ads typically have a transactional intent, while visitors from Google search results typically have an informational or navigational intent.

If you search "Bank of America log in" or "Nadal grand slams" you're probably not looking to buy anything, so advertisers are unlikely to run Google ads alongside those search phrases. But if you search "pizza delivery" or "hire digital marketing consultant" or "directors & officers insurance quote" you're looking to transact commerce, so those are the types of high commercial intent phrases that advertisers bid on. It's usually easier to rank in Google's search results for navigational and informational phrases than it is for transactional phrases.

So traffic that comes to your website from Google is either paid traffic from Google ads or organic traffic from Google's search results. And traffic from Google ads tends to be more transactional because the visitors searched a transactional phrase.

Referrals from Other Websites

Visitors who arrive from a link on another website need less convincing because they were referred. And who doesn't love referrals? Referral traffic is more qualified, because visitors consider links to be implied endorsement from the referring website. Getting reporters and bloggers to link to you from their articles and contributing guest posts to other websites are great ways to get referral links. But it's important that those links originate from sites that Google regards as authoritative and relevant to yours from a topical standpoint. More on this in Chapter 4 on SEO and Chapter 10 on digital PR.

Social Networks

If you're selling impulse purchases and you have the right followers, sharing links on social media is one way to drive traffic. Lindafeingold.com sells $14 million worth of highly offensive, novelty merchandise annually by sharing posts with their 165,000 followers on a private Instagram account. No ads. Just irreverent, organic Instagram posts designed to offend politically correct purveyors of cancel culture. With a single link from their Instagram profile to their website, they drive multimillion dollar revenue almost entirely through social media.

For the right customer in the right place at the right time, traffic from social networks can convert big time. The problem is you're reliant on the social network to reach your customers, so Lindafeingold.com walks a fine line because their merchandise is racy. If they violate Instagram's terms of service, they could be deplatformed overnight—they'd have to rebuild from scratch. They offset the risk of being wholly dependent on Instagram for access to their customers by actively building their email list as well. That way, if they get shut down, they can launch a new Instagram account and email their customers to let them know they've moved.

Social media is a good fit for them. But if you're a B2B making a complex sale, traffic from social media is one way to get people to register to download white papers or attend webinars. But those leads are unlikely to convert at a high rate. With the exception of recruiting new hires through LinkedIn, social media is not where software companies like Salesforce or SAP, whose business involves serving the needs of larger entities and not individuals, are going to generate their most qualified leads.

Email Campaigns

When people sign up to receive email from a brand and that brand nurtures them with a combination of useful, valuable insights and offers, traffic from those emails can be an excellent source of leads and revenue. We'll cover this in Chapter 6 on email marketing. For B2Bs, email marketing generates qualified leads, whereas for consumer marketers, emails generate e-commerce sales.

Direct Traffic

Direct traffic is either someone typing your URL into their browser, or traffic from an unknown source. In most cases, assume the latter because most people don't type out entire URLs. They search and click. It's quicker and easier. And browsers are set up to process whatever you put into the address bar as a search, because that's how they make money. If you go straight to website without loading search results, they can't display their ads.

You can minimize the percentage of visitors that fall into the direct traffic category, and you want to, because direct traffic is of an unknown origin. It's a wild card. Traffic from social media and email marketing are difficult to track. If your website usage analytics platform can't figure out the traffic source, it lumps those visitors into the "direct" category. So direct traffic is mystery traffic.

The way to measure email and social traffic accurately is by adding UTM parameters, which sounds scary, but it's not. I'll cover UTM parameters in the section on email. They're just snippets of information you append to a URL to see where the person who clicked it came from, and they're easy to set up. I'll show you how in Chapter 6.

Because of privacy rights, there's no way to eliminate direct traffic entirely. Some of your traffic will always originate from an unknown source. Once you have a healthy website with analytics in place, you can see the dollar value of each of these traffic sources so you know how much revenue came from search versus email and social media. But if you're just preparing to pivot and don't have enough traffic to draw meaningful conclusions, here's how to leverage the data in your analytics platform.

Reading the Tea Leaves

To get a sense of which channels are most likely to start producing revenue first, you need to make certain assumptions based on the products or services you sell. If you're a B2B provider selling a high ticket product that customers take time to research and try before they buy, look at the relationship between new to returning visitors. Enlisting in the armed forces, applying to a university, and opening an individual retirement account are typically things people spend a good deal time thinking about before they actually do it, so marketers at these types of organizations would want to see a lot of return visitors. The same is true of local businesses that service repeat customers, assuming they serve them at least partially online. So for considered purchases, there's a direct relationship between return visits and transactions. And for local businesses, there's a direct relationship between return visits and repeat customers.

If return visits—as a percentage of all visits—are low, you need to increase return visits. Common tactics for driving return visits include email newsletters, surveys, guides, white papers, webinars, and social media shares about the broader topics your potential customers are interested in, such as the benefit they derive from whatever it is you sell. This is in comparison to simply sending content about the features or benefits of your products, which will lift unsubscribe rates. You need to be more clever than that.

One way companies sell subscription services to products like Zoom, Dropbox, and Blue Apron is through product-led marketing. By offering a scaled-down version and free trials, they get you dependent on their product or service. Once you realize the benefits, they convert you into a paid subscriber. Every time you return to their site, they get a chance to try and convert you.

You might decide to spend $89 impulsively on a product you only use once or twice in your life. But you'll take months to decide on whether to buy a service for $9 a month, because it's an ongoing expense for the rest of your life and that adds up. Semrush, the search analytics platform I use, costs $200 per month. I thought long and hard about that subscription before I converted. If there's no sales cycle for whatever it is you sell, return visits aren't as important. But if there is, that's the metric to keep your eye on in the beginning.

Before we get any deeper into other patterns to examine at the onset, a quick word on statistical relevance. Would you rather eat at a sushi bar with a 5-star rating and seven reviews, or one with a 4.3 rating and 1,000 reviews? I'd go with the 4.3-star rating, because seven is just not enough feedback for me to feel confident in the accuracy of the rating.

That said, the more traffic you have, the more confidence you can have in your data because the volume minimizes deviations. Whoever has the most data about their customers has greater insight into their preferences and behavior. So there's no data like more data, which puts the tech giants like Amazon, Facebook, and Google in the catbird seat. Amazon's product recommendation engine—people who buy this also buy that—is only useful because they have mountains of data.

As a baseline, you don't have enough data to make assumptions with certainty until you have at least 1,000 visitors a month. The more traffic you have, the faster you can course correct. This is one reason why companies turn to paid media. You can buy traffic and use it to run experiments and see what happens. And you can apply what you learn without having to wait for enough visitors to show up to generate statistically relevant data.

To understand what customers respond to, you try out two or more pages with the same offer and see which one performs best. You might have two sign-up pages for the same email newsletter, and experiment with different headlines and images to see which one performs best. This is called A/B testing, but there are often C and D versions that get tested as well. The more versions you test, the more traffic you need to get statistically relevant the results.

The irony of website analytics is that you need data to grow traffic, but without traffic, you have no data. And if you have no data, you have no insight. That's the dirty little secret of digital analytics no one talks about. And it's why marketers who can afford it use paid media early on to expedite growth.

If you have fewer than 1,000 visitors per month (and if you're launching a new website or trying to relaunch an existing one, that means you) make sure you're measuring your traffic accurately, and then focus on content marketing. If you don't set up your analytics correctly at the beginning, you can't go back and recapture that data retroactively. That's why you're learning this at the beginning of this book. It's the key to the set-up.

I was working with a client that had a Shopify store and a WordPress site linked together. Shopify is a popular service for building and managing an online store. WordPress is the leading web content management platform. When it became clear that COVID-19 would force many retailers to shut down, Shopify's stock rose 300 percent over the next eight months. The service is popular among small and midsize businesses that compete against the likes of Amazon. Because, let's face it, these days everyone in e-commerce is competing against Amazon.

My client had a Shopify store selling gazebos and a WordPress blog where they published articles that answered frequently asked questions their customers had when they were deciding whether or not to buy one for their backyard. To appreciate why setting up your analytics correctly is so important, imagine that you purchased a custom, top-level domain (TLD) from GoDaddy. A top-level domain is a unique URL that you buy and use as the address of your website. As a hypothetical, let's say theirs was gazebo.com.

Now let's say my client's WordPress website was parked online at the URL www.gazebo.com, but their Shopify store was at www.store.gazebo.com, which is a subdomain of their TLD. And TLDs are unique website addresses. You can't put two different sites at the same TLD. Stay with me here, because this is important. In this case, both sites live on different servers. Because Shopify is a hosted service, your store lives only on their servers.

When someone visits www.gazebo.com, they click effortlessly from the WordPress blog to the Shopify store at www.store.gazebo.com. And when they do, they have no idea they're going from the server hosting www.gazebo.com to Shopify's server, which is hosting www.store.gazebo.com.

To them, they haven't changed channels. They're still watching the same TV show. But if you set up two analytics accounts and are measuring the usage of these sites separately, you have no way to track the customer journey. And this is a very common scenario.

Website visitors are anonymous. Unless subdomain tracking is set up properly at the onset, you'd be stuck having to analyze how people use www.gazebo.com and www.store.gazebo.com on separate website usage analytics dashboards. This defeats the purpose, because you can't track the customer journey with the WordPress blog and the Shopify store measured in different dashboards. You can't see whether or not your content is driving traffic to your store. To solve this problem, we hired a developer to implement subdomain tracking to monitor user activity across both sites in a single session.

Until you get to 20,000 visitors per month, A/B testing is tough. It's going to take weeks, if not months, to collect enough data for a worthwhile analysis between different pages, and even then you may not have enough traffic to get a statistically relevant result.

But once you've got website usage analytics tracking accurately and you've either bought or attracted enough traffic, these are the key questions you should be using your analytics to answer:

- What traffic source stays the longest?
- What traffic source visits the most pages?
- How does social compare to organic search traffic?
- How does organic search compare to referral traffic?
- What traffic sources join my email list, book a call, or make a purchase?

Ultimately, the real question you're looking to answer is this:

- Based on the sources of traffic—organic search, social media, referrals, email marketing and advertising—that convert best, how do I most effectively allocate resources in terms of time and energy invested to attract visitors?

The goal is to use your website usage statistics to keep tabs on which traffic sources deliver the best visitors and allocate resources accordingly. To do that, you need to understand a few more key concepts.

Average Pages per Session and Visit Duration

A session is a website visit. Pages per session are the number of web pages visited in a session. Duration is how long a website visit lasts.

Examining duration and pages per session by traffic source tells you which ones you should be focusing on. If you're spending half your time on social media but visitors who click through to your website from that source only visit one page and stay for ten seconds, you shouldn't be investing too much of your time in social media marketing.

If traffic from social media isn't converting, it means one of these things:

- Visitors aren't seeing what they expect when they click through.
- Visitors can't find what they want after they click through.

- Your ideal customers aren't seeing your posts.
- Your website is outdated or looks untrustworthy.
- Your site is too slow and visitors are leaving before the page loads.
- Your site doesn't look or load right on mobile devices.

These are all common reasons that traffic sources don't perform well.

Of the pages on your site that get the most visits, which ones have the longest session durations? Pages with the longest session duration are your top performing pages. They tell you what type of information on your site resonates best with your visitors. From that, you can see which topics your visitors are most interested in.

Bounce Rate

Google Analytics invented a useful metric called the *bounce rate*. If you visit a web page, don't find what you're looking for, and click the back button in your browser, you're *bouncing* off that page. Your bounce rate is the percentage of single-page sessions on your website. A web page that *bounces* visitors is like a trampoline rather than a funnel.

Instead of enticing you to click deeper into the site to make a purchase, download a white paper, or register for an offer, visitors bounce off the site without penetrating through the first page.

Not all bounced visits are bad. For example, a single-page visit with a four-minute session duration would be tracked as a bounce. But if you're operating an advertising-supported website, what matters is time on the page because it means people see the ads for a longer period of time.

In most cases, though, a high-percentage of single-page visitors is a bad thing. Before we dive deeper into getting customer insights from analytics, let's look at the difference between measuring analog versus digital marketing campaigns.

Cash vs. Credit

The big difference between digital marketing and analog marketing is kind of like the difference between paying with cash versus credit. If you buy something with cash, the only record you have is an analog, paper receipt you might lose. It's tougher to keep records of cash transactions. In fact, people tend to pay for things in cash when they don't want a record.

By contrast, if you buy something with a credit card, it's automatically recorded. The byproduct is a digital record of your transaction. Digital records are easy to collect and store. And when you get enough of them, you can analyze your spending patterns.

My accountant prefers that I buy everything on a credit card so it's easier to file my taxes at the end of the year. Instead of fumbling through a stack of receipts of all different sizes with the purchase description, amount, and dates in different places, the credit card company gives me a single, end of year report listing my transactions by category.

American Express takes all my purchases and gives me a report that shows me the trends behind my spending on business services, merchandise, supplies, travel, transportation, communications, entertainment, and restaurants. They give me a pretty report with charts and graphs.

Like credit card transactions, website usage data is structured. You can use a measurement platform to analyze organic traffic versus social traffic without having to sort records into different categories first. On the other hand, social media comments, chat session records, or notes taken by customer service reps are unstructured because it is difficult to sort conversations, notes, transcripts and other text descriptions into categories. User session replays, which are video recordings of individual visits to your website, are unstructured as well.

I tell you this because there's a new area of technology evolving rapidly called natural language processing that uses artificial intelligence in an attempt to understand and analyze unstructured text. And it's getting better all the time. Imagine what an enterprise could learn by analyzing their call center records. They'd be able to tell the most common problems customers are having with their products. Natural language processing is already used, for example, to look at customer reviews and rate their positivity or negativity as well as to analyze social media posts to determine the emotion expressed by the poster.

Now back to the cash versus credit metaphor. Digital marketing is like paying with a credit card because everything's measured. With that level of visibility you can evaluating your performance. You're no longer guessing; you have hard numbers.

John Wanamaker, a marketing pioneer who lived at the turn of the 20th century, famously said, "Half the money I spend on advertising is wasted; the trouble is, I don't know which half." This inefficiency spurred the mass media business. The logic was that, since only a small percentage of people who see an ad will convert, you need to buy ads in media outlets with the largest audiences.

Back then, all marketing was strictly analog. You had to guess what worked and why. Then came Google Ads, which allowed you to advertise in search results against a specific phrase or word and pay only if someone clicks. Now, instead of having to pay up front to put an ad in front of a million people in hopes of a small percentage converting, you could only show your ad to people actively searching for answers to problems you solve. The approach was much more efficient than buying broad reach to convert a small percentage. Now for the first time, you could go directly to the small percentage.

By inventing a more efficient advertising model, Google became one of the largest and most profitable companies in the world.

I hope by now I've convinced you that you can't improve if you can't measure, and that the byproduct of digital transactions is data. In the next section of this chapter, we'll dive deeper into how to interpret digital analytics. But if you've heard enough for now, this is a good point to take a break.

Let's talk about visits to your website that result in single-page sessions. Here are the most common causes:

Old Site Design - If your website appears out of date either in how it looks or works, it may give the visitor the impression that you're struggling to keep up with technology. That implies it might be risky to do business with you as you may then also struggle with order processing, shipping, returns, customer service, and cybersecurity, all of which rely on technology. If you haven't updated your website in a long time, chances are the rest of your systems are obsolete too. That's why antiquated websites bounce visitors. If all pages on your website have high bounce rates and your site isn't up to current visual standards, it's time for a redesign. Update the layout, language, graphics, colors, calls to action, and conversion path.

Confusing User Interface · If your site is difficult to navigate, people can't figure out where to go. There's no clear path to purchase or conversion. It's amazing how little patience we have for websites other than our own. If we can't find what we're looking for on someone else's site, we bounce in seconds. But when it comes to our own website, we judge it by softer standards. We think that since we care about ourselves, others will too. But we have little patience for someone else's bad website. So why would they have patience for ours? You can see if your visitors are finding their way through your website with customer experience–monitoring analytics that create heat maps. We'll talk about heat maps later in this chapter, but they're visualizations of user mouse movement, scrolling, clicks, and taps you can use to spot usage patterns and make data-informed decisions.

Poor Site Performance · Your site takes too long to load and everyone's hitting the back button because they don't want to wait. Or maybe it loads fine on the desktop, but it's painfully slow on mobile because it lacks some features, and most of your traffic is mobile. It could be that your images are too big. If you have a web page with twenty images that are 1MB each, it's going to load slower than a page with ten images at 350KB each. It's simple math. The more data on the page, the slower it loads. This is the problem with using an off-the-shelf WordPress theme. If it's a bloated template, hire a developer to streamline code so you're not forcing browsers to load a bunch of code that's not being used. This is called minification, by the way.

Wrong Content Focus · Visitors like your content, but they're not interested in whatever you're selling. Your content is misaligned with your commercial intent. You're producing articles, white papers, reports, and guides about what you think your prospective customers want to know, rather than what they actually want to know. They have different questions. This often happens when you're generating content that's too advanced for your audience. It's a common mistake. If you're selling an online service that's useful to salespeople, your content should focus on solving their pain points, rather than the chief financial officer's. Dumb it down and focus on creating content to attract buyers into the top of your digital marketing funnel. In most cases, simple content outperforms advanced, nuanced content every time, especially for complex topics. Also remember that people decide which content to consume based on how much time it takes to read.

If you'd like to use competitive intelligence to benchmark your session time, pages per session, and bounce rates against your industry average, search Google for "website session time by industry" or "website bounce rate by industry" and review the category that applies best to you. There are all kinds of great research studies on the topic being released all the time. There are all kinds of competitive intelligence analytics platforms like SimilarWeb for that, too. If you know what to look for, it's that simple.

"You should be testing stuff every week to see how it flies," says Derek Skaletsy, CEO of Sherlock, a service that tracks software utilization. "Tomorrow's marketer will be way more comfortable with and dependent on data not just to make decisions, but to perfect their messaging and home in on their target customer as well."

Monitoring the Performance of Web Design

"You can have the greatest product in the world, but if the user experience is poor, you'll lose out on sales," says Darren Krape, senior UX designer at Amazon. UX stands for user experience, which is a customer experience that happens online.

Krape was a guest speaker at a two-day seminar on digital diplomacy that I led for the US Department of State. Before he joined Amazon, Krape was at the US Embassy in Cairo where he played a critical role assisting with digital communications during the Arab Spring. Now he works at Amazon where he makes their web pages easier to use. Krape emphasizes that online conversions are directly related to ease of use. (Think one-click ordering.) The easier a web page is to use, the more it converts.

Amazon is the e-commerce gold standard. They've meticulously optimized their UX against terabytes of website usage data. User experience and customer journey are similar concepts. User experience is more obscure because it's the sum total of how people feel about the branding, design, usability, and functionality of your website.

User experience designers test different versions of the same page to see which convert better. They swap out buttons, text and colors, images, headlines, page layouts, and use session monitoring software and heat maps to see which web pages perform best.

Website usage statistics require a lot of visitors for meaningful customer insights, but you don't need a large sample to spot usage failure trends in user interface design. "If you have a user test with five or six people and three of them struggle, it's pretty clear evidence that that particular thing needs to be fixed," says Krape.

There are many reasons why people choose one product over another. But if your ideal customers are consistently going to your competitors, you need to identify and neutralize friction points that are obstructing their path to purchase. The secret to a low-friction customer experience is removing unnecessary bumps in the road of their customer journey. "The less information you collect during the sign-on or purchase process, the better. Any additional bit of information is additional friction to the user," says Krape. Let's take a look at friction points and how to minimize them.

Minimizing Friction Points

If you're trying to attract email newsletter sign-ups, make it as easy as possible. All you really need is an email address.

If you're offering a free demo or trial, don't ask for credit card information up front. Nothing kills product-led marketing quicker than requiring a credit card. You don't need a credit card to try Zoom or Slack.

Use graphics like progress bars to manage the user's patience threshold.

Friction points are the enemy. We'll go deeper into strategies for neutralizing them in the next chapter. However, when it comes to customer experience, the goal is to transform friction points into selling points. Customer experience analytics software creates heat mapping and capture session recordings that you can replay to spot friction points.

Heat mapping software shows you how people consume your web pages. Heat maps collect data on where users look and what they do on your site with an overlay showing clicks, taps, and scrolling behavior set off using color. The more someone clicks, the redder or hotter that area of the page is. The less someone clicks, the bluer or cooler that area of the webpage is. These actions are indicators of your visitors' motivations and desires.

Figure 2.1 Heat map of the homepage at ericschwartzman.com generated by Hotjar from over 1,000 visitors to the page.

Session replay software records videos of what people do when they visit your website. It's as if you are looking over their shoulder as they manipulate their phone or computer keyboard. You can see when they scroll, how they move their mouse, when they click, and when they exit. So instead of making assumptions based on numbers, you get visual proof allowing you to deduce why the behavior occurred. If they're bouncing because the page takes too long to load, you can see that. If they're getting frustrated because your images aren't clickable, you can see that, too.

I use a customer experience analytics platform called Hotjar. Hotjar is invisible to site visitors, but site admins get access to a private dashboard they can log into to see heat maps and session replays. If you're a WordPress user, you can install it yourself by signing up for an account and activating a plugin. At this time of writing, there's a free version of Hotjar that you can try first. They are product-led marketers. The video session recordings are anonymous. You get no personal information about the user that makes them identifiable. And Hotjar blacks out any screen elements or text that could compromise visitor security.

Session replay videos are tagged with:

- Country of origin
- Date of visit
- Device and screen resolution
- Browser type
- Operating system

Modern websites are "responsive," which means they're smart enough to detect whether the visitor is on a desktop or mobile device and respond by presenting that visitor with a page layout designed for their screen resolution. If your site isn't responsive, it desperately needs an update. If you're launching a site, make sure it's responsive. At the very least, you can compare how your site performs on desktop versus mobile—hugely valuable information, as you'll want to mold your UX to type of device.

Hotjar lets you run polls as well. You can ask visitors questions and get answers about what they want from your site. Do they want more information about certain products, features, or volume pricing? By figuring out what they're looking for that you're not giving them, you learn how to increase conversions.

Heat map and behavioral analytics research also improve content performance. Blogger Neil Patel used session replay videos to discover that his visitors read the headline and introduction first, and scrolled right to the bottom of his posts after that. They were scanning to get a sense of how much time it would take to read the article. Most scrolled to the button and bounced.

So Neil added a conclusion to the bottom of each post teasing rather than summarizing the key takeaways. He added conclusions more to tell the reader what they'd get if they read the whole piece than to give them the Cliff Notes for the article.

Sure enough, adding a conclusion lowered his bounce rate. Visitors dwelled longer at the bottom of the page, and scrolled back up to the beginning to read more. Blog post conclusions teasing the benefits of reading the full post are now a standard operating procedure for Neil. Without videos of his users' sessions, he never would have known.

When my clients Jennifer and Ross Halleck at Halleck Vineyard, a Sonoma Coast winery, launched their new website, we noticed from the website usage stats that mobile visitors were bouncing at a very high rate. When we checked the session recordings, we saw the reason: pages were loading too slowly on mobile devices.

If we didn't have web analytics and session recording tools in place, we would have been guessing why mobile visitors were bouncing. Together, the bounce rate metric and videos eliminated the guesswork, and we removed that friction by asking our developer to improve mobile site load speed. So it's important to get website usage and customer experience analytics up and running before you invest too much time tweaking your site. But there's one more area you need to keep your eye on as well.

Website Performance Analytics

How many times have you been out and about somewhere without great cell reception and try to use your phone to find something online? Waiting for pages to load on a mobile phone is painful. On the desktop, it's shameful. Guess what? It can also hurt your page rankings. "We, as a search engine, do not want to frustrate users. So for us, it makes sense to consider fast websites a little more helpful to users than very slow websites," says Martin Splitt, a developer at Google.[1]

Page speed is no substitute for good content. Content is a much more important ranking factor in organic search. But between two pages on the same topic with good content, the faster page will outrank the slower one.

Don't overestimate your visitor's patience threshold. According to research from Google on mobile phone usage, "53 percent of visits are likely to be abandoned if pages take longer than three seconds to load."[2] But keep in mind that entire web pages don't load instantaneously. They load sequentially, which means that some parts of the page load before others. On average, the amount of time between when a user clicks and a page starts to load is 1.28 seconds on the desktop, and 2.59 seconds on mobile.[3]

---

1   https://www.youtube.com/watch?v=XUOD6pcvnso

2   https://www.thinkwithgoogle.com/intl/en-154/marketing-strategies/app-and-mobile/need-mobile-speed-how-mobile-latency-impacts-publisher-revenue/

3   https://www.machmetrics.com/speed-blog/average-page-load-times-for-2020/#:~:text=Often%2C%20the%20hosting%20provider%20that,a%20time%20under%201.3%20seconds.

Loading the part of the page you see on your screen before the part you don't speeds up the user experience. You don't need the whole page to load to start your session, only what you see on your screen. To increase page speed, developers use a technique called lazy loading, which basically defers loading the part of the page you can't see until the user scrolls down.

The longer your pages take to load, the greater the likelihood a visitor will abandon your site. As technology improves and we habituate to faster loading times, patience thresholds only continue to lower. But if you're looking for some benchmarks, here's more research from Google[4] on the impact of mobile page speeds on bounce rates.

As mobile page load time goes from:

- to 3s, the probability of bounce increases 32%
- 1s to 5s, the probability of bounce increases 90%
- 1s to 6s, the probability of bounce increases 106%
- 1s to 10s, the probability of bounce increases 123%

Not everyone has the same type of phone, so load times vary. One way to monitor load times is by looking at your bounce rates in your website usage statistics by device type. High bounce rates are a clue that your site is loading too slowly on that device.

The best way to test and improve from that point is to actually buy one of those devices and test it yourself. But there's also a

4   https://www.thinkwithgoogle.com/marketing-strategies/app-and-mobile/
mobile-page-speed-new-industry-benchmarks/

testing platform you can try called BrowserStack (google it) that lets developers test a simulation of how websites load across all browsers, operating systems and mobile devices. But that's just an estimate. To know for sure, buy and test the device.

Website Performance Scoring Tools

There are plenty of free website performance scoring tools that you can use to evaluate the technical performance of your website. A few are Google PageSpeed Insights, Pingdom, and GTmetrix. Remember, you can find any of the platforms I mention in this book online.

Google PageSpeed Insights is probably the harshest. Like the others, PageSpeed Insights analyzes the content of your website, spits out a score, and makes suggestions for how to improve load time. You get a mobile score and a desktop score, which are different because Google maintains a mobile and desktop index. If you do the same search on a desktop and a mobile device, you'll get different search results. If you think your mobile score isn't important because you're selling enterprise products to business customers, think again. In 2019, Google switched to mobile-first indexing, which means your site performance on mobile impacts your desktop search visibility.

"Mobile-first indexing means Google predominantly uses the mobile version of the content for indexing and ranking. Historically, the index primarily used the desktop version of a page's content when evaluating the relevance of a page to a user's query. Since the majority of users now access Google Search with a mobile device, Googlebot primarily crawls and indexes pages with the smartphone agent going forward," according to the website Google Search Central.[5]

But if this is supposed to be a discussion about the technical performance of websites, why am I switching gears to how Google searches and indexes pages? How is that relevant to page speed?

Well, you're not the only one who wants to provide your website visitors with a positive customer experience. Google does, too. And a good customer experience for them means visitors find what they're looking for easily on the first try.

If a visitor searches for "dry white Zinfandel" and Google recommends a page in their search results that loads so slowly on mobile devices that visitors hit the back button and try again, that's a failed customer experience. And while it may not be the most important ranking factor, Google's algorithm does consider page speed because it impacts user engagement and conversion.

If your developer says the reason your site is loading slowly is because of third-party code that supports Google Analytics and Hotjar, find another developer. Google Analytics and Hotjar are standard tools of the trade. If your site can't track usage and performance, you need a new site. Maybe a new web host? But more likely a new site. What's the point of a website if visitors can't access it easily? The most common reasons websites load poorly are images that are bigger than they need to be or relying on your website software to resize images when pages load.

This is easy to solve by reducing your image file sizes when you upload. Imagine an e-commerce site with a catalog page

5   https://developers.google.com/search/mobile-sites/mobile-first-indexing

showing one hundred different product thumbnails. If all those thumbnails were 1MB files being resized by the browser when the page loads, it's going to be painfully slow. For WordPress users, there are plenty of useful media library management plugins you can use to handle this. I use a plugin called Smush that handles image optimization and lazy loading, but there are others. Search "image optimization tools" for a complete list.

A good image file size is less than 500KB, which is half of 1MB. But a better rule of thumb is to make your images as small as possible without compromising display resolution on a digital screen. Screens are limited by how much information they can display anyway, so why have huge image files?

Another way to increase page speed is with a content delivery network or CDN, which is a network of servers that puts the bigger files on your website on servers closer to your visitors. CDNs have data centers all over the world, and they distribute copies of your images and videos to servers near where your website visitors actually are. You'll need a developer to get it set up correctly, but this is a common way to improve site performance. Jeremy Fremont at Multidots, a WordPress development shop, installed CloudFlare to accelerate my content delivery speed—but you can just search "content delivery networks" for more options.

You don't need to know how to set up analytics, media management tools, or content delivery networks to improve site performance. You just need to know they exist.

Ideal Customer Profiles and Personas

Max Altshuler leads growth marketing at Outreach, an outbound sales platform. He's an inbound marketer selling an outbound sales tool. Outreach sells multi-user software licenses by the user, so his ideal customers are the companies that will buy a large block of user seats. He profiled those companies with large sales staffs to better understand how to attract them to his website.

An ideal customer profile (ICP) is a templated, single-page document that lists the characteristics of your best accounts so you have a way to decide what type of content marketing materials is most likely to resonate with your target audience. An ICP is an outline that lists criteria distinguishing of the companies you'd like to attract and sell to, such as:

- **Industry Focus** · Which industries can I help most?
- **Annual Revenue** · Can they afford me?
- **Headcount** · Do they have enough employees for me to sell to?
- **Budget** · Is the problem I solve big enough that they'll spend?
- **Geography** · Am I set up to do business in their country?
- **Technology** · Is my product compatible with what they're already using?
- **Size of Customer Base** · Do they have enough customers to get value from what I sell?

Include anything else that can be used to distinguish and isolate the organizations you want to sell to. ICPs are supported by historical data and customer interviews, but instinct plays a role as well. "If I had asked people what they wanted, they would have said faster horses," remarked the legendary carmaker Henry Ford.

If you're selling new-to-the-world products like reusable straws, wearable tech, or augmented reality, you're looking forward, not backward. Analytics are historical. If a product never existed, and no one's ever bought it, there's no historical data to consult. If your product is truly unique, you're going to have to guess who your ideal customer is. You're going to have to trust your gut.

ICPs describe accounts, not people. So they are supported by persona buckets, which represent the people you're selling to by role. Executives, managers, and employees have different pain points, so they respond to different messages. Thus, salespeople need to vary their message, depending on whom they're talking to. Marketers create battle cards with all the relevant messages they may need at the account and role levels to guide their content marketing by keeping them on message.

Personas help you tailor your messages to different roles at target accounts. Home Depot sells building materials to general contractors, wire to electricians, and pipe to plumbers. Each of them responds to a different message. Personas outline the characteristics of the people most likely to want, benefit, and buy what you're selling. We buy what we want, not what we need. So unless what you're selling solves a problem they're aware of, tapping desire is impossible. Personas articulate perceived needs, rather than actual needs.

Customer personas are fictional character profiles that distinguish people who are most likely to benefit from your product or service. Personas explain the needs, wants, and goals of your site visitors and include:

- Age range
- Gender
- Level of education
- Networks: college alumni, Facebook or LinkedIn group memberships
- Interests: sports, activities, or travel destinations
- Job title, role, and level of work experience
- Professional background and work history
- Reason they come to your site
- Other destinations they visit online
- Technologies they use
- Desktop or mobile visitor
- Relevance of the problems you solve

If you're selling software solutions to business customers, you'd want to create a persona for chief technology officers. Marketing to the CTO requires an understanding of who they are and what they do. If you identify potential customers with this sort of rubric, you have a better chance of making a professional and personal connection.

Let's say you had a way of automatically generating and attaching descriptions to recorded music files. When anyone played a song on a mobile device or desktop, your technology would automatically display the name of the artist, album, and track. And let's say you're looking for ICPs to license your music information service.

You could sell it to end users, but they're not going to pay much for a service like yours. Also, it's going to take forever to scale revenue if you try to sell licenses onesie–twosie. A better approach would be to sell to companies that deliver music to a large customer base, since more customers means more revenue. In this case, your ideal customer profile is streaming music providers. But since copyright compliance and digital rights management practices vary from country to country, you'd also want to zero in on media companies in countries where your service is compliant.

Jay Z's music and entertainment platform TIDAL is an example of a company that fits this ideal customer profile. They have a technology platform that delivers exclusive access to music, videos, livestreams, tickets, merchandise, and other experiences to fans on desktop and mobile devices. They also produce original content for subscribers.

Next, we need personas for the various stakeholders we're going to approach, so let's start at the top. Recording artists get taken advantage of by record labels. Jay Z created TIDAL so artists have a way to connect directly with fans and better control their destiny. If you were selling to TIDAL and you got in the room with Jay Z, you'd want to use your CEO persona to focus on what matters to him, which is the mission of empowering artists. And since he's the CEO, you'd also want to be ready to talk prices.

But before you get in the room with Jay Z, you'd need to convince his chief technology officer that your music identification service is a good fit. For that, you'd need a CTO persona that identified this role's pain points, because their pain is very different from the CEO's. "A CTO is a sort of ombudsman for all parts of an organization's technologies," says Ty Roberts, who runs strategic partnerships at TIDAL.

Ty is the former CTO of Warner Brothers Music. Before that, he was CTO at Gracenote, a music information service like the one in this example. I did their digital marketing and public relations for nearly a decade. Your CTO persona needs to be focused on why they decide to adopt new technologies and products and what it takes to get them to buy.

A CTO is also different from a chief information officer. CTOs are focused on data and technology in support of product development whereas CIOs focus more on security and internal systems management. If the nitty gritty details of maintaining security were part of your product, you'd need a CIO persona, because you're not selling to them. So personas are really about understanding the purchasing committee stakeholders, and tailoring your message to their individual pain points.

In order to sell new technology to a CTO, the CTO has to be able to sell it to the CEO. So the most successful CTOs are those who are able to win and maintain the trust of the CEO. CTOs do that by nailing these key performance indicators:

- **Uptime** - Is the system available?

- **Security** - Is the system secure from breaches?
- **Performance** - How efficiently does the system perform?
- **Milestones** - Does system development happen as scheduled?
- **Budget** - Does the CTO stay on budget?

This is how the CTO is measured, so your CTO persona should include messages that articulate how your product helps them achieve these goals.

In order to deliver the goods to the CEO, CTOs manage distributed development teams composed of internal employees and external developers. And while they may supplement their own development operations by licensing third-party software like yours, there are some things they cannot outsource. CTOs hire developers who reinforce their company's core competency. If it makes sense financially, CTOs minimize risk by outsourcing standard technologies so they don't have to build them from scratch.

Understanding the relationship between what they build in house, what they outsource, and what they license prepares you to empathize with the CTOs pain points. The goal in sales and marketing is to show the prospect that you understand their business and can provide what they need. Personas help you do that by breaking down what motivates your stakeholders.

Personas also help you communicate in your target customer's language. If you try and get a CTO to license software that does what they're developing internally, you're not going to get the sale. If you talk about internet security or data compatibility to a CEO who's focused on revenue and margins, your message will not resonate. And if you talk about speed and reliability to a CFO who's focused on operating costs and making payroll, you'll also miss the mark. Different roles speak different languages. Personas map all that out so you can use digital systems to scale your sales and marketing operations.

If you're selling a music identification service, your ICP would be streaming music providers in the countries you're set up to operate in. And your personas would be for the CTO, the CEO, and possibly to CIO depending on security vulnerabilities. At TIDAL, you'd want to start with Ty.

"To connect with prospective customers, you need two things. First, you need data. But second, you need to speak their language," says Jonny Bentwood, head of data and analytics at Golin, a global marketing agency serving the biggest brands in the world. You have to analyze and communicate the data in a way that resonates with your stakeholder. Jonny specializes in mapping customer journeys for enterprise clients. He earns his seat in the boardroom by focusing on the customer journey and each individual's role in it because the path to purchase drives revenue. In the boardroom, you focus on the bottom line.

Digital customer insights are about collecting enough data and research to get ready to pivot. ICPs and personas are the framework that allow you to scale online by getting you ready to provide leads with different pain points the information they need at various stages of the buying cycle. By mapping out your ideal customer profiles and personas, sales and marketing know who wants to know what when. On the B2B sales side, you can use a digital asset management tool like Highspot to share presentations with your salespeople internally and see which ones gets used most and result in new business. This also gives you the insight to continuously improve your content creation efforts, because now you know on the sales side what messages get deals done.

Internal data about how your salespeople use your marketing collateral is just as valuable as how visitors use your website. "Engagement data tells you what salespeople are consuming, what they're reading, and what they're delivering to clients and prospects," says Mary Shea, principal analyst at Forrester Research. If you know which content works best at helping your salespeople close deals, that data tells you what content your marketing people should be creating.

And that data is also a good way to improve the performance of your sales staff. "As you get that data, you align it to your pipeline and your forecasts and you start to have more intelligence around what good looks like and how to get your B and C players to do the same things your A players are doing," says Shea.

This is primarily a book about digital marketing, but doing business digitally also requires cross-functional collaboration. And what separates the winners from the losers is back end technology that crisscrosses through every part of their organization. To make you a successful digital marketer and earn you a seat at the boardroom table, let's look at what it takes to build a digital sales pipeline and forecast revenue against the analytics.

CHAPTER 3

Stacks, Automation, and Funnels

It used to be you could just turn on the TV and it worked.

Want to watch TV?

One button. Done. Watch TV.

You had a dozen channels to choose from. Anyone could turn on the television and watch a show.

But now, it's much more complicated.

You've got three remote controls. You have to set the right input. There's cable, Wi-Fi, Netflix, Amazon Prime, Apple TV+, HBO Max, Hulu. You have to search them all individually to find your show.

You have to enter an exact phrase-match. Is it "The Oscars," "The Academy Awards," or just "Academy Awards"? Get every letter just right or you'll get no results. No autocorrect. No autosuggest. No nothing.

And there's no keyboard. You have to select the letters and tap out the show name with a remote control that needs a direct line of sight to the cable box. It's like sending out an SOS with Morse code. You've got 5,000 channels but can't find anything to watch.

I get panicked phone calls from my mother-in-law.

Help. I can't watch my show.

Can you blame her? You need an engineering degree just to watch *Key & Peele*!

Why can't it just be simple? We all want a simple customer experience whether it is watching a show or choosing a content management platform, regardless of the technology behind the scenes. That's what we want from software. We want it to be easy. If I need a slide rule and spud wrench, that's not easy.

Pivoting to digital is pivoting to software, and despite what some vendors may tell you, one size never fits all. So while you don't need an engineering degree, you do need to understand some basic principles. Even if you're just in marketing or sales, having an understanding of how systems fit together better equips you for a leadership role.

Without a basic understanding of the software you use behind the scenes to operate a digital business, it doesn't matter how creative or how good your ideas are. Without the right systems in place, you've got no digital infrastructure to pivot to.

The good news is you can buy everything you need off the shelf. No innovation is required. The tools have been developed already. You just have to configure a set of compatible technologies and get them talking to each other.

Technology is ever-changing. Every year, Apple releases a new iPhone. Sometimes they even change the plugs.

They're not changing the plugs just to make you mad or to get you to buy new cables. Well, that may be part of it. But the bigger reason is, the new plugs move data quicker.

Because technology is always advancing, you have to keep up with it or you're out of date. Just like your home theater rig needs a TV cable box and an over-the-top media box like Apple TV or Roku, you need different types of software to run a business. And each one is always releasing a new version, with new features and upgrades.

I hate it when they rearrange the shelves at the grocery store. All the hard to find stuff that defies categorization, like Q-Tips, butcher's twine, and the Manischewitz get tucked away in new places. The people who work there don't even know where some items are.

Software vendors are constantly rearranging their products too. Every time they release a new version, they move features around, get rid of some, and rename others. They're constantly rearranging the shelves.

We're aware of new versions of mobile operating systems for Google Android and Apple iPhone because we have to install them. But Google also upgrades its algorithm regularly. Unless you're in the search engine optimization business, those upgrades are invisible to you.

All this begs the question, "If tech companies know it's a pain to have to relearn their products, why are they always changing everything up?" It's a fair question, and there's a fair answer. Technological advancement all boils down to one thing: Better chips for faster processing of more—and more complex—data.

Software developers are always improving their products to take better advantage of faster microprocessors. So technology is transitory. Pivoting to digital is also an ongoing, ever-evolving process, rather than a one-time event. It's something you're always getting better at, rather than a box you check, a one and done.

Since the steps of a digital pivot are interconnected, you need components that integrate with each other. If any of those components becomes obsolete, you have to rejigger the whole system to get it working again. And migrating to new software is like getting an organ transplant; you have to be careful the rest of the system doesn't reject the new integration. One way to lessen the pain is to pick software you can use for as long as possible without having to migrate.

It may seem a little more technical than you bargained for, but you're about to get a primer in information technology strategy. So stay with me, because I'm going to explain in nontechnical terms how to pick the right software.

Tech Stacks

When you combine different software applications together into one solution, it's called a tech stack. A stack is a term developers use to describe the core technologies from which they build new technological solutions.

Pivoting to digital is not just about building a better website. That's the tip of the iceberg. Your website is where you present yourself to the world. It's the front end of your tech stack. It's the presentation layer where people interact with your business.

But below the waterline is a collection of applications you can't see that are hard at work processing live chat sessions, displaying conversion pop-ups, collecting email newsletter sign-ups, syndicating podcasts, serving white paper download requests, managing webinar registrations, scoring leads, processing credit card transactions, and recording everything so you can analyze, optimize, and improve.

You use software to publish information. Sometimes you publish to a website where everyone can see it, and sometimes you publish to a page where only you can see it. When you publish to a place where everyone can see it, you're usually publishing to your website, or the front end of your stack. When you log in and enter notes on a customer record or create an invoice, you're entering data into the back end of your stack.

A full-featured digital business capable of marketing, selling, and servicing customers online has much more than a website in place; it has a collection of interconnected software tools that are compatible with each another. And that collection is called a stack.

For our purposes, stacks are off-the-shelf software products integrated together to perform standard business processes such as maintaining an e-commerce site, managing email marketing initiatives, or optimizing a website for conversions.

The best stacks are collections of software applications that work well together, which means they can be configured to exchange information automatically. If you have to manually cut and paste newsletter sign-ups on your website into your email marketing list, you're not integrated. Software applications that pass information between them automatically are integrated.

But since technology is always changing, stacks require ongoing maintenance. As products change, integrations can stop working, data security can get breached, and your system uptime can be compromised.

Stacks reduce friction and make it easier to get things done. The less friction, the more agile you are. The more friction, the more vulnerable you are. The byproduct of an integrated stack is a seamless customer experience. Like a pirouette, when you get it right, it's a thing of beauty.

Disruptive Innovation

Technology shakes up markets, organizational hierarchies, and people's lives. Disruptive innovation forces workers to learn new skills. It creates new efficiencies that can eliminate some jobs and business sectors altogether.

A great example of disruptive innovation is the shipping container, which resulted in the end of longshoreman unions, the building of new ports accessible by road and rail, and gave life to global supply chains. Without shipping containers, just-in-time manufacturing never would have happened.

When I launched my first SaaS (software as a service) company, we struggled to help the public relations industry communicate on behalf of their clients online, while new digital agencies were springing up all around them. "We're in PR. We don't do tech," was the common retort. What we were doing was integrating the two for a better outcome.

Eventually, after Target, Toyota, and UCLA came on board as clients, it grew into iPRSoftware, a multimillion-dollar business. When we started, however, online communications was viewed as disrupting the PR industry. Back then, public relations professionals were largely adverse to technology and any sort of quantitative analysis. Many of them had gone into PR to avoid it.

At a sales meeting, a prospective customer once handed me a stack of press releases and asked me if I could scan them into their online newsroom, as though bits could be transformed into bytes as easily as bytes are transformed into bits. Today, press releases are born, live, and die as bytes. Eventually, everyone realized that being able to communicate effectively online was essential, and I spent a decade traveling the world leading digital marketing boot camp seminars for the Public Relations Society of America, the US Department of State, the United States military, the Government of Singapore, and many others.

Once marketing and communications people realized they had to learn digital communications, there was a mad rush to acquire these new job skills. Those who couldn't adapt were pushed into retirement or let go while a digital savvy generation of communicators grabbed the baton, and technology disrupted the PR industry.

After that, I wrote *Social Marketing to the Business Customer*, the first book on B2B digital marketing. I also built an online training company to help organizations close the digital skills gap and scale their reach online. Another important endeavor was helping train them to mitigate the risk of various social media meltdowns, which had become a newsbeat all its own as executives and employees began losing self-control on social networks. In fact, many of the lynch mob rioters who took selfies of the infamous Trump-inspired Capitol Hill Insurrection were later fired by their employers.

Next, I joined a $1 billion B2B as chief revenue officer, where I oversaw the implementation of modern CRM technology and mobile app development. So, it's safe to say that, over the years, I've seen firsthand how technology disrupts industries, organizations, and lives. When two applications can automatically talk to one another, they often make the old way of doing things obsolete. If the people who did those things manually prior to the pivot can't be retrained and reassigned, they're going to be out of a job.

Integration is a threat to legacy business processes, and a threat to the people who perform them. Integrated stacks require less manual data entry, which means fewer data entry jobs. Stacks separate salespeople from their leads, making them more expendable. And they make companies less dependent on individuals to store and retrieve information. So from the organization's standpoint, stacks are a good thing. But for those employees unwilling to change the way they work, stacks are reviled and feared.

Technology not only disrupts organizations internally, it disrupts entire markets as well. Here are some examples of how technology has reshaped industry sectors.

Transportation

Uber and Lyft doubled the number of self-employed drivers, challenging the need for multiple vehicle ownership and redefining the way independent contractors are legally classified by the United States government after a decisive win for the ride sharing apps in their legislative battle against paying payroll taxes and giving their drivers benefits, overtime, and sick leave—at least in California. Early ride sharing app investors like Gary Vaynerchuk and Jason Calacanis pocketed millions. Uber and Lyft used disruptive technology to severely marginalize the taxi industry. And they put automakers on notice, because having your own car isn't as important anymore.

Hospitality

By launching an online bazaar where buyers and sellers could trade short-term lodging accommodations, Airbnb put pressure on asset-heavy hoteliers without buying or leasing real estate, despite transferring all the risk to the buyer. Since the likelihood of repeat business between the same buyer and seller in an online marketplace is much lower than it would be between a buyer and a hotel chain and since motivating the seller with the threat of a bad review is offset by the seller's ability to slam the buyer with an equally bad rating, sellers have no economic incentive to perform. The more important ongoing relationships are to successful transactions, the more risky peer-to-peer transactions are. But despite their business model that connects buyers and sellers without resolving disputes unilaterally, buyers have proven willing to assume that risk, and Airbnb is a juggernaut that has skyrocketed to gargantuan heights nonetheless.

Could they someday become the booking system of choice for hotels too?

Tax Prep

In the US, do-it-yourself tax prep software continues to eat away at assisted filings, many of which are now being prepared overseas as the internet continues to globalize professional services. As artificial intelligence improves, will tax prep one day become a free, automated service that banks offer to incentivize customers?

Subscription Models

Dollar Shave Club, which sells subscriptions to a never-ending supply of razors and shaving accoutrements has grown so quickly that Gillette launched their own subscription service. Now, you can subscribe to an ongoing supply of almost everything that's expendable, like underwear, fashion accessories, even your marijuana stash. Don't get me started.

Music

By introducing single song sales online, Apple iTunes killed the record album and record stores and brought the entire music business to its knees. Phonographs and cassette players are obsolete. We traded audio fidelity for random access to any song any time and reshaped the music and home audio equipment businesses.

Books

By assembling an online bookstore with the world's deepest catalog at competitive pricing, Amazon first drove retail book sellers out of business, then became the e-commerce everything store. Now, they're opening local community bookstores. Who would have thought? As a result, publishers who use Amazon's Kindle Direct Publishing service can be blackballed by retail book sellers.

Disrupting Industries with Technology

Industries are always changing. That's nothing new. But startups displacing incumbent market leaders by leveraging disruptive technology is new. Market leaders without a good digital strategy are more vulnerable to disruption because you can't turn a large ship on a dime. Consider Tesla versus any legacy car manufacturer like GM, or Instagram versus Kodak.

When a market is disrupted, the common factor we see coupled with innovation is the speed at which disruption occurs. Innovative disruption happens too fast for competitors to keep up. One company wields technology to introduce a new product or service, and the others can't migrate quick enough to compete.

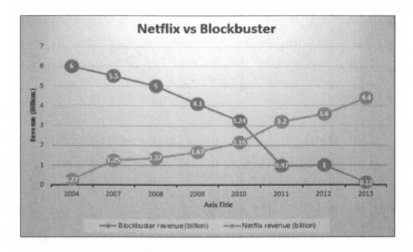

Figure 3.1 Revenue in billions of dollars at Netflix and Blockbuster from 2004 to 2013. During that period, Netflix put Blockbuster out of business. Change + Velocity = Disruption. Source: Mary Meeker

From 2009 to 2010, Blockbuster saw more than $2 billion in revenue evaporate. During that same period, revenue at Netflix climbed by more than $1 billion. Blockbuster couldn't turn their ship around quick enough. They took a torpedo from Netflix and sank. In the age of disruption, the fast eat the slow.

First, Netflix disrupted Blockbuster with a DVD subscription model that delivered movies more slowly, but which made the process of renting movies easier, and removed the risk of late fees—the major friction point of DVD rentals at the time. In a free market, whoever can play you the song you want to hear, get you a ride to where you want to go, or help you find a job easiest, fastest, and with the least amount of risk, wins.

When it comes to disruptive innovation, it's not just the easiest customer journey with the least amount of risk that wins. The behind-the-scenes work that gets done to serve customers matters, too. Disruptive innovators make it as easy to sell as it is for customers to buy. It's got to be just as easy for companies to sell, create, collaborate, plan, expense, procure, outsource, and hire.

The seller's experience—which is the path the seller takes to process a transaction and serve a customer—needs to be as seamless as the customer's. So the path to process and the path to purchase are equally important, because both together are how you achieve velocity. And an integrated stack is the tool that gets the job done. So choosing and configuring a tech stack that can handle the front end and the back end of your business is foundational to the digital pivot.

Killer Tech Stacks

Why is it that some tech stacks are so novel that they become competitive differentiators while others fail? What is it that successful innovators do that others don't? Tech stacks that kill off the competition do one thing better than everyone else. They make it easy to do business with a company from beginning to end in a digital environment. You can get all your needs met without talking to anyone if you don't want to through an end-to-end tech stack. You can do everything yourself, when you want, where you want.

End-to-end tech stacks are integrated software applications used to transact online business with customers from beginning to end.

Everything that needs to happen can get done without resorting to phone or email. There are no analog workarounds to slow down or interrupt your business processes. Everything happens online.

Analog workarounds like these are friction points that suppress velocity:

- Requiring a customer to call or email to complete a transaction that begins online.
- Requiring a document be printed, signed, scanned, and returned.
- Requiring information to be rekeyed, cut and pasted, or manually exported and imported to maintain separate systems.
- Requiring customers to email or fax anything at all. End-to-end solutions let you communicate and exchange documents electronically in one place.

Analog workarounds are manual tasks that frustrate your ability to complete end-to-end business processes in a digital environment. End-to-end solutions expedite the pace of commerce for the buyer and the seller. On the seller side, these systems let people in different roles collaborate and complete business transactions online.

A small business that uses Google Docs to draft proposals and contracts, QuickBooks for billing, and a calendar application for project management is plagued with redundancies; they have to manually cut and paste customer information from one place to another. And keeping documents in sync to avoid version confusion is a productivity drain.

First, they have to draft and send a proposal. If they land a new account, the customer has to sign, scan, and return a contract. Next, they have to rekey the customer information from the contract into the accounting software to generate an invoice. And after that, they have to take the scope of work from the proposal and enter milestones into their project management software to manage their resources against the deliverables. If there's a change order, it must be recorded and keyed in a bunch of places. All this extra work slows them down.

When I oversaw media relations for the 30th anniversary of *Star Wars* at the Los Angeles Convention Center, my team had to provide roughly 500 journalists with press materials, images, and video to augment their coverage. Rather than rely solely on physical press materials which are expensive, cumbersome, and harder for reporters to work with than digital media, we used iPRSoftware, the SaaS PR stack provider I founded, to provide registered members of the media with access to digital press materials through an online newsroom that could be managed by our own, nontechnical staff without the need for a web developer. It was as easy for us to upload content and approve registrations as it was for the media to get what they needed.

In small businesses, people with different responsibilities need different software applications to get their jobs done. End-to-end solutions give them a way to collaborate cross-functionally.

When you place an order on Amazon, it isn't processed manually. They don't get an email with your order details that they print out and hand to the shipping person. And the shipping person doesn't have to check a separate inventory system. These different roles collaborate in an end-to-end solution.

Depending on what you're looking for, the customer journey begins on Google, Amazon, or Yelp. From there, it moves to a company's website. If they have what you want, the price is right, and the experience is low-risk, you might convert and order a new iPhone case or a burger and fries for delivery.

A killer tech stack is an end-to-end system that lets you respond to leads and process orders in a low-friction environment with no analog workarounds. So an end-to-end solution is your goal. Let's look at the two basic ways of building one.

Vertically Integrated vs. Best-of-Breed Stacks

You can either build an end-to-end solution with different software applications from a single provider, or you can put one together with software from different companies. An end-to-end solution from a single software company is a vertically integrated stack.

Vertically integrated software providers like Microsoft, Oracle, and Adobe that do everything are a relatively new phenomenon. Originally, most end-to-end solutions were built from a hodgepodge of different software products that were stitched together with custom code or other homegrown solutions to fill in the gaps.

Best-of-breed software applications—such as QuickBooks, Microsoft Word, and Adobe Photoshop—do one thing really well. Best-of-breed stacks use APIs—application programming interfaces—to make leading software applications from different companies interoperable, resulting in a single coat of many colors. Vertically integrated and best-of-breed stacks both have benefits and drawbacks, depending on the size and type of business you're in, so let's break them down.

The benefit of going with a vertically integrated stack is the promise that the applications are already integrated with each other. All you have to do is turn the different applications on, configure them, and pay your bill.

Software companies that offer vertically integrated stacks usually have more limited feature sets than best-of-breed applications. Another thing to keep in mind is that vertically integrated solutions are often cobbled together from former best-of-breed applications that have been acquired.

In an effort to expand their offering, vertically integrated software providers buy up best-of-breed providers, and those acquisitions are driven by the best-of-breed provider's customer base. A big software company usually buys a little software company more for their customers than their technology. Sometimes, they buy a small software company just to migrate its customers over to their platform. Salesforce bought a best-of-breed social media monitoring platform called Radian6 and a social media advertising platform called Media Buddy, and integrated those products into what today is the Salesforce Marketing Cloud.

If they keep the smaller software company's product alive after the acquisition, that product is not going to be 100 percent compatible with the bigger company's software. The takeaway is that vertically integrated solutions are sometimes poorly integrated. So you might think you're getting an end-to-end solution, but after you settle into the stack and start trying to use some of the more advanced features, you realize that the integration isn't what it's cracked up to be.

In the early days, the only way to build an end-to-end solution was by stitching together best-of-breed applications from different software companies. Over time, the market leaders emerged with the best applications in their niche. Adobe got good at graphics, Microsoft at productivity, QuickBooks at accounting, and JIRA at software development project management.

They got so good that graphic designers, support staff, and book-keepers became reliant on them to do their jobs. Specialists and the organizations that employed them got so much value out of these best-of-breed applications that knowing how to use them became a sought-after job skill. Employers started listing them as a condition of employment, and specialists started putting them on their résumés.

Best-of-breed applications do what they do better than anything else. The problem is, they only do one thing. They're stand-alone solutions. But organizations operate collaboratively. And even independent consultants who only do one thing still have to write proposals, send invoices, and pay their bills.

If you rely on different applications that don't talk to each other, it takes you longer to get things done. You have to manage all these different applications. You've got a bunch of all-star players but not necessarily a cohesive team.

You can't build a cross-functional, collaborative workflow with a bunch of independent applications. And even if they are integrated with each other, stitching together best-of-breed applications is like conducting a series of hand-offs from one application to the next, with no overarching analytics. We've all seen that guy at the industry conference juggling two phones, a tablet, and a laptop attempting to do a product demo to close a sale only to suffer the epic failure of not being able to find his deck or access his virtual private network from the trade show floor. That is what poor integration and lack of big picture thinking looks like in the real world.

Frankenstacks

By now, you get the value of end-to-end solutions. You can move customer email addresses and phones numbers seamlessly from your customer contact software to your accounting and project management applications which means you can do more with less and serve customers faster.

You're also probably aware from unhappy experiences that integrating best-of-breed applications by mapping how data gets transferred from one application to another is a Faustian bargain. You get an end-to-end solution, but the only way to spot an issue is when the system fails.

Best-of-breed applications operate independently. They each have their own database. When you integrate them, you tell them how to pass information between one another. So you're on the hook for maintaining those integrations. You're going to have to preserve them when employees come and go or a new version is released.

It's easy to see why people get excited about simplifying the software they use at work by integrating best-of-breed applications. For employees, getting different tools to talk to each other means less cutting and pasting and less mind-numbing work. For small business owners, it results in more revenue per employee, because each employee can operate more efficiently and service more customers meaning fewer staff overall. But that promise disappears if the best-of-breed solutions aren't as interoperable as you thought.

Scoping

The way to insure your stack does what you need it to do is by figuring out and documenting your requirements before you start shopping for software. Interview managers and employees in every department and ask them what they need from an end-to-end solution. This is called scoping, and it's usually done by a business analyst who gathers the business requirements your end-to-end solution needs to satisfy. You can hire an analyst. But you can also do it yourself too. Just search "scoping questions" on Google, and you'll get numerous lists of questions.

Scope studies result in a scope-of-work (SOW) document that describes, from both functional and nonfunctional standpoints, what you need your system to do. It includes the milestones and deliverables expected from whomever you hire to build your stack. To manage web and software developers on a project, you need a scope-of-work document. When you hire a developer to build your stack, your SOW is your insurance policy that they'll build you something you can actually use. And it also ensures your employees have buy-in because they helped inform how the finished system needs to work.

If your end-to-end solution delivers the functionality outlined in the scope study, the likelihood of getting everyone to adopt your stack is high. If not, people are going to be frustrated and develop their own, less efficient analog workarounds to get their jobs done.

For an employee morale standpoint, unmet expectations are resentments waiting to happen. Scoping helps with expectations management, because people outside the software development world usually think integration means everything works with everything, or that all features can be seamlessly combined. Sadly, that's almost never the case.

Integrations are always limited, and those limitations are often not fully understood prior to scoping. And even after all that, small details may still get overlooked.

Stacks for Projects in Flux

My brother, Jamie Schwartzman, runs an award-winning boutique visual design and marketing agency called Flux Branding. He wanted to upgrade to a modern CRM integrated with a project management application so he could scale new business development without losing sight of his capacity to achieve his client deliverables.

He had been using a CRM called Daylight and a project management application called ProWorkflow. These tools were far from perfect—but very familiar to him so they were easy to use. He knew how they worked and he was comfortable with them.

But these best-of-breed applications didn't talk to each other, which was precisely the problem. His goal was an end-to-end solution that would improve the flow of information between the new business development, operational, and creative sides of his agency. We decided to try using an online automation tool called Zapier to get ProWorkflow and Daylight talking to each other. I also added in Slack, an internal collaboration platform, to streamline internal communications.

Given the sheer volume of information people exchange to get work done, Slack would help by parsing communications into smaller, bite-size chunks that are easier to digest. We've learned through social media to attenuate ourselves to activity streams by dropping in and pulling out the information we need when we need it.

Creative agencies are always juggling resources against shifting deadlines, so better communication is an ongoing goal. Our plan was to integrate Daylight, ProWorkflow and Slack. But since Daylight and ProWorkflow were stand-alone solutions that couldn't talk to each other, we needed some way to tie them together. The customer success team at ProWorkflow suggested we try using

Zapier to set up integrations. This required manually configuring a series of "if this, then that" rules to pass information back and forth, so accepted client proposals created by the business development side could easily be converted into a project plan and task assignments on the operational side.

When a project deadline changed in ProWorkflow, we set up a zap to notify everyone via Slack. That way, ops could notify the creative team without them having to leave Adobe Creative Suite or spiral into email.

It wasn't until after we set it up that we learned that the browser alerts couldn't display exactly what had changed. They just said that something changed, without saying what. So designers still had to leave Adobe Creative Suite to check the details. Sure, Slack was a bit easier and faster than email. But it didn't solve the problem.

We also learned that while you could configure a zap to send a notification via Slack when a task changed in ProWorkflow, there was no way to send Slack notifications only to specific assignees when new tasks were created.

Notifications for tasks with multiple assignees would need to be handled with employee-specific filters, which meant we'd need twenty filters to handle new and updated task notifications for ten employees, and we'd have to maintain those rules manually as employees came and went.

Digging a little deeper, we discovered that ProWorkflow sends out messages with bold and italicized text. You can't turn that off. And Slack displays that text as gibberish because, for whatever reason, ProWorkflow's text was not ASCII compliant, which basically means it's not interoperable.

If the only way to integrate best-of-breed apps is through Zapier, be very, very careful. Because the devil's in the details, the details are exceedingly tough to anticipate, and you may be getting on a hamster wheel you'll never get off.

We could have used Zapier to integrate Slack and ProWorkflow, but the level of integration was nonfunctional and Olympian to keep up to date. At the end of the day, it didn't improve speed or performance at Flux Branding. We just wanted the applications to integrate but the solution we had chosen, with no scope study, was not a major improvement.

Had I done a proper scope study, we might have foreseen some of these failings in advance. But we thought we could shortcut the process and save my brother time and money. Fortunately, our genetic bond outweighs the disobedience of Daylight and ProWorkflow, and I still make the dinner party guest list.

A more current best-of-breed project management application called Asana integrates directly with Slack and requires no intermediary like Zapier. Asana sends messages to Slack that include the reason for the update without requiring users to click through to see the details.

The Asana/Slack integration sends notifications from different Slack channels or users with the specifics about what has changed. If you consider the many different types and states of tasks and subtasks that make up a client project, sending the info to assignees with the substance of the change in the Slack notification enhances velocity.

Software applications provide many ways to complete tasks. When you link two software applications together, your hope is that the "stacked" applications will integrate seamlessly. But they never do. Integrated best-of-breed applications offer fewer options together than they do by themselves.

Assume that best-of-breed integrations are going to be limited, that you need to know the requirements before you choose applications, and that migrating to a new system will always be a challenge. Even after all that, there may still be some functionality you want that you don't have because it's difficult to anticipate how to improve processes that aren't yet in place. It takes a few months of driving a new car before you can tell whether or not you like it. You learn what works and what doesn't through use.

Getting comfortable with a new stack requires training for everyone, not just specialist employees. People need to be taught how to use software integrations. My brother said he felt like his new stack was a house he didn't know how to live in. "I was living in a tent and you moved me into a modern two-story house," he told me. "I knew how to take care of the tent. I don't know how to take care of a house. I don't know where the air conditioning is. And I can't go back to my tent, because it's all packed up."

The moral of this story is that deploying an end-to-end solution without a scope study is very risky, even for me, and I'm experienced. Small businesses often skip this critical step to save time and money, but unless their businesses are rigid and process-oriented and their people highly adaptable, failure rates are high.

If you're considering extending the functionality of one or two best-of-breed applications into a full stack, compare the value those apps give you to the value of the cross-functional collaboration capabilities that an end-to-end solution provides. Does the part of your business that relies on best-of-breed applications outweigh your need for velocity? If it does, stick with best-of-breed. Consider the integration and maintenance challenges. Can a vertically integrated, end-to-end solution sufficiently replace the best-of-breed apps that you currently rely on? Are you willing to trade best-of-breed functionality for the ability to automate cross-functional business processes, increase velocity, and get better metrics on your results?

For nearly a decade, vertically integrated solution providers like Microsoft, Oracle, and Salesforce have been building, acquiring, and integrating best-of-breed providers in a race to stack the ultimate, one-size-fits-all, end-to-end business software solution.

These tech giants offer a collection of applications that are already integrated. Their applications may underperform the best-of-breed offerings. Specialists may complain about having to use less functional tools. And the migration and configuration may be a heavier lift, but if the goal is cross-functional collaboration, vertically integrated stacks are the way to go.

Unlike best-of-breed applications, there's much lower risk that an application in your stack will become incompatible or obsolete because vertically stacked providers are in the end-to-end solution business. They want to keep their customers dependent on them, so it's in their best interests to support their integrations. Another big advantage is a common infrastructure. Whereas stitched-together, best-of-breed applications hand off information between systems, vertically integrated solutions live on one system.

Common Infrastructure

Sridhar Vembu, CEO of Zoho, a leading vertically integrated solution provider to small and midsize businesses, says common infrastructure is a real benefit. To enable faster, tighter integration between applications and give companies an easier way to build cross-functional workflows, he says the benefit of going with a vertically integrated provider is a common database. One database means fewer interdependencies because information doesn't need to be passed from one database to the next, and fewer integrations need to be maintained.

Data stored in one place is easier to analyze, spot issues before they arise, and find patterns with artificial intelligence. If AI separates tomorrow's winners from losers, and it appears increasingly likely it will, a common database is an advantage. You need less computing power to analyze one database then you do to analyze many. Since best-of-breed applications have their own databases, actionable business intelligence is harder to discern.

Getting Your Specs in Order

You wouldn't build a house without plans. And as you now know, you shouldn't build a tech stack without specifications.

Here's what you need to know to write an SOW.

Functional and nonfunctional requirements

These are just what they seem, a list of the things you need your system to do. The functional specs describe the business process you intend to use your stack to perform. And they also cover your administrative, transactional, corrective, certification, and reporting requirements. Nonfunctional requirements are things like processing time, number of concurrent users a system can support, uptime, and ease of use.

Workflow Narratives

User stories describe how people in different roles will use the stack. Here's an example of a user story from a scoping study I did for James Kinnaird, CEO of OTP DesignWorks on processing inbound phone orders that are driven by email marketing campaigns. Not everybody converts online. Some people receive promotional emails and call in.

Email Marketing Driven Phone Orders

Marketing notifies customer service that an email campaign has been scheduled. The notification includes a description of the campaign, the campaign date, and the campaign coupon code. After the campaign has been sent and calls start coming in, customer service asks the inbound caller for their coupon code. If a sales rep is associated with the coupon code, customer service transfers the call to the sales rep. If the sales rep is not available or if no rep is associated with the coupon code, customer service takes the order and either processes the credit card transaction or marks the order to be billed via mail.

Requirements

Here, I translate the user story into business requirements, score each one for prioritization, and include the person who provided the requirement.

System should be able to generate unique campaign/coupon codes that can be used to trigger special offers for e-commerce transactions and track relationships between sales reps and existing accounts. Priority 1. Raised by Gwen.

System must generate unique campaign/coupon codes that include a unique identifier in email marketing campaigns to expedite the customer identification process. Priority 1. Raised by Felix.

System must generate unique campaign/coupon codes that include a unique identifier in email marketing campaigns to expedite the product being promoted. Priority 1. Raised by Gwen.

If the caller is phoning in from a number that's on their customer record, it should trigger a pop-up that displays their customer information automatically on the screen of the customer service or sales rep receiving the call. Priority 2. Raised by Alice.

These requirements describe how customer service, sales, and actual customers interact with a tech stack. And since sales and customer service are different departments, it's a cross-functional workflow. Here are more examples of cross-functional processes:

- **Marketing Materials Updates:** R&D, Marketing, and Sales
- **Returns:** Customer Service, Operations, and Shipping
- **Online Orders:** Operations, Accounting, and Shipping

When you're designing a new system, it's critical to distinguish needs from wants. Pivots fail when companies are too ambitious and try to launch a system that can do everything. You can't boil the ocean.

Business Process Maps

You've probably seen these before but didn't know what they were, so let me explain them to you. Business process maps are diagrams with symbols that map out workflows using a standard business process modeling and notation language.

In addition to having a narrative description of how people collaborate to complete different business functions, these diagrams organized by job function express how people at work collaborate to get tasks done.

There are plenty of tools that make it easy to build business process maps. To show you what a workflow chart looks like, figure 3.2 gives a sample workflow which maps how an email campaign beginning in the marketing department becomes an order and generates revenue.

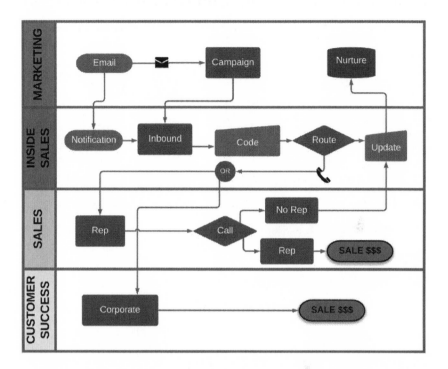

Figure 3.2 Business process map showing how four different departments collaborate in a digital environment to process a phone order stimulated by an email marketing campaign. Each of the four departments has their own lane, frequently called "swim lanes." The workflow process begins in the Marketing department, moves to Inside Sales, then to Sales, and concludes in the Customer Success department, a moniker for customer service departments at companies that sell subscriptions.

Like swim lanes in a lap pool, workflows are organized in departmental lanes with cross-functionality indicated by lines that traverse across different lanes. Business process maps are useful because they show you who does what, reveal areas for improvement, and help manage change by showing everyone what processes will be instituted before they actually are in order to avoid surprises. A business analyst sits with representatives from each department to create these maps, so everyone agrees on what the stack needs to do.

Once you've documented your business requirements, that specification becomes your scope-of-work document. And your SOW becomes the backbone of the request for proposal, or RFP, that you distribute to web or software developers to solicit bids. Since you know what you want your stack to do, the bids will be comparable, and you'll have an insurance policy against winding up with a system that doesn't meet your business requirements by delivering the functionality you specified.

Like a couple remodeling a bathroom who make impulsive, last minute changes that delay completion and increase costs, not having a plan or changing a plan mid-execution can be disastrous. In the world of software operations, the more requirements you layer into your specifications, the lower your chances of success. When a specification document has too many requirements, the result is scope creep.

It's best to keep the scope of your initial build as manageable as possible. As long as you've anticipated all your needs and scoped your solution properly, your stack can be improved and expanded over time. A strategy for managing scope creep is building yourself what's called a minimum viable solution. Instead of guessing what you need and building out features you may not actually use, the idea is to get a bare-bones but stable, iterative solution up and running and fine-tune after that, adding features and functionality based on actual user feedback.

Don't skip this step. You're not just building a website. You're building a revenue engine. If you want to know why digital companies outperform others in their sector, go to www.builtwith.com and look under the hood at their tech stacks.

Industry Solutions

One way small businesses avoid having to deal with scoping a custom stack is by going with a solution built to work for a specific industry. There are solutions for dentists, country clubs, vintners, gyms, hair salons, and almost anything else you can think of. You get a preconfigured solution for your use case. It may not be as modern as best-of-breed applications or as flexible as a vertically integrated solution because it's been standardized to provide the core features required for an industry-specific use case, but it does most of what you need out of the box.

If yours is a lifestyle business and you're comfortable with your annual billings and have no world domination ambitions, go with an industry-specific solution. But if you're looking to scale and out compete in your sector, go with a best-of-breed or vertically integrated stack.

Another reason to avoid industry-specific solutions is to mitigate the risk of obsolescence. Salesforce.com has a market cap of $225 billion; that buys a dedicated army of engineering talent. How could any small industry solution provider possibly compete? If you want to deploy a stack that's going to be around for a long time, get onto software being supported by the world's top engineers.

Homegrown Solutions

The riskiest of all courses companies take is building or configuring their own solutions from scratch. Often to save money, they take the penny-wise, pound-foolish approach of constructing a solution piecemeal. Almost always, these solutions are obsolete before they're even operational. It makes zero sense to maintain software for a customer base of one. How could you possibly stay competitive in whatever your core competency is and maintain a software solution at the same time?

Definitely get yourself onto a stack maintained by a team of software engineers. Sometimes companies are on homegrown solutions because they've been around for a long time and modern solutions did not exist when they got started. These days, it's the amateurs that deploy homegrown solutions. Don't learn this lesson the hard way.

Web Content Management

You bought this book because you want to pivot your business or your career to digital. And before you started reading this chapter, you probably thought that just meant having a good website, but now you see that a website is just a facade for a digital business and it has to play nice with all the other applications in your stack. So let's turn our attention to the leading content management system on the web, a free solution called WordPress.

By making website development easy, WordPress is the best-of-breed content management platform with a whopping 64 percent market share.[1] WordPress is not an end-to-end solution, but it can be integrated with e-commerce platforms like Shopify, Magento, Big Commerce, or Woo Commerce.

WordPress is a content management platform that's so popular that third-party software developers build integrated applications to extend its functionality. These are called plugins. Sometimes plugins are free, and sometimes they cost a few bucks, but the price is usually low to moderate and affordable for most small businesses.

My site runs on WordPress and I have worked on dozens of migrations with clients who are moving from other content management systems to WordPress. Media outlets like The New Yorker, BBC America, and Bloomberg all run on WordPress, which is notable because they're media companies meaning their websites are a big part of their business. When you build a site and publish content to attract customers, you're competing against the news media, so you're in the media business. If you're on a platform used by top media companies, you're in good company.

A detailed account of the expanse of the WordPress ecosystem is well beyond the scope of this book. If you're a small business looking for a WordPress developer, however, there are a number of community-organized, local WordCamp events happening in the real world and online where you can build relationships and connect with developers. But let's remember that, since WordPress just powers the presentation layer of your digital business, it's just your content management system. You're still going to need a full stack.

1   https://w3techs.com/

Marketing Stacks

Just as a business needs an end-to-end solution to compete, digital marketers need tools to attract, nurture, and convert awareness to consideration to evaluation to transaction.

There are literally thousands of marketing technology solution providers out there. At *chiefmartec.com*, Scott Brinker categorizes the options by:

- **Advertising & Promotions** · Paid search, paid social, display advertising, programmatic advertising, native advertising, video advertising, mobile marketing, public relations technology, and e-commerce print shops that make analog brochures and banners.

- **Content & Experience** · Marketing automation, lead management, content marketing, email marketing, SEO, website personalization, surveys, video marketing, digital asset management, and mobile apps.

- **Social & Relationships** · Customer relationship management, account-based marketing, influencer marketing, review sites, social media monitoring, social media engagement, conversational marketing, chatbots, community sites and advocacy, loyalty, and referrals.

- **Commerce & Sales** · E-commerce platforms, e-commerce marketing, sales automation, sales enablement, proximity marketing, IoT marketing, channel marketing, partner marketing, local marketing and affiliate marketing.

- **Data** · Consumer data, marketing analytics, data visualization, mobile analytics, website analytics, customer data platforms, data management platforms, data security, and data compliance.
- **Management** · Product management, project management, workflow management, talent management, lean management, agile management, vendor management, and collaboration.

Some of these providers creep beyond the scope of marketing, but if you map out how they get used cross-functionally, they all overflow into the digital marketing swim lane at some point.

Marketing Funnels

Whereas the customer journey is the experience people have doing business with you, the marketing funnel is the digital path they take on your website before they either purchase or engage with a salesperson.

Digital marketing is about finding and attracting customers into the funnel. As we've seen, there are many rivers through which leads flow into your website, and many ways to generate demand and drive growth. The next chapters of this book explain each one of them. But first, let's look at what a marketing funnel is and why you need one before you generate demand. Conversion optimization—maximizing sales efficiency—is dependent on having a funnel in place to collect and convert leads.

Hosting Website Visitors

Not only is my wife's mother, Cheryl, an amazing cook, she's also a great host. Whenever we visit, she puts out a beautiful cheese plate. There's hard cheese for me, soft cheese for my wife, Celia, and fresh butter for my son, William.

She takes the butter out of the fridge a few hours before we arrive so it's soft and easy to spread. There's something for everyone. Cheryl expresses love through cooking. She is socially graceful.

Marketing funnels are socially graceful too. They anticipate the needs and wants of your customers before they arrive so the experience they have is positive. If you invite someone over for dinner and your house is filthy with no hors d'oeuvres to serve while you're pulling the meal together in the kitchen, your guests probably won't enjoy themselves.

Unsophisticated digital marketers fail because they invest all their time and money inviting people to their website, but when their guests arrive, the place is a mess. It's not clear where to go or what to do. Some links are broken or there's no clear path to purchase.

Rather than leading a horse to water, you faked them out and led them to a mirage. And this is the most common reason companies fail online. They're doing backflips to get people to their website, but their website sucks. There's no cheese plate. No nuts. Nothing. Nada. So they bounce to a website that's more comfortable.

Before you invest in social media, first make sure you have somewhere nice to invite people. Set the table. Make it easy for customers to get the information they need to decide if you can solve their problem. Make it easy for them to do business with you.

Good funnels anticipate your customer's wants and needs, so they stay longer and convert at a higher rate. Amazon shows you the delivery time for things you might want to order without having to place an order. In the old days, you wrote an ad, sent it out, and if it worked, the phone rang. A good salesperson answered the call and told the customer what they needed to know to make the sale. It doesn't work that way anymore. Now you run an ad and buyers go to your website and self-educate online. If they don't find what they want by themselves, the site doesn't convert, and the phone never rings. So you need a funnel to convert visitors into leads first.

A good marketing funnel converts in no more than three clicks. Visitors land on an information page and click through to a conversion page. If they convert, they move to an acknowledgment page. That's a funnel.

Behind the scenes, the order goes into a tech stack which sends out an email confirmation with a link to your CRM where you can get more information about the status of the lead.

You design marketing funnels the same way you map workflows. And you can have different funnels for different goals. You might have one funnel to acquire email newsletter registrations, another for generating e-commerce transactions, and a third for scheduling introductory meetings.

Enterprise Case Study – Cision

Cision sells software for public relations. The company was acquired in late 2019 for $2.74 billion. They're a SaaS (software as a service) provider, so it's a considered purchase with a sales cycle rather than an impulse buy. David Cardiel was head of global demand generation at Cision. And while he has since moved on, he built the marketing funnels Cision uses to acquire leads.

Cardiel has over ten years' experience building and optimizing funnels, and his process starts by building different funnels for different kinds of leads. He likes to keep things simple, so he segments his leads into two groups. Tier 1 leads come through his demo request funnel, and everything else is Tier 2; leads from white paper downloads, newsletter subscribers, and webinar registrations.

Tier 2 leads get scored and routed to his customer development team, who contact qualified leads within twenty-four hours. At Cision, he lifted the lead-to-opportunity conversion rate for Tier 1 leads from 42 to 87 percent. And he raised the lead-to-opportunity rate for Tier 2 leads from 3 to 23 percent.

Rather than chuck leads over the fence to the sales team, Cardiel believes in passing his demo request leads to market development reps to enrich and qualify those prospects first. This is part of the lead scoring process, so salespeople can see at a glance which leads have the greatest propensity to convert.

Accounts are scored based on ideal customer profile criteria—industry, number of employees, and revenue—coupled with the way they got to the website and their engagement level.

Leads are scored based on persona criteria—title, seniority, demographics, and professional association memberships—coupled with the way they got to the website and their level of engagement.

Cardiel has tweaked his integrated stack to prioritize leads based on engagement. Before a website visitor converts, they're just an anonymous visitor. But after they convert, he can measure how many times they come back to his site, which pages they visit, and how long they stay in one place.

This is a great example of how meaning is found at the intersection of disparate data points. Unless you can see the relationships between your website usage, email marketing, chat sessions, product utilization, and lead pipeline data on one dashboard, it's difficult to get any useful business intelligence from those metrics.

Cardiel can see which email campaigns are opened, which leads click through, where they went after they arrived, and how long they stayed. If the visitor works for an existing account, he can even see all service requests and chat sessions with other people at that company. Since his marketing funnels are built on an integrated stack, all that activity is stored on their customer record in his customer relationship management system.

As you can see, you couldn't do all this with just a website. You need an integrated stack. And if you think all this is beyond you because you're just a small company, you used to be right. But you're not anymore. I've overseen development teams on major software migrations that I could not do myself. But today, any small business can get an integrated stack up and running with one or two freelancers.

I got my current stack up and running that way, and I'm not a software developer. While I did need a little help here and there, no innovation was required, only configuration. My stack consists of off-the-shelf solutions. I augment a vertically integrated CRM solution from Zoho with best-of-breed digital marketing applications (my core competency, and hence an area in which I want to outperform) because Zoho's digital marketing applications don't satisfy my requirements.

For Cardiel, if a lead is with a major account with which Cision has an existing history, that contact record is added to an account record, and the account profile is handed off to a sales rep who can review the history before contacting the lead. Enterprise customers buy more user seats, generate more revenue, and get assigned a higher priority in his digital queue. This is called account-based marketing.

At Cision, if anyone signs up for a demo, Cardiel assumes those leads are actively shopping and talking to his competitors. During business hours, his team responds to demo requests within five minutes.

Here are commonly used applications in marketing stacks, organized by funnel stage.

Awareness Stage

- **Google Analytics** - website usage analytics
- **Google Search Console** - search visibility analytics
- **Semrush** - search engine research
- **Talkwalker** - social media monitoring
- **Mailchimp** - email marketing and autoresponders
- **Muck Rack** - journalist/blogger contact database
- **Hootsuite** - social media engagement dashboard
- **INK** - content performance optimization
- **Lately** - social media marketing automation
- **Google Adwords and Social Media Advertising**

Consideration Stage

- **Hotjar** - user experience analytics
- **WordPress** - content management
- **Yoast** - search engine optimization
- **Google Optimize** - A/B testing for webpages
- **Uberflip** - user engagement optimization
- **Opt-In Monster** - lead capture forms
- **Blubrry** - podcast distribution
- **Vimeo** - video hosting
- **Zoom** - webinars

Evaluation Stage

- **Salesforce** - CRM (customer relationship management) leader

- **Microsoft Dynamics** - CRM for Microsoft shops
- **Zoho** - CRM leader for small and midsize businesses
- **HubSpot** - inbound marketing platform with CRM
- **Outreach** - outbound sales sequencing platform
- **Zoom Info** - customer enrichment data
- **Intercom** - digital messaging platform
- **Highspot** - sales enablement platform
- **Gong** - sales call analytics platform

Purchase Stage

- **Shopify** - customizable e-commerce platform
- **Woo Commerce** - WordPress e-commerce platform
- **Amazon** - e-commerce platform for third-party sellers
- **Square** - retail e-commerce gateway/payment processor
- **PayPal** - e-commerce gateway/payment processor
- **Venmo** - e-commerce gateway/payment processor
- **Stripe** - e-commerce payment gateway/processor with one the best APIs
- **Payoneer** - e-commerce payment processor with escrow services
- **Authorize.net** - payment gateway service only (requires bank merchant account)
- **Braintree** - e-commerce payment processor only

Tech Stack Hedging

The reason small businesses are small is because they struggle to standardize their business processes. If they could standardize the way they service customers, they wouldn't be small. They'd scale up and grow up.

The main reason digital pivots fail is that scoping, implementing, and learning to use stacks requires experience and time that a small business is either unwilling or unable to invest.

I oversaw the development of a two-sided online gig economy marketplace application where businesses could hire interns. Choosing applications to handle the purchase stage of our process was more challenging because we had to hold funds in escrow for clients and let them release funds against milestones. In that case, none of the standard e-commerce payment/gateway providers would suffice.

We went with Payoneer, because at the time, they were the only provider we could find that would allow companies to pay via credit or ACH in any country, escrow the funds, and give interns a way to transfer their earnings to their bank account, e-wallet, pre-paid credit card, or international payment in over 150 currencies.

Figure 3.3 shows a collection of screenshots from the marketplace application we designed that we put on to Payoneer for e-commerce.

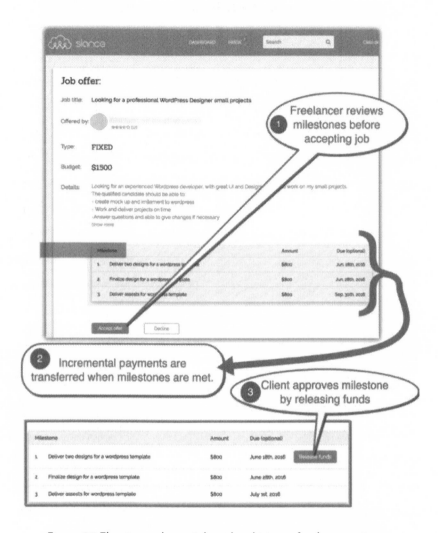

Figure 3.3 The steps a buyer takes when hiring a freelancer using a product I developed with Billy Howard, Jr., Adam Thornton, Eric Bush, and Alex Saavedra at the Center for Digital Innovation at Howard Industries. Payoneer was the right e-commerce provider for our use case because they allowed us to hold the buyer's funds in escrow and make incremental distributions against milestones.

Processing an e-commerce transaction may sound simple at first. When you start thinking more about what kind of payments you want to accept, how you want to process transactions, and how you want to pay out those funds, some e-commerce providers are going to be a better fit than others.

Square is a good solution for small business retailers because you can just plug their little square credit reader into your phone and swipe a credit card. Plus, you pay a lower processing fee if you swipe a physical card.

But regardless of the e-commerce provider you plug into your stack, you hedge your bet by selecting an application that can deliver the functionality in your scope study and by choosing a provider that has the funding, revenue growth, and engineering staff to keep their product current.

Once your tech stack is up and running, you need to teach people how to use it. "When you demo new integrations to clients, keep it simple," says Rand Singer of Los Angeles–based Singer Consulting, which helps entertainment companies deploy and maintain tech stacks. "Don't overwhelm users with the details of what it can do. Show them the easiest way to get their job done. Let them pick up advanced features on their own, as they acclimate," says Singer. He also happens to be an amazing jazz saxophone player, so he knows how to improvise under pressure.

Now that you have a sense of the scope of a digital business, let's get into the single most foundational of all the digital marketing skills, search engine optimization.

CHAPTER 4

Search Engine
Optimization

'm not much of a sports fan, or cook, for that matter. But every
year on Super Bowl Sunday, I make chili and watch the game.
Nobody eats it but me because it usually isn't very good. One
year, I decided to try and make a chili so good that my wife would
not just eat it, but come back for seconds.

There used to be a great restaurant in Venice Beach called
72 Market Street. That was their address. It's not there anymore
because little in LA withstands the test of time. It's a town fasci-
nated with the latest, rather than the oldest.

Snapchat moved into 72 Market Street years later. But when the
location was a restaurant, they had a dish on the menu called Kick
Ass Chili. Celia and I are both Angelenos, and she remembered
it. So I asked her, "If I can make the Kick Ass Chili they served

at 72 Market Street, will you eat it?" And she said, "If you can make the Kick Ass Chili from 72 Market Street, I'll eat it." The *Los Angeles Times* had published the recipe years ago before the restaurant closed, so I went to their website to get it.

Now, I may be a fair weather sports fan and a half-baked cook, but I'm fluent in Boolean and know how to write advanced queries online. Yet I couldn't for the life of me find the recipe. I was searching backward and forward, every which way I could think of. But no matter how I searched, I just couldn't find it.

So I opened a premium research tool called LexisNexis and finally found it. It was under the headline, "Almost Angus." Now, "Almost Angus" may have worked in print with a sidebar listing the ingredients and a picture of a guy stirring a pot. But with search, all you have to go on is text. When they posted the recipe to their website, they didn't rewrite the headline and subhead with the right keywords, so there was no easy way for a search engine to understand what it was. Search engines choke on irony, wit, and humor.

So I decided to do a test. I'd take the recipe, write a blog post about my experience, and see if I could start ranking in search results under "72 market street kick ass chili" on Google. I wrote a blog post titled the "Finding 72 Market Street's Kick-Ass Chili Recipe Online." Sure enough, after a couple of weeks, my blog about the chili recipe was outranking the once mighty *LA Times*.

In some ways, it kind of saddened me. Ever since the internet became a news distribution channel, the *Los Angeles Times*—and the entire newspaper industry for that matter—has been struggling. With the rise of Craigslist, classified advertising revenue has declined steeply. Display advertising was migrating online. The *Los Angeles Times* had been in and out of bankruptcy several times and let some of my favorite writers go. I still subscribe, but just so I have a way to start the barbecue.

And here they had an opportunity to get in front of me with their archival content (of which they had over a century's worth) and generate some ad revenue. But they failed to convert. All they would have had to do was change the headline before posting it online, which wouldn't have been that tough. It made me wonder how many millions of advertising impressions their archives were missing out on—and the associated revenue. But since they hadn't retitled the chili recipe before putting it online, I couldn't find the recipe on their site.

Think about an advertising channel like outdoor billboards. You're driving by on the freeway at sixty-five miles an hour. What's the likelihood that you're going to notice a billboard and buy what they're advertising? But there I was, jumping up and down, raising my hand and begging for content I knew they had. Since they never edited the story to make it easy for Google to index for relevance, I couldn't find it.

It made no sense. Their advertisers were defecting to Google, Amazon, and Yelp. Here was a way to recapture and sell attention to advertisers. And they fumbled it.

It's like going to CVS to buy a specific brand of shampoo. There are literally hundreds of options. Asking an employee if they have it is pointless. They don't know where anything is either. If you don't find your shampoo, CVS loses the sale. No wonder Amazon is eating retail's lunch. Giant stores with no help and a bunch of merchandise you can't find are like websites with content you can't find. Like CVS, the *Los Angeles Times* has this vast archive of evergreen, historical content but no one can find it.

I'm not suggesting that search engine optimization would have fixed all their woes. They still needed to lower their costs and keep producing interesting content, which is a bigger challenge. But the notion that this once great newspaper's original content couldn't be found in the modern age was sad.

While the *LA Times* was asleep at the wheel, an entire industry of food-driven media brands used search optimized recipes to grow their outlets and generate huge returns from advertising impressions. As I mentioned earlier, I did find the recipe. And I did make the chili, which I thought came out pretty good. My wife liked it, too, but she said it was a little too spicy.

And years later, I still rank for "72 market street kick ass chili." Try it and see. I even rank for "kick ass chili." But for years, the *Los Angeles Times*, which was the original source of publication for that recipe, was nowhere to be found.

It's really a shame, because every great city needs a great newspaper. But what good is news if you can't find it? Which brings us back to the idea of creating content that's easy for Google to index for relevance, as well as examining how their algorithm—a set of rules they use to retrieve links from their search index based on a query—decides who should rank first.

Most people think marketing is about finding customers. But instead of searching for customers, search engine optimization or SEO is about helping customers find you.

Search Engine Marketing (SEM) vs. Search Engine Optimization

Google is a media company. They sell advertising alongside editorial content. But instead of producing original content like the *Los Angeles Times*, Google's content is created algorithmically by engineers. Their editorial content is their search results. And their advertising units are their pay-per-click ads.

Prior to Google, "advertising was like a rude stranger interrupting a conversation to sell you something you neither wanted or needed," wrote Ken Auletta in his book *Googled*. By giving advertisers a way to match ads to relevant search queries, "the buy was more efficient because it was cheaper, more targeted, and Google only charged when the customer actually clicked on the ad."

At the same time, Google cut out the middleman, in this case traditional ad agencies who marked up the ad spend, because for the first time you could just go online and buy ads yourself. Google ads are the sponsored results that appear on search engine results pages.

In 2020, advertisers spent $61 billion advertising on search engines, and that number is expected to reach $77 billion by 2024.[1]

---

1   https://www.statista.com/statistics/456181/search-advertising-revenue-device-digital-market-outlook-usa/

SEM is paid media with a twist. Advertisers use a virtual auction platform to bid on search terms. The highest bidder gets their ad displayed when someone searches their term. But, and here's the twist, they only pay if their ad gets clicked. So it's much more efficient than mass media. Search engine marketing requires cash and clever copy.

Unlike SEM, search engine optimization or SEO refers to creating content in a way that makes it more likely to appear in Google's editorial which is their algorithmic search results. That's done by using the right keywords in your text and getting backlinks to your pages, and I'll drill down deeper into these concepts in this chapter.

The benefits of being mentioned in the editorial content of a publication versus in the advertising are unmistakable. Ads are bought and sold, so we consider them to be biased in favor of the advertiser whose claims could be untrue. But we consider editorial content to be an impartial, third-party endorsement of sorts.

In the news business, the editorial content is an attempt by journalists to capture and relay truth. Ads are an attempt to sell you something. You can win hearts and minds with advertising. But trust and confidence comes from editorial coverage.

Since Google's editorial content is their search results, they have tremendous influence over popular perception. The top search result is Google's preferred brand. Such top-ranked searches are what the world's most trusted search authority considers the best information source for that query. But how does Google decide who to rank first?

The Google algorithm is the Coca-Cola formula of the modern ages. No one knows what's in it for sure. Google uses proprietary technology to rank search results. There's no rabbinical panel that weighs in. The process is fully automated and constantly changing. And it's kept a secret.

Google likes it that way. Coca-Cola has a secret formula for their syrup, and Google has a secret formula for their algorithm. It's secret by design. If it got out, unscrupulous marketers would be able to artificially manipulate Google's search results. (This happens all the time; marketers trying to game the system and Google correcting and adjusting in a never-ending cat-and-mouse game.) That means it would be harder to find the best content. We wouldn't trust them as much. And they'd be vulnerable to being disrupted.

"We are, to be honest, quite secretive about what we do," says Udi Manber, VP of engineering search quality. "There are two reasons for it: competition and abuse. Competition is pretty straightforward. No company wants to share its secret recipes with its competitors. As for abuse, if we make our ranking formulas too accessible, we make it easier for people to game the system. Security by obscurity is never the strongest measure, and we do not rely on it exclusively, but it does prevent a lot of abuse."[2]

Search engine optimization is more like public relations than advertising, because the way you go about earning a page-

2 https://googleblog.blogspot.com/2008/05/introduction-to-google-search-quality.html

one search rank is more like getting a front page article in the press than buying an ad. You can't buy a front page story in the *New York Times* or the cover of *Vogue*. Similarly, you can't buy organic search rankings. For that reason, SEO is considered earned media.

SEO is the process of earning search rankings. The goal is to appear in the first page of Google's search results for relevant, high-volume terms because most people never go beyond that first page of search results. A page-one ranking is Google's impartial, third-party endorsement for the web pages listed. And it drives qualified traffic to top ranking sites.

Search Sessions

To understand how an online search can lead to gaining a customer or a lead, consider how a marketing funnel relates to searching for information online. Not all searches have commercial intent. Searching for the definition of a word, the capital of a country, or the birthday of an elected official are unlikely to result in a sale.

But search sessions with high commercial intent typically play out something like this. You have a problem you need to solve. Let's say you're working from home, and you want to free up desk space by mounting your monitor on the wall.

You're problem-aware. You search "monitor mounts," and the first result is a link to Amazon. Click that one, and you'll be faced with hundreds of options. You know that. The second result is a link at nytimes.com that says "The Best Monitor Arms | Reviews by *Wirecutter*." You like the promise of an impartial recommendation so you click that one, which takes you to an article titled "Best Monitor Arms."

A-ha! It wasn't a monitor mount you wanted after all. It was a monitor arm. You've advanced to the next stage of the search session. You're solution-aware.

Wirecutter's top pick is the Fully Jarvis Monitor Arm. You click the link and transit over to the Jarvis Monitor Arm product page on fully.com. You're now brand-aware. But you're not necessarily done.

You might try searching "Fully Jarvis Monitor Arm" again on Google to see if you can find it for a better price. You might watch a product review on YouTube or read what people have to say about it on Reddit. Or you might be satisfied with the *Wirecutter* recommendation and buy it.

SEO is about your product/service/entity/organization getting found by searchers at all stages of the funnel, from problem-aware, to solution-aware, to brand-aware. You want to keep showing up for as many relevant search phrases as possible. But in order to do that, you need to know what problems, solutions and brands your customers are searching for.

Keyword Selection

Search terms express or capture varying degrees of commercial intent. A keyword like "b2b growth marketing" has a tad more commercial intent than "what is b2b growth," which is a more informational query. But a solidly commercial intent is expressed in a phrase like "b2b growth marketing consultant" because it means the person searching is looking for someone to hire.

At SalesHacker.com, they want to rank for bottom funnel search terms like "sales training" and "sales consulting." Bottom funnel terms have transactional intent. These are the final searches you do before you buy. A search for a coupon or promo code is a bottom funnel search. At SalesHacker.com a search for a phrase like "I need sales training" or "I need sales consulting" are bottom funnel searches. Searches like "what is sales development" or "what does a sales development manager do?" are informational. They have a lower commercial intent so they're top funnel searches.

At the time of writing, you can broaden your awareness of potential keywords by checking out "related searches" on the bottom of Google's search results page. I say "at this time of writing" because like the supermarkets I mentioned earlier, Google—and all online services for that matter—are constantly rearranging where things are, just like retailers are constantly rearranging their shelves. So if, when you're reading this, you can't find "related searches" at the bottom of the page, just look around because they probably moved it. Related search queries tell you that people who search the phrase you just searched also search these related terms.

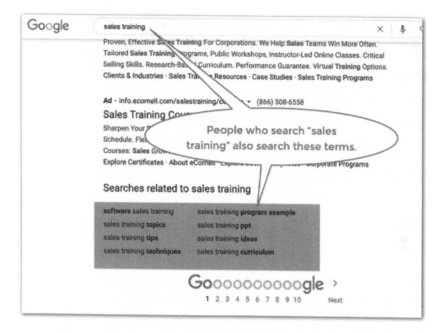

Figure 4.1 Google displays "related" searches at the bottom of their search results pages. This is essentially a window into how Google determines relevance because they are telling you that they consider all these searches to be related. Therefore, if you have the best content for all these terms, you are likely to rank for them in queries as well.

The objective in SEO is to drive qualified traffic to your website by ranking for search terms that are relevant to the problems your products or services solve. But since other digital marketers are trying to rank for those same terms, SEO is very competitive. When you're just starting out with a new website and you're not ranking for relevant terms, you begin by trying to rank for terms that are less competitive. There are keyword research platforms like Semrush that you can use to get estimates on search volume for most phrases. Semrush shows you how many times a term gets searched per month.

What you tend to find is that ranking for a single word like "pizza" is more difficult than ranking for a phrase like "best thin crust pizza delivery beverly hills." It's easier if you begin the process of SEOing a website by trying to rank for longer search phrases with more keyword modifiers, because there are fewer web pages online that have been created to rank "best thin crust pizza delivery beverly hills" than "pizza."

To find descriptive words you can add to a search term, search the phrase "keyword modifiers" in Google and you'll get a bunch of suggestions of descriptors you can add to a seed keyword if it's too difficult to rank. That way, if you can't get ranked for the competitive term, at least you can get ranked for a phrase that includes that term. For example, it's easier to rank for "SEO digital marketing consultant los angeles" than "digital marketing consultant," so start with a longer phrase that you have a chance of ranking for.

If you can get ranked for a longer search phrase that includes the keyword you ultimately want to rank for, you can peel off the modifiers one at a time and go for the high-volume keyword. You might start with "best thin crust pizza delivery beverly hills." Once you're ranking for that, you might go for "best pizza beverly hills." And if you can pull that off, then you'd go for "pizza beverly hills." If you start with that phrase, it's going to be much more difficult because Google knows next to nothing about your website. So get some easy wins on the board first. Then, you can start to peel away the modifiers and go for more competitive terms.

This approach is sometimes referred to as a long tail keyword strategy, the idea being that it's actually better to rank for the hundreds of keywords that make up the long tail of a graph than it is to rank only for the spike.

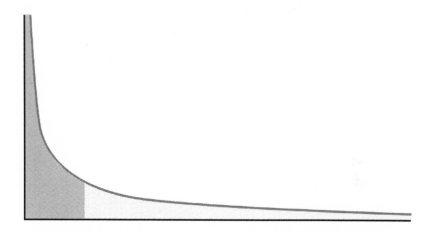

Figure 4.2 Long Tail Theory - Since store inventory space is limited, they stock best selling items, represented by the green spike. If this showed sales by product, a retailer would stock more top sellers to generate higher returns. But if you were selling digital music performances on a jukebox like my client Ecast, your inventory costs are zero; the long yellow tail of the graph becomes just as lucrative as the green spike. Retail is about best sellers. In e-commerce, a deep catalog can be just as lucrative, and in SEO, it's just as effective to rank for hundreds of long tail keywords as it is to rank for high-volume seed keywords.

The Long Tail is a term coined by Chris Anderson, former *Wired* magazine editor-in-chief, and the term actually grew out of a meeting I set up for him with Robbie Vann-Adibe, who at the time was CEO of Ecast, a digital jukebox company.

The Theory of the Long Tail says when the boundaries of time and space disappear, selling small quantities of products from a deep catalog is just as profitable as selling large quantities of products from a small catalog, which is why Amazon can justify selling some products below cost to grow market share. E-commerce removes the physical restrictions imposed by retail and gives life to a new way of doing business.

Long Tail Theory says instead of just targeting one or two high volume search phrases, you're better off generating demand through hundreds of keyword phrases that are relevant to the products you sell. But search engine optimization isn't just for e-commerce. Let's take a look at some other applications.

SEO in Public Affairs

We filter digital information with keywords. SEO strategy is foundational to digital marketing and communications because messages are made of keywords too. Search engine optimization is used in military information operations, investor relations, and public affairs as well. Let's take a look at how a euphemism undermined climate policy action with disastrous consequences.

When I served as special advisor on social media communications to the US Department of State, search volume for the term "global warming" far exceeded searches for "climate change," a term that GOP climate change deniers in the House and Senate saw as far less threatening.

It is unfortunate that climate has become a partisan issue in the US. Fossil fuel industry proponents, plutocrats, and petrostate actors with deep pockets fund the political campaigns of Republican lawmakers, who reciprocate by strategically undermining science to delay regulatory action that addresses global warming.

Meanwhile, Rupert Murdoch's right-wing media empire promotes misinformation on behalf of the Saudis who are major News Corp shareholders. Meanwhile, Mark Zuckerberg plays the innocent bystander role while his platform amplifies lies with impunity. "Facebook's goal of showing people only what they were interested in seeing resulted, within a decade, in the effective end of shared civic reality," writes Jia Tolentino in her book Trick Mirror: Reflections on Self Delusion.

As a result of an unrelenting stream of misinformation, there's a disconnect between the scientific consensus on global warming and public opinion. How it happened is straight-out nefarious. To downplay the dangers of greenhouse gas emissions, GOP lawmakers intentionally popularized a more ambiguous keyword cooked up by a political pollster to mislead voters into believing that global warming is a hoax.

Despite the fact that 97 percent of climate scientists agree that human activity is the cause of global warming,[3] conservative Republicans "are evenly divided over whether to prioritize alternative energy (49 percent) or expand fossil fuel production (49 percent)," according to research from Pew.[4] This is the result of a premeditated keyword strategy.

The litany of public affairs smear campaigns that have undermined regulatory action are painstakingly documented in

3   https://climate.nasa.gov/scientific-consensus/

4   https://www.pewresearch.org/science/2019/11/25/u-s-public-views-on-climate-and-energy/

Merchants of Doubt, a book by Harvard professor Naomi Oreskes and Caltech science historian Erik Conway about how the tobacco, fire retardant, pesticide, and aerosol packaging industries used lies and deception to foster doubt in the minds of voters, so these industries could keep making money from their products without being regulated.

Given the overwhelming scientific consensus, if a US voter says that global warming is inconclusive and that no one knows for sure if or why it's happening, they've been snookered by the fossil fuel industry's war against science, which goes so far as to use focus groups to test language that best alleviates the perception of risk, bot armies to amplify lies on social media, and stolen emails leaked on Wikileaks to try and discredit climate scientists.

Like the tobacco, fire retardant, pesticide, and aerosol packaging industries, fossil fuel proponents leveraged the same group of politically conservative, academically respected scientists they used to cast doubt on the dangers of smoking to deceive the public into believing that climate change is a hoax.

According to the Center for American Progress Action Fund, there were 150 members of the 116th Congress—all Republicans— who said with straight faces that they did not believe the scientific consensus that human activity is making the Earth's climate change. But now, with the undeniable extreme weather impacts of climate change undeniable, the forces of inaction have realized that they can no longer convince enough people that climate change isn't real. So they have turned to a new array of tactics which includes the use of bot armies to game social media, the attempt to distract climate advocates by getting them arguing among themselves about how best to solve the crisis as well as efforts to convince progressives that it's too late to turn back and that the only thing we can do is learn to adapt. "Marco Rubio tries to tell his fellow Floridians that yes, climate change is real, but the solution is to adapt. Does he mean that they should grow gills and fins? Because that's the only way that the millions of people around the world who are displaced by sea level rise will be able to cope with the inundation of the coastlines," says Michael E. Mann PhD, a distinguished atmospheric scientist at Pennsylvania State University who has been vilified for decades by fossil fuel interests and Republican climate deniers for his research, which makes clear to people outside the science community that emissions are causing global warming.

In 2002, a confidential memo by Republican pollster Frank Luntz got leaked to the press. It advised against using the "frightening" phrase "global warming." Up to then, President George W. Bush had used the term in speeches. But after Luntz's memo, he shifted to "climate change." Luntz also wrote, "Voters believe there is no consensus about global warming within the scientific community," which, of course, was not true. "Therefore, you need to continue to make the lack of scientific certainty a primary issue in the debate," he advised. As a result, using the term "global warming" became politically unsafe at the State Department. If you wanted to keep your job you used the term "climate change." Otherwise, you could expect GOP lawmakers to come gunning for you. As a result, the department started using the term "climate change," which was a much lower volume search phrase, on their website.

The "safer" term acknowledged that our climate is changing. But isn't it always? And over the next decade, "climate change" became a higher volume search phrase, while searches for "global warming" dropped. In 2007, there were five searches for "global warming" for every one search for "climate change," a ratio of 5:1. But by January 2021, those numbers flipped. Searches for "climate change" exceeded "global warming" by nearly 3:1. Instead of protecting the planet by regulating the fossil fuel industry, lawmakers regulated their terminology instead.

Doublespeak—a term coined by George Orwell in his book *1984*—is on the rise for the same reason Orwell predicted, to misconstrue the truth. Whether it's euphemism, jargon, gobbledygook, or hyperbolic language, doublespeak is used to distance us from the truth. And it impacts not just what we say and think, but what we search for and how as well.

"We talk about spin," says American linguist William Lutz, "and it's all right to be a spin doctor. But what are we really saying about a spin doctor? A spin doctor sits there and says, 'Oh no, no, no, you didn't hear what you thought you heard. Let me tell you what you really heard,' and proceeds to put a spin on it. And the spin turns out to be something entirely different than what was said." Lutz wrote the Security and Exchange Commission's *Plain English Handbook*, and sixteen other books on the use of clear language.

In a democracy, we decide what policies and candidates to back by listening to the public discourse. If the discussion is carried out in doublespeak with organizations deliberately misleading the people so they don't really know what's going on, we wind up making decisions on the wrong basis. Climate deniers hid the dangers of global warming by using a euphemism to detach science from the truth.

This underhanded strategy effectively neutered the State Department's website from appearing in search results for the term "global warming." The prohibition extended to other US government agencies as well, which made the search results that came up for that term less credible, because at the time, Google considered .gov sites more trusted than .com, .org, or .net domains. The noticeable absence of government-sponsored content only served to confuse people more about the conclusiveness of climate science that proved the planet was warming. Fossil fuel interests promoted doubt into the public consciousness by substituting a less threatening keyword, impacting search results and changing popular perception.

SEO in E-commerce

If you're in e-commerce, you want to avoid doublespeak and embrace popular language. Call yourself whatever words most people associate with what you sell. Using a euphemism like "low-cost leader" when everyone's searching "cheap" is like calling kick ass chili "Almost Angus." Promote yourself as the "low cost leader" in paid media all you like. But when it comes to SEO, or SEM for that matter, embrace high search volume keywords.

If people are inserting the keyword modifier "cheap" before whatever it is you're selling, and you don't optimize for that by using the word "cheap" in your web copy because you think it disparages your brand, you're going to lose that customer to whomever is willing to optimize for that keyword. When you pivot to digital, the keywords you use impact both popular perception *and* profitability.

An HR manager wants to differentiate her company from other employers by saying her company doesn't just give you a job; it gives you a career. She thinks it sounds better. But it doesn't because for every five searches for "jobs" there's only one search for "careers." It's fine to embrace both terms. But from a SEO perspective, she should lead with the higher volume phrase.

How do you know what "high volume" is? There are all sorts of free and paid tools online that you can use to measure the volume of search phrases. Google the term "keyword research" for a current list of providers. These tools tell you which keywords get searched most. You can compare mortgage to loan, couch to sofa, and coffee shop to diner and see which ones get searched most by geography.

SEO requires letting go of corporate lingo. We search how we think. There are 50,000 searches a month for "kids movies new." There are only 1,300 searches a month for "children's movies out now," and only twenty searches a month for "new children's films" with or without the apostrophe.

When I was SEOing a web page for the home entertainment division of a Hollywood movie studio, our keyword research showed us that "DVD kids" was the phrase to rank for. But no one says "DVD kids," they say "DVDs for kids" or "DVDs kids love."

But the phrase we wanted to rank for wasn't "DVDs for kids" or "DVDs kids love." It was "DVD kids." So I included the phrase "... a DVD kids love ..." in the headline, and we were coming up on page one of Google search results for "DVD kids" in a couple of weeks.

Of course, there is a caveat to all of this thinking, and that is quite simply the speed and nature of change when it comes to search technology and advances in artificial intelligence driving them. The jury is out on the degree to which keyword variations matter these days. As artificial intelligence gets better and becomes more important in Google's algorithm, we may find that these sorts of tweaks will ultimately become insignificant. No one knows for sure. But one thing is certain. SEO starts with keyword research. And the goal is to get found when people search the terms and phrases they associate with what you sell.

SEO in Media Relations

When Congress was preparing to put Medicare Part D into effect in 2005, which was a federal program to help seniors with out-of-pocket expenses for medications, I put an SEO strategy together for AARP to get local healthcare reporters outside DC covering the proposed legislation in order to raise nationwide awareness of the program. My client wanted local reporters, rather than just national healthcare reporters, covering the proposed regulation, writing about Medicare Part D.

I analyzed the text from the previous three months of articles written by local healthcare reporters. I did the same thing for the national healthcare reporters in the US. And I ran the text through a keyword density analyzer to see what words each group used most frequently. (Search "density analyzer" online and you'll find a bunch of free tools you can use to create word clouds from raw text.)

By visualizing the keyword density, I learned pretty quickly that local reporters didn't cover healthcare policy at all. The keyword "healthcare" almost never appeared in their coverage. Instead, local reporters were covering what was happening in their local hospitals. For local reporters, the keyword "hospital" was the most popular term in their coverage.

So before AARP sent their experts to Capitol Hill to testify on Medicare Part D, I went through their congressional testimony transcripts and added the keywords "hospital," "hospitals," "patients," "children's hospital," as well as the names of many major metro hospitals. Back then, repeating keywords several times was a best practice, as long as you could do so without negatively impacting readability. Today, keyword density is less of a factor. Whoever says the same thing in the most different number of ways generally scores highest for relevance. But again, the Google algorithm is secret so the degree to which these types of thing matter is in constant flux.

Generally speaking, written testimonies to Congress can only be submitted electronically. So after the AARP experts testified, we submitted testimonies optimized for local healthcare reporters. Under the Freedom of Information Act, those testimonies must be shared publicly, which means they are available online.

Sure enough, local healthcare reporters found them. And we saw a flurry of local mainstream media news coverage on Medicare

Part D outside of the DC beltway. News about the impending program spurred a whirlwind of discussion and widespread awareness among seniors, and Medicare Part D became a benefit. Now, seniors can enroll in a supplemental drug plan that lowers their prescription drug costs, a real benefit to those living on a fixed income. And SEO played a role.

So as you can see, search engine optimization is a foundational strategic communications discipline that can be used to support political agendas, e-commerce marketing and everything in between. But if everyone's using the same keywords, how does Google decide which sites to rank on page one?

Inbound Links

The most successful news break I was ever a part of involved a Silicon Valley CEO who was releasing groundbreaking technology that threatened to disrupt an entire industry.

This CEO, who will remain nameless, had previously founded and sold a company he'd built for a lot of money. The kind of money that pays for private jets and multiple homes all over the world. He was loaded, smart as a whip, and well-known by tech reporters.

Prior to releasing the news about his new technology, we briefed all the top industry analysts and journalists under a news embargo, which means they would get advance access to the news in exchange for agreeing not to publish their story before a certain date.

Under a news embargo, no one gets a scoop, but everyone who's anyone from the *New York Times* to the Associated Press is on it and has the time to prepare detailed coverage that they can release when the embargo lifts. On the day our embargo lifted, our news was everywhere, including page A1 of the *New York Times* and the cover of the Marketplace section in the *Wall Street Journal.*

Prior to our news break, when you searched the CEO's name, a story came up on page one accusing him of financial skullduggery at a previous business. My client had sued the business magazine over the article for defamation and won. But nevertheless, the story remained on page one when you searched his name, staining his reputation in the court of public opinion.

But we had a dozen national stories break on the day we lifted the embargo, which led to a snowball of news coverage. And after that, when you searched his name, the older, false story was nowhere to be found. All the new coverage from the embargo pushed the old story down so far down in the rankings that you couldn't find it anymore. We thought we were home free.

But six months later, that pesky article showed up on page one again when you searched his name because of a single, high-authority backlink. We've talked a lot about what makes content topically relevant. But we haven't talked about why some sites rank higher than others. The reason is backlinks. Let's get into that now.

Google beat Yahoo! at the search game by treating links from one website to another (called backlinks or inbound links) like votes and ranking sites accordingly. The more links to your site from other sites with lots of backlinks, the more authoritative you are in the eyes of Google. Yahoo! had been using keyword density to rank search results. But that was easily gameable.

Unscrupulous marketers would repeat a keyword a hundred times on the bottom of the page in white text on a white background and presto, they'd rank number one. And that meant the usefulness and relevancy of Yahoo's rankings declined, because dickhead marketers started keyword stuffing their pages making it harder to find good information.

When Larry Page and Sergey Brin were at Stanford, they realized that the best pages on the Stanford intranet were the ones people were linking to most. So they devised an algorithm that treated links like recommendations and ranked results accordingly. There were other factors too, but backlinks—which are the same as inbound links—were central to their approach.

Now that you understand the concept of backlinks, let's return to the embargo news break about the Silicon Valley CEO that temporarily pushed down the old smear story that had been showing up when you googled his name. We analyzed all the backlinks from other websites that were transiting to the negative article, and we saw that one of the backlinks was from Stanford.edu. We contacted the person who had published the link, made our case for removing it, and they complied. Once the inbound link was removed, the old story disappeared forever from that CEO's search results. Now, when you search his name, it's nowhere to be found.

If Google treats links like recommendations and we had links from the top news media organizations in the world, why would a single inbound link from Stanford be seen as more powerful than the combined links from all those news organizations? The answer is: not all inbound links are equal. Some links are more influential than others. Generally speaking .mil links beat .gov links, .gov links beat .edu links, and .edu links beat everything else. Try getting an inbound link from a .mil or .gov. Not so easy.

A link from a .edu is a little easier to secure, but still much tougher than getting a backlink from a commercial entity. But since Google was invented at Stanford.edu, my guess is there's no inbound link quite as powerful as an inbound link from Stanford.edu. That may be the coup de grâce. But again, as artificial intelligence improves, I expect these factors to become less important over time, particularly if Google is able to get smart enough to make truth a ranking factor. We're not there yet, but they're working on it.

By using keywords that Google considers topically related to one another—and you do that by searching a term, noting the related searches, and using those related terms on your text—you demonstrate relevance and make it easy for Google to index your site categorically. But attracting inbound links from other websites to your own is how you earn top rankings. And the more inbound links, the more authority you have. And a website with a ton of inbound links coming to it has more authority than a website with one or two backlinks. For that reason, links from sites that publish news are high-authority, because people talk about and link to news articles. And high-authority links lift your rankings more than low authority links. A backlink from the *Wall Street Journal* has much more authority than a backlink from my blog.

There's more to it than that. But at a high level, SEO is about researching and selecting the right keywords, using them on your site, and getting other sites to link those keywords back to you.

First, you need to choose the right keywords. And second, you need to get other people to link those keywords back to you by creating and publishing the very best content for that search term.

But it takes time, resources, and money to create the best content for a keyword. And it's hard work. People want quick and easy solutions, so there's a whole underground industry of deviant SEOs out there maintaining link farms they call blog networks, which are really just a bunch of sites with crappy or mediocre sites linking to each other in an effort to game search. Beware of vendors that sell backlinks because Google considers links from these types of sites to be toxic.

Inbound links from toxic domains can have a negative impact on your search rankings. Even if you don't buy inbound links from toxic domains, popular sites still wind up attracting toxic inbound links. Deviant SEOs publish backlinks to high authority sites to try and make themselves look legitimate to Google's algorithm. Semrush monitors your inbounds links so you can disavow the toxic ones, which is essentially a way of telling Google that the toxic domains linking to you are worthless.

If you want to rank number one for a term, search that term. Read the top four ranking pages and ask yourself, "Can I create better content?" The way to rank number one for a term is quite simply by having the best content for that term. If you've got the best content in a category, people will find it, link to it, and spend time on it. And all that boosts your search rankings.

Brand Search Optimization

In 2005, another guy named Eric Schwartzman launched a blog about his experience as the father of children that are legally and emotionally his own but not biologically. Before he was married, the other Eric Schwartzman "learned that his lifetime goal of becoming a father was slim, if not impossible." With help of medical science, a donor, and credit cards, he and his wife were blessed with children. On his blog, he called himself a DI dad. DI stands for donor insemination.

Back then, when you searched Eric Schwartzman, Google ranked my consulting website first, and his blog second. The other Eric Schwartzman and I have never met, but we have forwarded email that we've mistakenly received to one another over the years.

I am happy for the other Eric Schwartzman. And I respect his right to talk about his experience as a DI dad. But now and again, people would confuse me with him in meetings. I don't want to say it was embarrassing, because it wasn't. And it was an easily resolvable case of mistaken identity.

But what if it *had* been a case of mistaken identity that killed a business opportunity? Or, what if negative comments on some review site ranked just below your website when people searched your brand? If you call yourself a thought leader and someone's obituary outranks your website, will people be convinced you're the authority you say you are? If Google doesn't recognize you as an authority, are you really as well regarded as you think you are? Brand search optimization is a less-discussed part of SEO that has more to do with reputation management than e-commerce, but it's no less important.

When you search for an answer to a problem, Google shows you the best results it can find. If you search a brand name, Google shows you the best information it can find about that brand.

Since we trust Google to show us the most relevant results, brand search has a direct impact on our perception and opinion of that brand. Brand search drives first impressions. "With brand search, you're trying to present yourself in the best possible light when someone searches your brand name," says Jason Barnard, a Paris-based SEO expert specializing in brand search.

If a negative review about your brand ranks second or third, that tarnishes your reputation. Yet marketers invest heavily in search engine optimization of their sites for unbranded keywords without giving much thought to brand search engine optimization. If you're Dunkin' Donuts and people search "dunkin donuts" on Google, that's a branded search. But if they search "donuts near me," that's an unbranded search. While the unbranded term has greater potential to drive customers, the branded term has greater potential to impact popular perception. Instead of putting all your eggs in the unbranded SEO basket to get found by people who are problem- and solution-aware, realize that once they become brand-aware, you may need to clear that hurdle as well.

If you want to control your reputation, you want to dominate the entire first page of search results when someone searches your brand. It's not enough to just rank number one for your name. At a minimum, you want your website to rank first and your social media accounts to rank under it. If you can dominate your page one search results, you can push your competitors and questionable results to page two or three, which is a ghost town because almost no one looks beyond page one.

Some brands have much better search engine results pages than others. Search the word "Google," and check out their search results. I'm assuming that since they're the company behind search, they have the best brand search results.

Not only does Google.com rank number one, but they have sub-links under it to the different sections of their website so you can go straight to your Gmail, image search, or news search from their brand search results.

The second result is their corporate blog, where they write about their products, culture, and research and development. The third result is their Twitter account, and instead of just seeing a link to their profile, you see their last three tweets in boxes right there in the search results.

The fourth and fifth links both lead to www.about.google.com, a content marketing microsite with more company and product information. Sixth is their Wikipedia page. Seventh is *Think with Google*, where they share market research they conduct to promote their revenue-generating products.

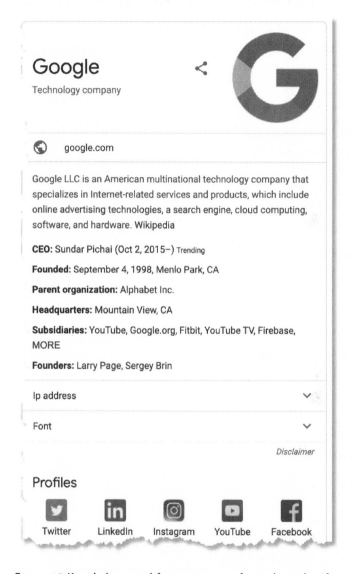

Figure 4.3 Knowledge panel from page one of search results. If you search the keyword "google," this panel appears in the upper right-hand corner of the search results page. Knowledge panels list factual information about brands.

On the right-hand side is a special box called the *knowledge panel* (see fig. 4.3) with factual information about Google, like the date they were founded, their CEO, and their social media profiles.

As expected, if you search the word "google," every link on page one of their brand search results is about them. They control it. But for most brands, at some point in the customer journey, people are probably going to search your name/company name, and what they find can kill or seal the deal.

Keep in mind, if you're logged into your Gmail when you search, Google customizes the results you see based on your search history. To check your brand search results, you have to do an incognito search.

Getting Your Social Profiles Ranking

You can help Google figure out which social media profiles are yours by adding what's called *structured data markup*[5] to your homepage. It sounds more complicated than it is. You're basically just adding some instructions to your website that make it easier for Google to understand which social media profiles are associated with your web domain.

If you have a WordPress site, you don't need a programmer. You can do it yourself. Figure 4.4 shows you where to add your social media account URLs to your user profile in WordPress.

---

5   https://support.google.com/webmasters/answer/3069489?hl=en

Figure 4.4 At this time of writing, you can find this WordPress 5.6 screen in the left-hand menu under Users. Next, select your user name.

If you use the popular SEO plugin Yoast, figure 4.5 shows you where to add links to your social media profiles to generate schema to help Google associate your social media profiles with your website.

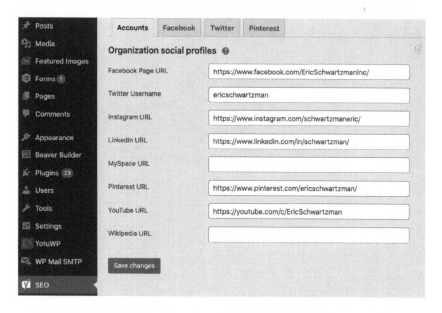

Figure 4.5 At this time of writing, WordPress users with the Yoast plugin installed can find this screen at SEO > Social.

WordPress translates your entries into code called schema that tells Google which social networking profiles to associate with your brand. Schema is Google's preferred language for indexing websites. Make sure you use your brand name as your social networking profile account name. Also, use similar images for your profile picture, the same description, and reference the same web domain.

Repetition is key. Keep all your profile information consistent so it's easier for Google to verify that they all belong to the same brand. If you've got a Knowledge Panel, structured data also helps Google add your social profiles to it.

Knowledge Panels

Only some brands have a box that appears on the right of their search engine results page called a knowledge panel, which showcases information about their brand that Google considers to be factual.

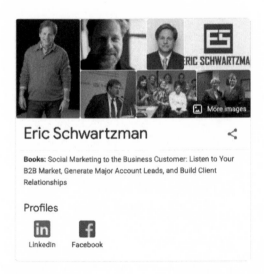

Figure 4.6 Eric Schwartzman's knowledge panel, which appears in the upper right-hand corner on Google when you search "eric schwartzman."

On brand search engine results pages, the organic links on the left-hand side are recommendations. The right-hand side displays factual information in a knowledge panel.

For more examples of what knowledge panels packed with factual info look like, search any major brand like Apple or Disney. But don't confuse a knowledge panel with a Google My Business listing. They look kind of the same, but GMB listings have ratings and reviews and knowledge panels don't. Anyone can set up a GMB listing. But not every brand gets a knowledge panel.

Knowledge panels are generated automatically[6] by Google's algorithm. Information that appears in them comes from various sources across the web.

One surefire way to get a knowledge panel is through the creation of a Wikipedia entry. But this is ill-advised because creating your own Wikipedia page is against their conflict of interest policy which plainly states: "Conflict of interest (COI) editing involves contributing to Wikipedia about yourself, family, friends, clients, employers, or your financial and other relationships." Furthermore, Wikipedia entries "must be written from a neutral point of view (NPOV), which means representing fairly, proportionately, and, as far as possible, without editorial bias ..." and none of that is possible if you violate the COI policy.

Wikipedia publishes no original information. They summarize "all the significant views that have been published by reliable sources on a topic." Without reliable articles to link to, there's no

6   https://support.google.com/knowledgepanel/answer/9163198?dark=1

justification for adding a new article. Wikipedia is an encyclopedia, not a vanity press.

This is one reason why there's tremendous value in retaining a competent public relations consultant when it comes to online reputation management. Earned media coverage is the public record behind a Wikipedia page, and Wikipedia pages are a surefire way to get a knowledge panel.

Securing news media coverage is a long haul. But a smart digital public relations strategy (more on that in Chapter 10) is getting press coverage to serve as source material for a Wikipedia page, which in turn gets you a Google knowledge panel. If

Figure 4.7. Zoom Video Communications knowledge panel appears screen right when your search "Zoom" on Google.

your public relations consultant can generate enough third-party news coverage, the visibility of that coverage may be short-lived in a Google search. But if it serves as source material for a Wikipedia page, its value is extended indefinitely. And it can also help you get more people backlinking to your site.

Keep in mind, you need to generate factual source material that Google trusts. In practice this means that online influencer blog posts and social media shares aren't as legit as articles published by recognizable news media brands or books with the imprint of a respected publisher. You can see which news outlets Google considers reputable by searching Google News and checking which sites are indexed. You can't force the knowledge panel to display something that's not corroborated by the majority of information on the web.

According to Amit Singhal, SVP of engineering at Google, "Google's Knowledge Graph isn't just rooted in public sources such as Freebase, Wikipedia, and the CIA World Factbook. It's also augmented at a much larger scale—because we're focused on comprehensive breadth and depth. It currently contains more than 500 million objects, as well as more than 3.5 billion facts about and relationships between these different objects. And it's tuned based on what people search for, and what we find out on the web."[7]

Featured Snippets & People Also Ask

Brian Dean of Backlinko coined the term *skyscraper technique*, which is an SEO strategy that involves analyzing high-ranking content and writing something better—often longer, fresher, and more comprehensive—on the topic.

The skyscraper technique is essentially about overwhelming the reader with an encyclopedia-style article that covers everything under

---

7   https://blog.google/products/search/introducing-knowledge-graph-things-not/

the sun related to that search term. For content creators, this approach is a significant investment. And the articles are often composed of dense copy blocks that can provoke a TL;DR (too long didn't read) response.

So while writing a definitive 10,000-word article can be an effective SEO strategy, it's not always so helpful to someone searching for quick answers. If you search "what is the skyscraper technique in seo" you probably want a quick answer, not the Magna Carta. So Google added feature snippets to their search results pages to save you from having to skim through long-form content to find a short, crisp answer.

Figure 4.8 shows a featured snippet I got for my client Halleck Vineyard, a Sonoma Coast winery that makes an award-winning dry White Zinfandel.

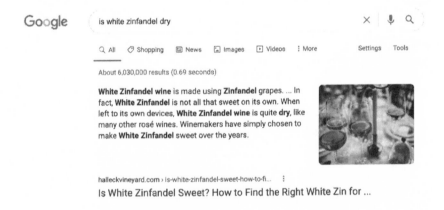

Figure 4.8 The featured snippet is the excerpt at the top of the search engine
page results screen, pictured when you search
"is white zinfandel dry."

A featured snippet (see fig. 4.8) is an excerpt in a box that appears at the top of the search results. Featured snippets are automatically generated by Google to answer the searcher's question right then and there, without having to exit the search results page. The publisher responsible for the excerpt gets additional brand exposure by means of the URL, which in this case is halleckvineyard.com. But the text included in the featured snippet is determined by Google.

You get featured snippets by creating content that answers questions like "what is ..." "how to ..." and "where is ..." that people search on Google. If you start typing a question into Google, the autosuggestions that appear are examples of questions people commonly ask Google. There's another feature that appears in search results called the "people also ask" box which gives you more insight into the questions people are searching. Featured snippets and "people also ask" results protect you from having to hunt through long articles for simple answers.

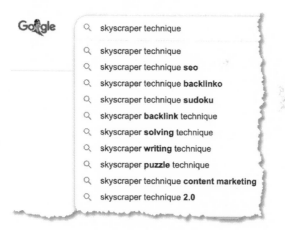

Figure 4.9 When you search a keyword like "skyscraper technique," Google autosuggest provides similar search phrases, any of which you can click on to search that term.

Being cited in organic search results, knowledge panels, feature snippets, and "people also ask" boxes as a source on topics related to your area of expertise is a powerful testimonial from Google because you're being recognized as a preeminent thought leader.

Video Search Engine Optimization

If you embed YouTube videos on your site, you can optimize them for brand search, too. If you get it right, your reward is a video carousel on your search results page. You can also get your videos ranking in Google Video search and YouTube. Since YouTube tries to increase user session time by automatically showing you more videos that are similar to the one you're watching, it's a good idea to also optimize the title, description, and tags of the videos you upload to YouTube against their autosuggest recommendations, which will be different from the autosuggestions in Google search. Jason Barnard, the brand SEO specialist I mentioned earlier has his videos ranking on page one of his Google search results (see fig. 4.10) when you search his name.

Figure 4.10 Videos of Jason Barnard appear in Google search results when you search his name.

Yoast, the WordPress SEO plugin I mentioned earlier, also has a video optimization feature that makes it easier for Google to associate videos with your brand by generating a video sitemap on your website. When you install their Video SEO plugin and re-index your site, it generates a video sitemap to help Google index your videos like this:

XML Video Sitemap

Generated by the Video SEO plugin for Yoast's Yoast SEO plugin, this is an XML Video Sitemap. Google

This sitemap contains 59 URLs.

Video	Title	Description
	B2B Marketing at SXSW through Keynotes and Panels	B2B Marketing at SXSW takes many forms, from trade show exhibits to parties to swag. But the best B2B marketing opportunities at SXSW come from influencing the influencers from the podium. To be most ...
	Harnessing Virtual Reality for High Impact Teachable Moments	Could virtual reality (VR) help is recover from trauma, enhance our empathic capacities, end climate change and someday even bring us world peace?
	Inside the Institute of the Future with Marina Gorbis	Marina Gorbis (@mgorbis) is executive director of the Institute of the Future and author of The Nature of the Future. In this podcast, she talks about how technology is changing the world of educatio ...
	3 Easy Ways to Boost PR Performance in Lean Times	The coronavirus pandemic will forever change how information workers collaborate. While we're all working separately from home, our fate as a species has never been more connected. What's the use of t ...
	Los Angeles PR Agency Leaders Share COVID-19 Communications Advice	For PR Tech Wednesdays this week, I organized a panel of Los Angeles Public Relations agency leaders featuring Bob Gold of Bob Gold & Associates and Kimberly Goodnight of Media Playground PR to ta ...

Figure 4.11 Video sitemap generated by Yoast for ericschwartzman.com. This page lives on my website, but isn't listed in the navigation, so you can't get there by visiting my site. That's intentional. This video sitemap is only there to help Google index the video content on my website for their search algorithm.

Video sitemaps (see fig. 4.11) help Google associate the videos on a website with a brand by publishing schema that makes it easy for Google to index the videos for relevance, kind of like structured data markup. More specifically, schema is a semantic vocabulary that makes it easier for Google to read and represent your site in search results. If you're using a modern content management platform like WordPress, Shopify, or Squarespace you don't have to do anything to publish schema. It's handled for you automatically.

Corporate vs. Personal Brand SEO

On the personal branding side, it's worth noting that you'll never be able to effectively SEO yourself without your own website. Unless the name of your company is your name, you and your company or employer are not the same entity. If it's a company you own and it has another name, Google will see you and your company as separate entities. If you're a thought leader or consultant, this is a really good reason to use your personal name as your site URL.

In this case, your name is your personal brand and people search it. Unless you have a personal web site—even just a one-pager—your personal brand is not being managed. Red Sox fans register their kids for season tickets the day they're born. I bought my son the URL for his name when he was one year old. I paid for it until he's eighteen. After that, he's on his own.

Your goal is to get your personal site ranking number one when people search your name. If you're active on Twitter, you get engagement from your followers, and you're publishing schema, that should trigger Twitter boxes when people search your name with your most recent tweets.

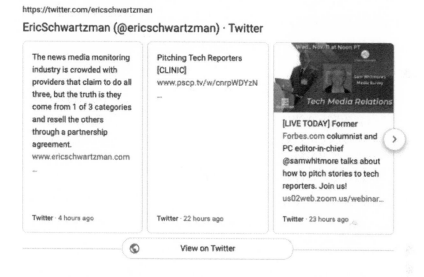

Figure 4.12 Twitter boxes showing my last three tweets appear in my brand search results when you search "eric schwartzman" on Google.

Putting It All Together

Gaetano DiNardi leads growth marketing at Nextiva, a company that sells voice over IP phone systems. His job is to get their site to come up first when someone searches "cloud phone system." It does now. But it wasn't always that way.

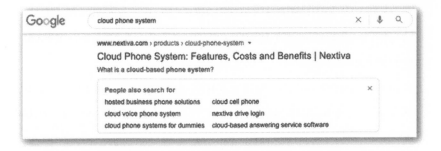

Figure 4.13 At this time of writing, nextiva.com has the number one organic ranking for the search term "cloud phone system" on Google.

He started by building out a landing page where he could convert traffic into leads. Because there's no point driving traffic if you're not set up to convert it. He wrote engaging copy for the page, copy that focused on the problems his cloud phone system solves. He did his research and made sure to use the right keywords. Anticipating the questions visitors to the page may have, he spelled out all the details about the features, cost, and benefits they might want to know.

Once DiNardi had an optimized landing page up and running, he went to work to try to get people to link to him. He reached out to other webmasters and asked them to link the phrase "cloud phone system" back to his landing page. Contributing guest blog posts to reputable websites that exercise editorial control over who gets published is a great way to get backlinks. It's the main reason why guest blogging is popular among digital marketers. Marketers write free content for other sites in exchange for a backlink. DiNardi links the phrase "cloud phone system" in his guest blog posts back to his landing page. Note that as a guest blogger, you are in a sense "borrowing" the authority of the blog, generating an organic backlink, and avoiding any issues with Google not trusting the site. A threefer.

Before you pitch guest post ideas to editors of high-authority blogs, it's a good idea to establish yourself as a competent writer first. I receive pitches daily from marketers who want to submit a guest post for my blog. But most of the time, their submissions are so full of nothingness that I can't use them. Unless I can find previous articles they've written that have some value, I usually don't respond.

Ideally, I want to see content they're publishing at the same domain as their email address. That way, it's more likely they actually wrote it, and that they're subject matter experts and not just SEO drudges at an overseas blog factory. I qualify guest bloggers by checking out their website first.

Next, I check their social media followers to see what kind of engagement they have around their content. Your followers are social proof that your content resonates with a community. I want posts from people with engaged followers because that improves the chances of their content resonating with my audience. Social media marketing comes after owned media marketing. Once they have a following and the other influencers in your space know them, I'm going to be much interested in their guest post submission.

Keep in mind that for DiNardi, a term like "cloud phone system" costs around $55 a click on Google Ads. If he can rank for that term organically in natural search results, he gets those clicks in perpetuity for free. It's not really free though, because he has to do a lot of work to get there. Still, instead of buying one click, he's investing in an annuity that will continue to pay rewards over time, and that annuity is a clickstream. So even when he runs out of advertising budget, the visitors will keep coming. It's like the difference between buying vegetables at the market versus growing them yourself, which is why it's called organic search—you're growing your traffic organically.

The goal is to dominate the search results for all keywords that are relevant to the problems you solve. Through repetition, your brand gets repeated exposure, which improves your chances of breaking through, getting noticed, and the visits, leads, and sales that go with that.

You want people to keep seeing your website over and over when they search different terms related to your space. They keep seeing you in their search results. They find your podcast, your videos, your tweets, and your blog posts. They just keep seeing your site come up. You become "top of mind." And through that process, they understand that you're a player in their space, and they click.

Hopefully, they buy something from you at some point. But people rarely buy a considered purchase on the spot. They do research first. If you're a realtor, what do home buyers want to know when they're looking for a house and what kind of SEO-optimized content can you generate to answer their questions when they search? If you're a B2B, what do you need to explain to those prospective business customers to prove your value?

SEO is really just about optimizing as many avenues of discoverability as possible. If you're generating high quality content marketing, you're going to win in the long run. But it's a marathon. And you can't give up too quickly.

Voice Search Engine Optimization

Voice search has been rising gradually over the years. With voice search enabled, you can do a hands-free search by asking a mobile device or a digital assistant a question. Voice search is an emerging technology, and voice search optimization is a moving target.

China and Russia have their own voice search platforms, but penetration there is still quite low. So English is the dominant language for voice search. The tech companies, algorithms, ranking factors, and information sources that power voice search are all in a continual state of flux that's not in the purview of a long-form business book like this. Nevertheless, at the time of this writing, one in every four searches conducted is a voice search, and half of all voice searches are for local businesses, according to research from Semrush, which publishes an annual voice search study.

Half of all voice searches are informational queries, like "how to," "what is," and "why are." The other half are for local businesses.

Voice search brands are Google Assistant, Apple Siri, and Amazon Alexa, which all use different algorithms to retrieve and play back answers they pull from various data sources. For answers to informational queries like, "How long does it take to boil an egg?", Google Assistant reads answers from the top three "people also ask" results. About 12 percent of all voice search answers on Google Assistant are taken from "people also ask" content.

When Google reads the answers to informational questions, it cites the source of that information by saying "according to" and naming the URL or publisher. So voice search is a brand authority opportunity, particularly for people or brands who want to be considered experts in a category.

When it comes to local business search, Google Assistant uses Google My Business listings and Google Maps for relevance, and determines rank based on proximity and star ratings.

Voice search is hardware specific. Apple Siri is exclusive to Apple devices. Google Assistant is exclusive to Android devices. Alexa is exclusive to Echo devices. They're all proprietary.

Siri provides informational answers by synthesizing results from Google and Bing organic search results. And it's the best voice search engine for finding music, according to the most recent voice search study from Semrush. For local business questions, Siri uses Yelp star ratings first and proximity on Apple Maps second to determine ranking. The number of reviews does not appear to be a ranking factor at this time. But star ratings are.

Google Assistant and Apple Siri are the leading voice search providers. Amazon Alexa is more for voice commands like turning on a light or searching for products on Amazon. "We asked thousands of queries to Google, Siri, and Alexa, and Alexa couldn't answer 23 percent of our questions," says Olga Adrienko, VP of brand marketing at Semrush. For local queries, Alexa relies on Yelp and Yext.

Spoken word answers average forty-two words. To optimize for voice search, focus on getting featured snippets and the Local

Pack (see fig. 4.14), which is a search results feature that appears on page one for any query with a local intent. Search any local business category like "dentists" or "accountants" and you'll see a pack of local results. To optimize content for voice search, try to keep your answers to forty words and make sure your site loads fast. Sites that load fifteen times faster than average websites are more likely to be included in voice search results.

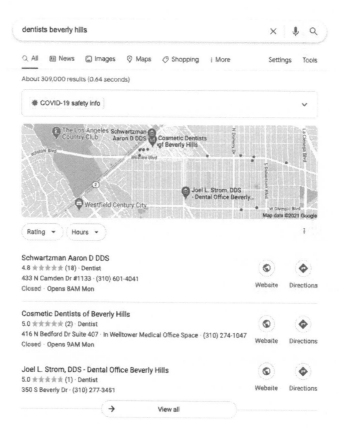

Figure 4.14 A Local Pack in Google search showing the top three results for the query "dentists beverly hills." Aaron Schwartzman is an excellent dentist who happens to be my cousin.

Now that you know the basics of SEO, let's take a look at what makes online content go viral.

CHAPTER 5

The Laws of Virality

It was not because of social media that Tunisian street vendor Mohamed Bouazizi set himself on fire. He did it to protest the confiscation of his wares by a municipal inspector who forbade him from setting up shop beside a government building.

But it was the viral nature of social media that made his self-immolation the spark that ignited the Tunisian Revolution and emboldened activists in other Arab nations to protest autocracy. On social media, posts about Bouazizi's self-sacrifice struck an emotional chord with millions of young digital natives who used their mobiles phones and Facebook, YouTube, and Twitter to trigger a digital protest that destabilized the governments of the region. If you share something on social media and everyone who sees it passes it along to their followers, your share goes viral. And that's precisely what happened. Protesters shared the news of Bouazizi's self-sacrifice with more than one of their connections, which sent it viral. Within a month, Tunisia's president had fled in exile while the rest of the Arab world watched.

Like a wildfire, social media fanned the flames as revolutionary fervor spread to Libya, Yemen, Oman, Egypt, Syria, and Morocco. It gave rise to the Arab Spring which saw more despots deposed amid violent uprisings, insurgencies, and civil wars.

The virality of the outcry on social media was the catalyst, but not the cause. As Steve Coll wrote in *The New Yorker*, "… youthful populations, high unemployment, grotesque inequality, abusive police, reviled leaders, and authoritarian systems" ignited the intifada.

But social media was the platform that turned one man's suffering in Tunisia into an uprising that spread throughout the entire Arab world. It was social media through which news about the movement was passed organically from one person to the next at a scale that made these anti-government protests impossible to ignore. And it was social media that fed the hopes and dreams of those hungry for opportunity and freedom.

Hundreds of thousands of Egyptians took to the streets to protest the injustices of President Hosni Mubarak. Even a state-sponsored internet blackout couldn't stop anti-government demonstrators from forcing Mubarak to step down in just eighteen days. According to a story in the *Economic Times*, the Arab states were caught flat footed but "… have since caught up in the digital arms race, adding cyber surveillance, online censorship and troll armies to their arsenals." But at the time, the so-called Arab Spring offered a glimmer of hope.

When a message goes viral online, it can make and break nations. In the case of the Tunisian street vendor, rampant injustice was the reality that led to the uprising. But as politicians get more sophisticated in the use of social media to promote their agendas, real injustice isn't required. Donald Trump used the virality of social media to amplify lies and deceive millions of Americans into believing that his 2020 loss to Joseph Biden was due to a rigged election.

Before his Facebook and Twitter accounts were shut down, Trump tweeted the word "rigged" seventy-five times in a campaign to gin up false charges of electoral fraud[1] that resulted in a failed coup d'état. Despite the lack of evidence and sixty-two failed legal attempts to overturn the election results, after months of stolen election claims, Trump assembled his supporters for a rally at the White House on January 6, 2021, which was the day Congress was set to certify the results of the US presidential election. In a fiery speech, Trump told the crowd, "We fight like hell. And if you don't fight like hell, you're not going to have a country anymore." He whipped his supporters into a frenzy and told them to go down to the Capitol and "make your voices heard."

His efforts resulted in a lynch mob that erected gallows with a noose and stormed the Capitol chanting "Hang Mike Pence" because Pence had rejected Trump's demand to overturn the election. Vice President Pence narrowly escaped, but the mob

---

1   https://www.usatoday.com/in-depth/news/politics/elections/2021/01/06/trumps-failed-efforts-overturn-election-numbers/4130307001/

temporarily halted the official counting of the votes certifying Trump's loss to Biden. Bizarre and grotesque as it is, in this example, no proof of wrongdoing was required. Instead, Trump was able to leverage the virality of social networks, the support of the right-wing news media, and fabricated legal claims that had been rejected by the courts to seduce his voters into believing a free and fair election had been stolen.

"There is no evidence that any voting system deleted or lost votes, changed votes, or was in any way compromised,"[2] according to a statement from the US Election Infrastructure Council on Cybersecurity, a US Federal agency led by Trump appointee Chris Krebs, who was dismissed for publicly rejecting Trump's fraudulent election conspiracy theories.

Out of the fear of a viral flogging from Trump on Twitter, Republican lawmakers in the House and Senate kept quiet, while Trump used the courts to mount legal challenges that went nowhere, even in courtrooms where he had appointed the judges. So powerful was his viral propaganda campaign in convincing his supporters that his loss was the result of a stolen election, that even after a recording of a phone call was released of Trump pressuring Georgia's top election official—a Republican no less—to overturn the state's presidential results,[3] Trump's supporters still believed that the election had been stolen. Social media was the bullhorn he used to amplify an unrelenting drumbeat of misinformation. Long

2   https://www.cisa.gov/news/2020/11/12/joint-statement-elections-infrastructure-government-coordinating-council-election

3   https://www.npr.org/transcripts/953012128

before Trump lost the US Electoral College, he was on the offensive on social media calling mail-in ballots "unconstitutional," "dangerous," and rife with "fraud."

A Tale of Two Viruses

To stop the spread of the coronavirus, states were expanding mail-in voting. Out of concern that making it easier to vote would result in his loss, Trump went on the offensive to suppress the vote distorting the facts about mail-in voting. His tweets sparked a viral deluge of misinformation online that was amplified by the social networking algorithms.

That's right, just like Google has a secret algorithm they use to determine their rankings, social networks have algorithms they use to rank the shares you see in your newsfeed. You're not seeing the most recent posts. You're seeing the most engaging posts as measured by the number of comments, likes, and shares they receive. Obviously, the more emotionally charged a post on social media is, they more likely it is to spark passions that result in engagement.

With social networks amplifying a firehose of misinformation, it's no wonder people were confused. In a video that was viewed 350,0000, Terrence K. Williams, a politically conservative comedian, told his three million Facebook followers "If you mail in your vote, your vote will be in Barack Obama's fireplace."[4] Anti-Muslim activist Pamela Geller told her more than one million Facebook followers, "Mail-in ballots guarantee that the Democrats will

---

4   https://www.salon.com/2020/07/19/outright-lies-voting-misinformation-flourishes-on-facebook_partner/

commit voter fraud," and Peggy Hubbard, a Navy vet and police officer warned on Facebook that "Your democracy, your freedom is being stripped away from you, and if you allow that then everything this country stood for, fought for, bled for, is all in vain."[5] The result was misinformation that incited civil disobedience and voter suppression, the latter of which is nothing new in the US. The weaponization of social media merely continued that thread.

A master of media manipulation, Trump, by stirring up his followers with carefully crafted, emotionally charged messages designed to infuriate his base, demonstrated that social media cuts both ways. While it was harnessed by pro-democracy organizers in the Arab world in pursuit of freedom, it was also used by Trump in his quest for autocracy. Today, we see demagogues using social media to promote doubt, spread conspiracy theories, game financial markets, and undermine the core tenets of democracy.

The virality of social media is a signal to the free world that it's time to make mainstream and social media outlets accountable to the truth. As long as commercial enterprises can profit from the spread of lies with impunity, the free world is at risk.

The period "which we are living through now, introduces epistemic chaos caused by the profit-driven algorithmic amplification, dissemination, and microtargeting of corrupt information, much of it produced by coordinated schemes of disinformation. Its effects are felt in the real world, where they splinter shared reality, poison social discourse, paralyze democratic politics and

5   https://www.propublica.org/article/outright-lies-voting-misinformation-flourishes-on-facebook

sometimes instigate violence and death." These are the words of Harvard Business School Professor Emeritus Shoshana Zuboff from an essay in the *New York Times* which argued presciently that we have an inalienable right to our personal hopes, dreams, fears, and desires, and that "Unless democracy revokes the license to steal and challenges the fundamental economics and operations of commercial surveillance, the epistemic coup will weaken and eventually transform democracy itself." That's the power of viral media. This stuff is a very big deal.

Under the laws of virality, social media can be used to make military commanders, CEOs, HR managers, product designers, engineers, college candidates, preteens, and everyone else a potential plaintiff or defendant in the court of public opinion. In fact, my editor discouraged me from including this section about viral media. This is, after all, a business book, and he felt I could objectively underscore Trump's apt use of social media and its viral tendencies without "politically tinged rhetoric." But the earth is round. Two plus two equals four. And Trump used viral media to try to overturn a free and fair election. This book will outlive me. I'm betting that history is on my side.

Politics aside, the laws of virality are everyone's business, not just world leaders and online influencers. Viral media is used by corporate marketers as well. "The reality is people make decisions based on emotion. They may whittle them down based on fact. But we all base what we do on emotion," says Greg Reeder, vice president of marketing at SAP National Security Services and former deputy director at the United States Marine Corps where he led social media communications. Col. Reeder served the US loyally. His quote is pulled from a podcast interview recorded nearly a year prior to the insurrection. Please do not consider him to be an advocate for my views on Trumpism. I have no idea how he votes. The point is, virality impacts policy and product makers alike.

Controlled Chaos

Traditional command and control—top-down management style practices, where the worker bees follow the bosses' orders, struggle to keep pace with the speed of viral communications. Organizations that operate by committee stumble in this environment. There's simply not enough time to circle the wagons and make decisions by consensus.

Brand marketers have always tried to control their corporate identity, just as public relations has always tried to control the message. But marketing and PR require premeditation that real time, social-media driven, conversations just don't allow. In a conversation, you don't have time to bring in the team to figure out how to respond to every question, thought, or idea.

Organizations that saddle their external communications apparatus with total authority over social media are typically the ones that get hamstrung by the velocity of viral media. Just as marketing and PR don't tell salespeople what to say in customer meetings, they are ill-equipped to serve as a brand's single mouthpiece on social media.

Just as we learned in Chapter 3, like workflows that traverse an organization, the laws of virality make social media engagement a cross-functional necessity as well. You can't use social media to optimize a customer experience unless everyone who plays a role in that journey participates in the dialogue. Customers that tweet a product issue aren't trying to find your phone number, so attempting to sequester them into a private direct message conversation isn't going to work. They want to resolve their issue publicly and use their followers to keep you honest.

Social media started out as the marketing department's concern and quickly spread to customer service, product management, and HR. Still, getting companies to embrace the use of social beyond marketing and PR isn't easy. Encouraging cross-functional engagement requires executive sponsorship, which demands enlightened leadership. That's you after you've finished reading this book.

Capitalizing on viral media requires pushing decision-making authority to the edges of the organization. In military parlance, it would be more about equipping service members to maneuver in the field than it would about protecting the fortress.

Under the laws of virality, reach is a factor of engagement, so enabling the broadest possible addressable market to communicate on your behalf increases your probability of success. If people share your message with more than one person, who in turn share it with more than one person, you go viral.

A practical alternative to ramping up extraordinary viral marketing campaigns is just getting your frontline representatives active on social media and getting everyone else out of the way. For most organizations, this is a more realistic, sustainable approach.

Reorganizing at that level requires a shift in thinking that impacts corporate policy and governance. It demands a level of social media literacy that does not currently exist in most organizations because they haven't read this book or otherwise been exposed to effective training.

Digital Illiteracy

If the sustainability of social media is the result of a growing community of messengers, then the more people who carry your message, the greater the likelihood of virality. The more people who like, comment, and share, the greater the likelihood of rising to the top of the newsfeed.

A branded Instagram or Facebook account used by an organization's public relations or marketing team is an important channel for maintaining a brand's public record. But it will never be as trusted as the conversations attributed to a diverse, engaged community of people like yourself. And the larger the community, the more likely we pay attention, and the more likely we believe.

To marketing and PR professionals who for years have served as gatekeepers of the brand message, the notion of ceding control in exchange for reach is counterintuitive. But the laws of virality are driven by a broad online constituency, who can serve as your brand's army of online ambassadors.

Blocking Social Media Access

What if instead of using marketers to handle your corporate Twitter account, you trusted all your employees to use social media to get their jobs done? The byproduct of all their sharing would be marketing. That's why prohibiting employees from using social media at work infringes on the laws of virality. The thing to realize is that when people use social media to get work done, they leave behind a trail of digital bread crumbs. Those bread crumbs can be discovered through search and shared through social media in perpetuity.

Without a reasonable corporate policy in place, the idea of scaling social media communications through unofficial spokespeople is risky. But if you've thought it through, the digital record that gets left behind transforms social media from a productivity drain into a productivity gain with social media marketing becoming the byproduct of just getting work done.

Instead of relying on public relations and marketing professionals to spin "authentic" content, useful insights are naturally created by employees and left online. When people use social media to get their jobs done, they transfer organizational intelligence to the social web and organically build awareness in stride. Zappos, the online shoe seller, is famous for providing amazing customer service via Twitter. Unlike phone support, when they answer questions on Twitter, there are leaving information online where everyone can see it.

Instead of just creating content marketing materials, the archival value of real conversation happening online brings economies of scale to social media marketing. Inbound customer service inquiries are deflected as people find answers to frequently asked questions themselves online. Despite the promise, this approach is uncommon. Organizations are afraid some numbskull employee will post trade secrets or share something that damages their reputation. Instead of teaching employees what they can share and what they can't, they use draconian social media policies to gag frontline employees. Official spokespeople do the tweeting while the real subject matter experts—folks with the actual intelligence customers want to help make purchasing decisions—are prohibited from using one-to-many communications channels. Unfortunately, this has become standard operating procedure, despite the fact that the risks are manageable through governance and training.

Most organizations do have digital media policies in place. But you need legal counsel and a divining rod to apply them fairly and effectively. If you'd like to see what an effective social media policy looks like, go to www.socialmediapolicytemplate.com. In the mass media age, organizations required their CEOs to do media training. In the network age, you need to social media train the entire workforce.

Social Media Security

To integrate social media into wartime communications, the US Department of Defense, one of the world's most risk-averse organizations, relaxed their social media usage rules by prohibiting command from blocking enlisted service members' access to social media, which boosted morale by giving soldiers down range a way to teleconference with their loved ones back home.

Loose lips sink ships. So as long as service members agreed not to share sensitive information or images with GPS coordinates, Admiral Mike Mullen, chairman of the Joint Chiefs signed a memo allowing social media use, recognizing that the benefits of this kind of communication outweighed the operational security risks. And with one stroke of a pen, the Pentagon shifted their communications strategy.

Information operations is defined as the use of propaganda and misinformation to gain a strategic advantage over an adversary. Al Qaeda was already uploading beheadings to YouTube to promote fear and psychologically degrade US allied forces. And the beheading videos were going viral.

Admiral Mike Mullen was aware that the Pentagon's conventional public affairs processes were too cumbersome to respond quickly in a 24/7 viral media environment. But he was handicapped by his own bureaucracy, which prevented the Defense Department from responding quickly.

"We were at the churning point, and we were moving away from hierarchical command and control communications to a more agile, networked structure," says Jack Holt, who was director of emerging media at the US Department of Defense. Beyond the more obvious use of social media as a public affairs channel, the bigger opportunity for command was winning support at home for the war effort. By issuing the order that prohibited command from blocking access to social media by lower ranks, Admiral Mullen seized the opportunity of viral media by making every service member a spokesperson.

Corporate social media blackout policies are usually the result of management's digital illiteracy. They are enacted by misguided leaders who believe that restricting information flows is the best way to control popular sentiment. In fact, they are missing out on the economies of scale that a distributed force of goodwill ambassadors brings to getting out a message, any message.

As long as leadership provides the frontline with clear-cut, easy-to-follow guidelines that can be used to distinguish between conversations that can happen in public and conversations that need to be kept private, even the most risk-averse organization can utilize the laws of virality to gain a competitive edge.

Viral Engineering

The truth is, for most of us mere mortals, engineering viral messages is a long shot. It's hard to put lightning in a bottle, and even harder to take it out. Most marketers are still scratching their heads trying to figure out the secret recipe to viral content. Although the goal of viral marketing is to achieve broad reach on social networks through engagement, more often than not, content that goes viral is naturally occurring, not masterminded by marketers.

If your business is selling your audience's attention to advertisers, the longer people spend consuming your content, the more inventory you have to sell. In an effort to amass more attention to sell to advertisers, social networks like Facebook, Instagram, TikTok, Twitter, LinkedIn, and YouTube use algorithms to automatically push the most engaging content shared on their platforms to the top of the newsfeed because the longer we stay, the more money they make.

Viral marketing is the creation of content authored to entice likes, comments, and shares. A virus spreads when a single infection leads to more than one new infection. If existing infections cause only one new infection, the disease stays alive, but there won't be an epidemic. If existing infections cause less than one new infection, the disease dies out. For something to go viral, those who see it have to share it with more than one person, who also pass it along to more than one person, creating a snowball effect.

Figure 5.1 Image by Gage Skidmore (cropped)
Creative Commons BY-SA 2.0

Sometimes a message gets passed along because it's cute or humorous, like the grumpy cat photo (see fig. 5.1) posted by Bryan Bundesen on Reddit that went viral. Sometimes it gets shared by design, like the Ice Bucket Challenge, a cause-related marketing initiative where people made videos of themselves dumping ice water on their heads and challenging three other people to either do the same or donate $100 to the ALS Association, a nonprofit searching for a cure for Lou Gehrig's disease. Their viral marketing campaign raised $115 million in donations, increasing their research budget by 187 percent.

But why is it some viral campaigns work and others fail? What makes a message go viral?

Lost Art of Rhetoric

Joe Romm has a PhD in physics from MIT. He served as acting assistant secretary at the US Department of Energy, and he is super smart. Early in his career, his brother-in-law lost his home in Mississippi to Hurricane Katrina. And that's when for him, climate change became personal.

Romm did a little research and realized quickly that despite the scientific consensus that global warming posed an existential threat, it had failed to result in any meaningful environmental protections. Why hadn't this news gone viral on social media? And wasn't everyone behind finding a solution to keeping our species alive? Joe wanted to know why, which led him to become a student of the lost art of rhetoric.

The term "rhetoric" has negative connotations in modern language because it's considered elitist verbal trickery, but that's not what it actually means. Rhetoric is simply "the art of effective or persuasive speaking or writing, especially the use of figures of speech and other compositional techniques." He learned that those skilled in rhetoric understand the laws of virality best.

To share what he learned, Romm wrote a book, *How to Go Viral and Reach Millions*, which is the single most useful book ever written on the use of rhetoric for viral marketing. In fact, the next section of this chapter is inspired by him. (But it is no substitute for the complete work. If you want a comprehensive book on the practice of rhetoric, put this book down and get his book right now.)

As he explains in *How to Go Viral and Reach Millions*, rhetoric was invented by the ancient Greeks for the purpose of persuading jurors in the courtroom when their nascent democracy shifted from magistrates to juries. It was then that the Greek philosophers pioneered the art of rhetoric.

Rhetoric remained the basis of Western education all the way up to the end of the Elizabethan era, when it was replaced by science in the Age of Enlightenment. At that point science, experimentation, evidence, and fact became the basis of modern argument, and rhetoric became a lost art.

Now, the internet and social media have shortened attention spans to the point where attention itself has become a scarce commodity. Social engineering has become so powerful, we're seduced by video games with 3D graphics and algorithms like TikTok's that are so good at vacuuming up our attention, they pull us into a time warp. We're locked into a serotonin-fueled, brain reward loop cyber trance without even knowing it.

As William Gibson predicted in *Neuromancer*, the book that coined the phrase "cyberspace" and inspired the film *The Matrix*, we "jack in" and check out. And virtual reality, which Gibson was referring to, isn't even mainstream yet. But as you're learning, virality has a downside that can't be ignored. Online media has become so hypnotic that behavioral addiction to it is a thing now. And while there's a good deal of video game industry funded research that doubts the relationship between digital media and attention deficit hyperactivity disorder, children with ADHD do have "a higher rate of compulsive video game use[6]." Just as ominously, since social networking became available on mobile devices, "the rate of US hospitalizations for preteen girls who have self-harmed is up 189 percent."[7] Jonathan Haidt, professor of ethical leadership at the NYU Stern School of Business, writes, "Heavy use (but not light to moderate use) of social media (as opposed to "screen time," more generally) is consistently associated with depression, anxiety and self-harm, particularly for girls."

By linking the quest for likes and comments to our feelings of self-worth, social networking platforms have become so good at hijacking our attention they are "tearing apart our shared social fabric," according to Tristan Harris. He is the producer of

6   https://pubmed.ncbi.nlm.nih.gov/29573063/#:~:text=Participants%20with%20 ADHD%2C%20however%2C%20had,video%20game%20use%20than%20 controls.

7   https://ajph.aphapublications.org/doi/10.2105/AJPH.2018.304470

The Social Dilemma, a docudrama that explores the dangerous human impact of social networking, and president of the Center for Humane Technology,[8] a nonprofit whose mission is partly to illuminate the harms and existential threats of persuasive technology. "As long as social media companies profit from outrage, confusion, addiction, and depression," says Harris, "our well-being and democracy is at risk."

Amplified misinformation, demagoguery, and manipulation is the world of social media today. As technology gets more immersive, social networks—which still create no original content themselves—will be even better positioned to monopolize our attention, manipulate our desires, and stoke our fears. In this never-ending popularity contest, it's only going to get harder to capture and keep someone's attention.

According to Joe Romm, on average, only one out of twenty things you share on social media get clicked and even fewer get read. That means 95 percent of the content created goes unread. It also means that the headline *is* the story, because people do read the headline, giving rise to the practice of clickbait, which is content whose main purpose is to get visitors to click a link.

But before we drill down on the importance of headlines, let's talk about the role of rhetoric in sharing messages that go viral versus messages that get ignored. First and foremost, messages that get noticed use the subtle art of rhetoric to tell emotionally compelling stories. We are programmed genetically to respond to

8   https://www.humanetech.com/

stories. They are how we make sense of the world. And emotions are what make stories memorable. Messages conveyed as stories are more memorable than messages conveyed with precision.

Emotionally compelling stories follow an "if, but, then" formula.

- "if" is the setup
- "but" is the conflict
- "then" is the resolution

Stories that trigger emotions catch and hold our attention. Romm says the most memorable emotions are awe, anger, and anxiety. Visiting your childhood home is an emotional experience triggered by deep memories. We remember how we felt much better than what actually took place there. Stories that get remembered, believed, and shared are the ones that trigger emotional reactions.

As an example of a short rhetorical story that conforms to this rubric, Romm offers attorney Johnnie Cochran's famous line in the OJ Simpson trial in reference to the glove with his blood on it "If it doesn't fit, you must acquit," said Cochran, stealing a page from the ancient Greek philosophy playbook.

If you've never been directly involved in litigation, you probably think decisions made in courts of law are evidential, that facts speak for themselves, and that the truth prevails. In litigation, it's often the deeper pockets that win because money buys legal protection and attorneys are skilled at cultivating reasonable doubt. Cochran's rhyme planted a seed in the minds of the jurors that blossomed into an acquittal verdict.

But you don't need to be a Greek philosopher or a trial lawyer to understand the power of persuasive language. Here are my favorite recommendations from Romm for creating memorable, viral content.

1. Short Words Win

Big words are less persuasive. Long, multisyllabic words require more effort to hear/process so they don't connect with readers as easily as short words do. The majority of these sayings are made from single syllable words.

- "Black lives matter"
- "Build back better"
- "Don't be evil"
- "Move fast and break things"
- "What's in your wallet?"
- "The buck stops here"

2. Repeat, Repeat, Repeat

Anaphora is a Greek term that means repeating the same words at the beginning of a series of sentences. Martin Luther King Jr. repeated the phrase "I have a dream" eight times in his speech. And in *A Tale of Two Cities*, Charles Dickens wrote the memorable parable, "It was the best of times, it was the worst of times, it was the age of wisdom, it was the age of foolishness, it was the epoch of belief, it was the epoch of incredulity, it was the season of light, it was the season of darkness, it was the spring of hope, it was the winter of despair ..." repeating the phrases "it was" ten times. Studies also show that if you hear something that's not true over and over again, eventually, through repetition, you start to believe it. Here are more famous products and slogans that penetrate our collective consciousness through repetition.

- TikTok
- Captain Crunch
- Maybe she's born with it, maybe it's Maybelline
- To be or not to be ...
- What happens in Vegas, stays in Vegas

3. Alliteration

This is putting together words with the same sounds. Memorable children's tongue twisters like "she sells sea shells by the sea shore" are alliterations. When Dr. Martin Luther King Jr. said "I have a dream that my four little children will one day live in a nation where they will not be judged by the color of their skin but by the content of their character" he combined the words *color*, *content*, and *character* to make his speech more memorable. Businesses incorporate alliteration into their brand names as well. Examples include:

- El Pollo Loco
- Best Buy
- Krispy Kreme

- American Apparel
- Mickey Mouse

4. Rhyme

Rhymes are a powerful memory trick. Lyrics from pop music get burned into our memory banks forever. Furthermore, statements that rhyme are more credible. According to Romm, research studies have shown that out of two statements that say the exact same thing, the one that rhymes is more believable. So save time and persuade with rhyme.

- Four more years
- Thank heaven for 7-Eleven
- Birds of a feather flock together

5. Metaphors

By involving us in the process of decoding their meaning, metaphors enhance memory as well. Comparing something we don't know to something we do know makes it familiar, easy to grasp, and stimulates the brain, which helps make it memorable too. Metaphors speak clearest to people who learn visually. They form a picture with words and those pictures are memorable.

Author Joe Romm is also the editor-in-chief of *Front Page Live*, a daily news site created to beat right-wing, conservative propaganda websites Breitbart News and The Drudge Report at their own game. At *Front Page Live*, Romm uses the laws of virality to make the truth more memorable and contagious on social media, but he acknowledges that rhetoric is not enough. In the world of viral media, persuasive language is table stakes. To elevate fact-based stories that discredit misinformation and propaganda, Romm uses a headline testing platform called Chartbeat to improve audience engagement and increase readership. The world's top media companies all maximize the business value of their written and video content with headline testing tools.

Analytics that quantify the viral attraction of online media have become so important that they even play a role in the editorial decision-making process. There's a popular saying in the news industry: "If it bleeds, it leads." For social media, it should be rephrased to: "If it rivets, pivot."

Viral Automation

In the male-dominated tech start-up world, Kate Bradley-Chernis is a unicorn. A former on-air host at Sirius/XM, Bradley-Chernis founded a company called Lately, a social media marketing platform that uses artificial intelligence to sift through long-form text and video content to locate and share the most "clicky and sticky" passages, as Romm puts it.

Lately uses AI to comb through blog posts, audio podcasts, and videos. It analyzes viral potential and auto-generates social posts—snippets most likely to go viral—that can be scheduled and released on social networks. "When you know what your customer cares about, why would you guess?" asks Bradley-Chernis. Instead of guessing what messages might stick in a vacuum, AI counts up all the digital engagement bread crumbs left behind and predicts what new messages are most likely to get noticed. Lately reverse engineers the message by analyzing and tapping into popular pockets of past interest.

The same algorithmic techniques used by social networks and mainstream media are starting to come within reach of marketers. An emerging class of content performance optimization startups are using AI-powered algorithms to automate virality.

While Lately automates virality by analyzing historical data, Michael Umansky and his partners, Alexander De Ridder and Gary Haymann, developed viral guardrails for content creation. Their company built INK for ALL, content performance optimization software for authoring sticky content.

Figure 5.2 INK Founders (l. to r.) CTO Alexander De Ridder, CRO Gary Haymann, and CEO Michael Umansky with their content performance optimization patent.

"We created INK to give storytellers control of their own destiny," says Umansky, whose language processor guides makers through the viral content creation process. Like Lately, INK uses artificial intelligence to give content creators better visibility over the story, substance, and style that's most likely to capture and retain people's attention.

Rather than create content first and optimize it second, INK scores your text for readability and search engine visibility as you write. A tool like this has the potential to make much of the conventional SEO process a thing of the past. Given the importance of capturing and sustaining attention in a world of infinite content choices, it is likely that their vision of a content performance creation tool will someday be integrated into products like Google Docs and Microsoft Word as well. Think of it as a logical extension of autosuggested word and phrase choices.

Viral SEO

Dale Bertrand is an Ivy League–educated search engine optimization specialist who says technical SEO is on its way out. A man on a mission, Dale leverages the laws of virality to build search authority. Google's getting better at using AI to separate the wheat from the chaff all the time. He devised a novel approach to SEO that puts a brand's message, or mission, front and center as a way of distinguishing brands from their competitors in the eyes of Google.

"Google doesn't live to reward technical people for the correctness of their code. That's not what Google is looking for. They're looking for the most useful content," says Bertrand. By putting the actual message before the math, he prescribes a mission-driven approach that beats technical SEO every time. "Optimizing canonical tags, sitemaps, and crawl budgets doesn't deliver the bang for the buck that it used to," he adds. He believes investing more than 20 percent of your time in technical SEO is the road to diminishing returns.

The basic aspects of technical SEO still matter. But if you're using a modern content management system like WordPress, HubSpot, or Shopify and you have a website with fewer than 10,000 pages, overinvesting in website performance isn't worth the time and energy. In modern content management systems, most of the technical stuff is handled automatically.

It used to be that you could just optimize for a keyword, and you would rank. Now, you need to optimize for keywords *and* have backlinks to rank. Writing about topics people are passionate about—and want to link to—increases the likelihood of going viral.

This is what Bertrand calls "mission-driven SEO" which is building authority by aligning with a common cause. Brands with a purposeful mission cut through the clutter. They get noticed. And they motivate online influencers to publish links back to them. Google uses those backlinks to rank results, so mission-driven SEO is building authority by pivoting to topics that trigger an emotional response.

"To leverage mission-driven SEO, you do need a purpose," he says. "It doesn't have to be a social mission. It could be craftsmanship, or quality, or a backstory, but it does need to be legit.

We've partnered with law firms advocating for a position that relates to our purpose, and built content around that. The law firm contributes to the content, links to it, and helps us promote it," says Bertrand, who advises clients to reach beyond bloggers for inbound links.

By creating mission-driven content that dovetails with the positions of other organizations, Bertrand builds authority by engaging subject matter experts from outside the digital world. The easiest way to spark viral conversations is by creating purposeful content that resonates with others who are passionate about your cause.

Earned Influence

Out of all the organic media channels (owned, shared, and earned), it's earned media that has the greatest potential to send a message viral. When an influential third party endorses a product or service, that endorsement is seen as an impartial, unbiased testimonial. The more influential the person making the endorsement, the greater the likelihood your message goes viral.

Talkwalker is a social media analytics platform that shows you sentiment, influencers, and themes happening on social networks. It also maps the virality of online messages so you can see how they wound up going viral. On a timeline, Talkwalker shows you the order in which individuals amplified your message so you can see who had the most impact.

On January 6, 2021, when President Trump incited a lynch mob to storm the Capitol and hang Vice President Pence, the most engaged tweet with the hashtag #MAGA came from Trump supporter Chanel Rion who founded a front group cleverly titled the "*National* White House Correspondents Association," a Trump-friendly alternative to the 117-year-old "White House Correspondents Association" which had barred her from the rotation in the White House briefing room.

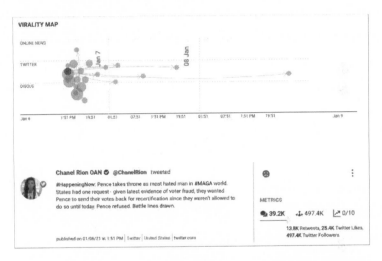

Figure 5.3 Virality map from Talkwalker with a timeline illustrating how a tweet gets republished and amplified to reach a larger audience.

Rion's tweet, which was sent at 10:51 a.m. alleging "evidence of voter fraud" and calling Pence the "most hated man in [the] #MAGA world" amplified Trump's big lie. Her tweet was liked 25,400 times and retweeted 9,100 times. This virality map from Talkwalker (see fig. 5.3) shows how the tweet went viral, with each bubble representing other Twitter users who amplified Rion's tweet. The bigger the bubble, the more retweets those users got. So it is possible to see who the propaganda operatives are that passed

Rion's lie along, which means it's also possible to charge them with defamation and violating national security.

But these types of tools are also useful to marketers looking to get their content to go viral. With a platform like Talkwalker, you can locate hot pockets of conversation that buyers are having about the problems you solve, and see who the influencers in those communities are. If you have intelligence about how, who, and where conversations break out, you can target your engagement efforts and strike where the iron is hot. The virality map identifies the online influencers who made the tweet go viral.

In addition to analyzing things like share of voice (how much your brand is mentioned versus your competitors) and message pass-through on social media (the number of people who amplify your message), Talkwalker can also ingest rich text and draw comparisons between external and internal data. "By analyzing customer service, customer survey, web chat, and sales data collectively, you can discover and validate all sorts of insights," says Todd Grossman, CEO of Americas at Talkwalker.

"Corporate decision-making is due for a major overhaul. At the moment it is dominated by internal data," writes Meltwater CEO Jorn Lyseggen in his book *Outside Insight*, which argues that companies need to start benchmarking their performance against their competitors using publicly available data like job postings, online news, social media posts, online advertising, and patent applications.

"While most companies have this data on their own website via Google Analytics, you can now see this information about your competitors' websites and benchmark your business against them," says Jessica Bohm, director of marketing intelligence at Similar-Web, a company whose tool lets you monitor the performance of your competitors. It's possible to get accurate estimates of how much traffic other sites are receiving from the five sources (search, social, referral, email, and direct) and much more. You can follow the customer journey on other websites, see what potential buyers click, where they drop off, and if they convert. You can use SimilarWeb as a tool to find gaps in your competitors' funnels and see how they're driving sales to specific products. Market intelligence is always relative to your competitors. Benchmarks are the intersection of external and internal metrics.

Growth Marketing

Growth marketers use the laws of virality to drive growth, sometimes at the expense of profitability. Growth marketing is growth at all costs and it is used primarily in winner-take-all markets like internet search and web conferencing, where the network effect is critical to success.

"Profitability is not the be-all, end-all for startups. It might be as or even more important to grow your customer base and grab market share first, while you're still disrupting the existing market," says Andy Sack of Lighter Capital[9].

In its start-up days, PayPal lost money on a per-transaction level. The online shoe store, Zappos, a lean start-up that put market share before efficiency, lost money on shoe sales when they

9   https://www.lightercapital.com/guide-8-saas-metrics-that-matter/

were just getting started. And even today, Amazon uses predatory pricing to drive competitors out of business, putting market share before gross profits. They may lose money on e-commerce sales in order to grow their customer base, and make that money back through Amazon Web Services, their infrastructure as a service platform, or Amazon Prime, their subscription service.

Black Friday retail promotions use low prices to attract customers. Customers attract more customers, who buy more than just discounted items. The cookies are sold at cost, while the milk is full retail. If prices drop below a given threshold, people talk, and offers go viral.

Retailers have been underpricing one or two select items (called loss leaders) to bring in foot traffic, with the intention of making it back on the overall sale for decades. Like the brick and mortar retailers that came before them, Amazon is willing to lose some battles to win the war for global domination.

Growth marketers have different priorities. Instead of vanity metrics like website traffic, bounce rate, search rankings, or the number of leads generated, growth marketers use customer acquisition and churn rate as their key performance indicators.

The specific metric could be trial user growth, customer growth, subscriber growth, revenue growth, or product utilization growth. But they stay focused on actual growth metrics, instead of the metrics that lead to growth. After all, what's the true value of a lead that never closes, or web traffic that doesn't convert?

B2Bs have to persuade purchasing committee stakeholders, who need nurturing and educational content in order to arrive at a consensus. Consumers, on the other hand, are more likely to make purchasing decisions independently and impulsively, so growth there is more about streamlining the path to purchase with e-commerce.

Growth marketers use end-to-end solutions with closed-loop reporting so they can measure and attribute revenue to every digital touchpoint in the customer journey. There are many books on growth marketing, but if you only want to read one, make it *Blitzscaling* by LinkedIn cofounder and executive chairman Reid Hoffman and *New York Times* reporter Chris Yeh. Hoffman is also a venture capitalist with privileged access to Silicon Valley growth marketing insiders at major tech brands who gave him valuable privileged information. No one understands the business case for growth before profit better than Hoffman, who uses Uber as one of many growth-driven start-up examples. Like Amazon, Uber is willing to lose smaller battles in order to win the larger war.

"Uber often uses heavy subsidies on both sides of the marketplace when it launches in a new city, lowering fares to attract riders and boosting payments to attract drivers. By paying out more than it takes in on those early trips, Uber is able to reach critical scale faster than a more conservative competitor. Given the winner-take-all nature of the ride-sharing market, that wasteful spending has helped Uber achieve a dominant market position in the cities in which it operates."[10]

It's worth pointing out that, with no inventory costs, it's easier for software companies to deficit finance growth than it is for

10   Blitzscaling

manufacturers. Tesla Motors lacks the infrastructure to meet the demand for its vehicles, so it would be pointless for them to invest in growth by undercutting their competitors on price. So far, Elon Musk has been unable to bypass supply chain limitations. But when those restrictions disappear, growth can be driven by realigning sales, marketing, and service against common KPIs.

"If you look at sales and marketing as a revenue engine or a system, it affects the way you make business decisions. You don't make siloed decisions. You make decisions that help the system," says sales and marketing alignment specialist Jeff Davis.[11]

The basic argument is that, when cross-functional disciplines like sales and marketing come together in service of revenue growth, the outcome is always going to be better. Why? Because they're focused on corporate, rather than departmental growth.

For a growth marketing strategy to be successful, folks from marketing, sales, and customer success have to operate as one system, and be accountable to shared KPIs. This underscores the importance of an integrated stack that accommodates cross-functional collaboration.

"You cannot look at data in department silos. You cannot say marketing has a handoff to sales. That is fundamentally flawed. That concept of a handoff implies a silo. Your data cannot be separate. You have to look at the entire customer life cycle," said InsideSales.com CEO Dave Elkington on *The Alignment Podcast* by Jeff Davis. This is why, from a practical standpoint, stand alone,

11   https://www.jeffdavis2.com/thealignmentpodcast

departmental software solutions that aren't integrated into the rest of the company frustrate alignment.

Integrated, end-to-end solutions mean everyone has to work together. "Reps are the people closest to the customer and their group knowledge around what prospects want is invaluable," says Outreach CEO Manny Medina.[12] It doesn't matter who's right. What matters is growth.

Product-Led Growth

Another way start-ups drive growth is by building virality into their products. Instead of creating products and marketing them, they build products that market themselves. Product-led growth is the strategy of engineering growth by design into the product itself, and it appeals mostly to companies where the value a customer gets is proportionate to the number of people on the platform. Obviously, the more buyers and sellers there are on Airbnb, or the more people there are texting on WhatsApp, the more value these services deliver.

Product-led marketers offer an introductory version of their product for free that provides enough value to lure trial users. And once those users are hooked, they try to upgrade them to paying customers by offering more bells and whistles. LinkedIn used product-led growth to establish their dominance, and introduced subscription services with added features after that.

12   https://www.amazon.com/gp/product/1119584345?ie=UTF8

Product-led growth is a go-to market strategy that relies on using your product as a vehicle for acquiring, engaging, and retaining new customers. Slack and Dropbox are examples. In this model, there's no traditional B2B sales cycle. You don't download a whitepaper, attend a webinar, and get contacted by a sales rep. Instead, demand is a result of your experience using the product, or your desire to connect with someone via the product. The idea is to get the product itself to go viral.

Venture capitalist Sean Fanning of Napster fame maintains a list of product-led growth companies, including Shopify, Atlassian, Zoom, Twilio, and Slack, which all use product-led growth marketing strategies. Fanning believes, "The valuation gap between public product led growth businesses and the rest of the public SaaS landscape will widen ..."[13] His Product-Led Growth Index shows how gross revenues and enterprise value-to-revenue multiples at product-led growth SaaS companies are roughly double that of non-product-led growth SaaS companies.

According to HubSpot's VP of marketing Keiran Flanigan, it wasn't until HubSpot introduced an entry-level, freemium product that their business really took off.

Dangers of Virality

AI, advanced algorithms, and big data have ushered us into a new era of marketing and consumption. We've seen viral technology impact consumer behavior and revolutionize our

13   https://openviewpartners.com/product-led-growth-index/

capabilities as marketers. And we've seen it used by and against autocrats.

The dark side of virality is addiction. How do we live peacefully in a world with millions of messages competing for our attention? How do we resist the never-ending stream of emotional triggers? And how do we find a balance without relinquishing these technologies that monopolize our attention and enjoy them at the same time?

This is a question best-selling author, digital anthropologist, and futurist Brian Solis, who currently serves as global innovation evangelist at Salesforce, is focused on. And it's a question more people started asking after the release of the Netflix documentary *The Social Dilemma*, which examined the consequences of viral engagement. The challenge is that the social networking algorithms use so-called "bubble filter" algorithms, which increase utilization by showing us more of what we're already watching. And they insulate us from different points of view; one result is the aggravation of a state of hyper-partisan political polarity.

Is the current state of affairs simply a trailer for more of what's to come? AI, algorithms, and the social networks behind them use our own insecurities against us while simultaneously making us feel in control. "Social networks align content and advertising around what the algorithm deems important to us. They stoke our cognitive biases and our said or unsaid vulnerabilities. And they create engagement and activity around those things because they are extremely charged. As you share, others share back. And make no mistake, that's all by design," says Solis.

But rather than blame social media or those who exploit it, Solis says, we need to become literate, deliberate, and honest about what we chose to engage with online. What we see online is a result of how we submit our attention. With that awareness, we can take responsibility for how we engage by avoiding echo chambers and taking personal accountability for our clicks.

For example, if you think it's unfair that celebrities have to deal with invasion of privacy but spend lots of time consuming paparazzi images online, you're part of the problem because you're supporting a media product that is the result of invading someone's privacy. If you don't want to see hateful content, don't engage with it. If you want to see alternate points of view, consciously engage with those instead.

Taking personal accountability is remembering that we can decide what we engage with. Instead of considering ourselves passive victims of AI, we need to retrain the algorithm. We can show the algorithm what we want to see by liking and engaging with content that fills our lives with value and purpose. Solis explores this approach in his book *Lifescale: How to Create a More Creative, Productive, and Happy Life*.[14] "You get back what you put out into the world," he says. So the ethics of AI are not universal. Instead, they're a result of personal choice.

Viral marketing is about capturing and keeping our attention. But with AI, we may not understand the social, economic, and political repercussions until it's too late.

---

14   https://www.amazon.com/Lifescale-Establish-Rituals-Routines-Achieve/dp/1119535867

In the early days, social media was heralded as the channel that would democratize information once and for all. The wisdom of the crowd would collectively problem-solve to debunk misinformation. And the transparency of the internet would be the ultimate disinfectant. But that's not the way it turned out. In the world of viral media, sunlight also drives growth.

It's time to take a step back, to think about how we got to where we currently are before we think about where we want to go. Brand marketers want to create a better customer experience. But we have to remember that connected customers are in a more chaotic world. Consider the headspace they're in when they interact with your message. Instead of simply stoking awe, anger, and anxiety, craft your message from a place of empathy. Put the individual ahead of your target persona's customer experience.

As you forge into the future of viral marketing, evaluate whether your company is truly striving for innovation or simply iteration, and course correct accordingly. And never forget what it means to be a human being when you leverage the laws of virality.

CHAPTER 6

Email Marketing

'd much rather get a Christmas card in the mail than an email from Paperless Post. Email is more of a chore to sort through. I can put a Christmas card on my mantle and enjoy it for the entire holiday season, whereas a Christmas card email gets opened once and deleted. A beautiful Christmas card from a company I do business with is appreciated. A Christmas card via email, not so much. Direct mail is a better way if you want to build awareness.

Email campaigns are designed to trigger a reply. I'm more likely to reply and say thanks to an email than I am to snail mail, so email has higher response rates than direct mail. In business, email is the channel we use to follow up with people. And the more personalized the email, the greater the likelihood they'll reply. So bulk email campaigns need to be personalized to be effective. You can send anyone direct mail if you have their address. But if you want to send them email, it's best if you have their permission.

Out of all the digital media channels, email marketing is the most effective and underutilized. Email marketing campaigns take longer and require more advance planning than social media posts. But since email has predictable response rates, email marketing campaigns generate more consistent returns than social media posts. In the digital pivot, email marketing is the channel through which you nurture prospective customers who have signed up to receive notifications from you.

Planning an effective email marketing campaign starts by locking in on the action you want the recipient to take. If you want them to book a discovery call, attend a webinar, or buy something, your campaign should be designed with that action in mind. Email is a much better for direct marketing than it is for building brand awareness. Email marketing campaigns begin by creating a landing page with an offer or conversion opportunity.

A landing page is what it sounds like. It's a page through which people enter your site. Not everyone enters your site through the homepage. A "squeeze page" is a type of landing page that's not linked to any other pages on your site. It has no menu or footer links, and the entire page is visible on the screen without scrolling. Squeeze pages have a form and a submit button, so the only action you can take is the one intended.

Brian Dean of the SEO website Backlinko creates landing pages for his online courses that are roughly 10,000 words long with screenshots, testimonials, videos, graphic icons, and an FAQ. As a frame of reference, this chapter is just over 4,000 words.

If someone clicks through from your email to your squeeze page, you fulfill the users' expectation by keeping the email and landing page copy consistent. The landing page copy should align with the email marketing campaign copy. Using the same headline and image shows the recipient they're getting what they clicked for. In addition to the creative content in the email message, you have to name your campaign, write a subject line (or multiple if you plan to A/B test), add sender details, choose your recipients, send it to yourself to make sure it looks good, and schedule it.

If your email lists are segmented by account, industry, or role, you can personalize your message based on those parameters. You've got to write the email with a call to action that speaks directly to a known problem the recipient has that they're willing to acknowledge and are trying to solve. There are lots of little steps, and they're all important. But in order for an email marketing campaign to be effective, it has to get opened.

Autoresponders, Campaigns, and One-to-One Emails

Autoresponders are emails set up to go out automatically, based on a web form submission, user activity, or time decay. When you sign up to receive a coupon code or submit a lead form on a website, the email you get in return is generated automatically by an email marketing platform. If you get additional emails from that same company, those emails are part of an automated campaign to try and upsell and cross-sell over time.

If you abandon your shopping cart on an e-commerce site before you complete your transaction and get an email reminding you about it, that too is an autoresponder email. Autoresponder emails are set up in sequences, where user activity triggers different email responses. The next autoresponder you receive may be triggered by the link in the previous autoresponder you clicked.

If you subscribe to the B2B Lead Gen Podcast, you get an autoresponder welcome email. In that email is a link to the white paper *Essential Digital Marketing Skills*. If you click on that link, but don't download the white paper, you get another autoresponder reminding you to download the white paper. If you download the white paper, you get a sequence of autoresponder emails trying to get you to book a discovery call.

Email marketing campaigns, on the other hand, are created manually and include newsletters, product updates, and one-time promotions. These are what people usually think about when they hear the phrase "email marketing." Campaigns are more common than autoresponders, but the latter generates, on average, one-third of the revenue from email marketing.

One-to-one emails can also be used to generate leads and commerce by adding an auto signature to your emails with links to your landing page. Traffic from email is notoriously difficult to measure in a website usage analytics platform, so here's where you would apply the UTM parameters we learned about in Chapter 2. Just search "generate UTM parameters" to create a tracking link you can include in your emails to measure inbound traffic in whatever website usage analytics platform you're using.

Email Subject Lines

In email marketing, your subject line is your outer envelope, just like a direct mail piece. If the outer envelope isn't compelling, nobody opens it. When you scan your inbox, you use the subject line and the sender's name to decide what to open and what to delete. Most people delete a slew of emails from their inbox without opening them. In email marketing, the objective is to get your message seen and then to get the recipient to open and click; your email marketing campaigns live or die based on the subject line.

The top email marketing performance driver is creating a sense of urgency in your subject line, which means making them time-sensitive. If you offer free shipping, it should expire in twenty-four hours. If you're announcing a software beta program, have a deadline to sign up. Whatever you're promoting, there needs to be an expiration date.

After that, the next best way to drive performance is with suspense-related or teaser subject lines. Email subject lines that ask a question that's relevant to your audience, like "Who will be the leaders in your industry?" or "Top Downloads for <Month>," work well because they have to open the email for the answer.

Single word subject lines like "meeting" or "follow-up" that get the recipient guessing get opened too. But the word has to relate to the contents of the email itself. Don't trick people, or they'll open it, see that you wasted their time, and unsubscribe.

SubjectLine.com is a free tool for testing email subject lines. It's been used to check over 8 million email marketing campaigns. And it scores the potential performance of subject lines based on dozens of parameters and variables. Subjectline.com also dispels many of the myths about triggering spam filters with words like "free," all caps, exclamation points, and emojis. These are all fair game, and they can actually improve open and click rates.

If you're sending out newsletters, steer away from standardized subject line formats like the name of the newsletter and the date, or the word "newsletter" in brackets in front of every subject line.

Mix it up. Don't repeat the identically worded subject line with a new date. It's a common practice that doesn't work.

Avoid static subject lines, and say what your content is about. Take the time to be specific. Put your offer front and center in your subject line, and you're open rates will rise.

Death of Email

Experts have been predicting the death of email since it was invented. They predicted Twitter would replace email because it's permission-based. They said Slack would replace email because it's easier. There's always a newer communication channel that's going to replace email. But email hasn't gone away and is unlikely to anytime soon.

Email is a legacy channel that's become the digital marketer's forgotten stepchild. But email marketing brings a level of predictability that's tough to achieve through other channels. Based on the size of your list, you can forecast conversions with a higher degree of certainty. For lead nurturing, particular for companies selling complex products, email marketing remains an important arrow in your quiver.

Small business owners wear so many hats that they're among the most avid downloaders of free white papers, checklists, and cheat sheets. They're easier to target because their interests are broad. If you're trying to break through with enterprise customers, getting your email to the right person takes much more time.

In tough economic times, email marketing campaigns with free offers work particularly well at building relationships. Anything free does really well in a recession. "Free content, free webinars, free checklists, free offers, free anything does extremely well on the consumer side," says Jay Schwedelson, CEO of Worldata, a direct response email marketing services provider with a research division that analyzes the results of hundreds of millions of email marketing campaigns.

You don't need the best email marketing platform with every little feature, so don't spend too much time agonizing over which one to go with. Interoperability with your stack is critical. But the major players like Marketo, HubSpot, Eloqua, Constant Contact, and Mailchimp are all reasonable options. And if you get really good at using any of these platforms, you'll always have work.

The reason interoperability is so important is that you want your salespeople to be able to sort the leads in their sales pipeline software by email marketing campaigns, opens, and clicks, so your email marketing software needs to be able to sync up with your customer relationship management software. After that, you don't need all the bells and whistles, so look for an email marketing platform for a competitive monthly price. Specifically, you want a service that's not going to nickel and dime you if you want to send an extra 5,000 or 10,000 emails. That shouldn't cost exponentially more.

Another reason to go with one of the major email marketing players is you want a platform that has the resources to maintain a good sender reputation. If you go with a platform that lets anyone upload a list and carpet bomb the world with no checks and balances, their servers are going to get blacklisted. Since you're sending email through them, your email deliverability rate—the percentage of emails you send that reach the recipients inbox—is at risk.

Apple Mail, Gmail, and Yahoo! Mail all have buttons that make it easy to report spam. The risk of letting anyone upload a list to an email marketing platform is that someone sends a campaign that triggers a spam rate of more than one complaint for every 1,000 messages sent. Servers dispatch emails from IP addresses, and once an IP address gets a high number of spam reports, their emails sent from that IP get tagged with a warning message or get sent to the recipient's spam folder.

The last thing you want to do is send email campaigns from your own server because you don't want to damage the IP reputation of the server you use to send individual emails. Email marketing platforms have their own IP addresses, and segregating the two is a good way to off-load the management of bulk email deliverability to specialists. So don't try to do your own email marketing without a provider because delivery is complicated and tricky. And if you get it wrong, you can get your domain name blacklisted, which is fixable but will suck up hundreds of hours of your life to repair.

Biggest Email Marketing Mistakes

One big mistake people make when they're sending offers is including social media sharing buttons in their email marketing templates. Have you ever shared an email marketing campaign on social media? Even if you're sending breaking news, getting someone to share it from an email is a long shot. Plus, it's more information for the recipient to process. Keep your templates simple with one obvious conversion opportunity.

The second biggest mistake in offer emails is linking your logo to your homepage. Don't divert them from taking the specific action you want them to take by allowing them to click away from the conversion opportunity you're seeking to make. If you're nurturing people who signed up to receive email from your company with a newsletter, and your objective is to stay top of mind without selling, including a bevy of links is fine. But even with informational email marketing campaigns, it's smarter to include a call to action alongside the editorial content. Keep it simple.

"The simpler the email, the higher the click-through rate, the higher engagement. If you want to build a relationship with your customers and leads, you want to make your emails look like they're coming from a person, not a brand. And people don't usually send emails with designs, screenshots and images," says Brian Dean of Backlinko. "The better you can simulate that your emails are not mass campaigns, the more likely you are to get an open rate or a click-through rate that's high. That doesn't mean you need to send plain text emails, because those can't be tracked. But try to keep design at a minimum," says Dean.

There are different levels of deliverability. Your email might get delivered, but to the recipient's spam, promotions, or notifications folder. Dean says keeping your email simple helps with deliverability as well. "Not only does it help engagement. It also helps your email get delivered to the primary inbox tab in Gmail. The bigger an email is in terms of file size, the more likely it is to land in the Gmail promotions tab, which makes sense because emails that are meant for just you personally usually don't have a bunch of art on them. So I think that's one ranking factor that Gmail uses to separate which emails make it to the primary, and which ones they show in the promotions tab," he says.

Offer emails should only link to conversion pages. The objective is to get people to open your message and click. So don't send them down a rabbit hole by confusing them with a bunch of ancillary links. Make it easy to get to the page and take the action you want them to take.

Numbers Game

I admire great salespeople. As leadership expert and author Matt Church says, "Some will. Some won't. So what?" It's the same attitude that makes for a great email marketer. Email marketing is a numbers game. If they don't open your message, you've been ignored. If they open but don't click, that's a maybe. And if they click and convert, that's a sale or a lead.

Email marketers try different subject lines and calls to action. Since it's a numbers game, performance is improved by making small changes and testing outcomes. You experiment with different subject lines to see which one performs better.

Before you start testing, benchmark your starting point because you can't improve if you can't measure. Start by measuring your deliverability rate. If you send out 10,000 emails, the percentage that actually lands in the recipient's inbox is your deliverability rate. Testing email marketing campaigns is widely misunderstood. You can only test one thing at a time, like a different subject line or with and without an image to see how that impacts your performance. If you test two variables at that same time there's no way to know which factor boosted your results. Be patient. The process is painstakingly methodical. Find a win, move on, and keep going down that list.

If you're dealing with a smaller email list, fewer than 5,000 emails, for example, focus on list growth. On an annualized basis, about 20 percent of your email addresses are going to go bad. Your entire list will become undeliverable over the course of five years.

So if you have a 2,000-person list, you're going to lose 400 people every year.

If your list is small, you may not be able to split your list in half and A/B test two versions of the same campaign. Instead, send a campaign to your entire list. Then, change one variable and send another campaign the following week. See how they do against each other.

If you want statistically significant results, you can't confidently test a segment with less than 1,000 emails. If you have a 2,000-name email list, you can test two subject lines in one campaign. If you have a 3.000-name list, you can test three headlines. The bigger the better because you're not going to get reliable information for a list with just a few hundred names. It's not a big enough control group. But everyone has to start somewhere. If you're sending to less than 1,000 names, validate your assumptions in multiple campaigns before you act on them.

In terms of how much is too much email marketing, determine your frequency based on your unsubscribe rate. If you have an average unsubscribe rate of .25 percent, and it jumps to .75 percent after you increase your frequency, that's an indicator you're sending too frequently. Use your unsubscribe rate as your campaign frequency barometer.

Next, look at your email open rates. But be skeptical. There's a new phenomenon in the email marketing world, which is particularly prevalent in B2B markets. To block malware, spyware, adware, and viruses, more businesses are filtering their incoming mail before they distribute them internally.

In your email marketing campaign report, server-side malware scans might wind up registering in your dashboard as an open or a click. But it's a false positive. If you don't realize it's their cybersecurity software triggering your "open" rates, you might think more people are opening your emails. But it's actually just bad data.

"If you see your open rates jump and your response rates decline, then you likely have a bot traffic problem. Send out a test campaign at 3 a.m.," says email marketing expert Jay Schwedelson. If you see "opens" from the same, alleged superusers you saw before, those aren't real opens. Show the results to your email sending platform and ask for help. If you don't get it, migrate to another platform.

As you work to build your email list over time, you're going to get some strange email sign ups from addresses that don't look like real people. They're not. These are bots trying to hack into your website through your registration forms. These are injection attacks and they happen to everyone. It's not at all uncommon to pick up these kinds of spammy registrants, so let's take a look at strategies for keeping your lists clean.

List Hygiene

There are two things you need to do to maintain data hygiene. First, you need to keep bots from signing up for your list, which is an ongoing challenge. There are a lot of bots out there are designed to look for forms with poor security that they can use to infiltrate websites and networks. So it's important that the company behind the web sign-up forms you use to collect registrations on your website is able to keep their technology current. Hackers are working round the clock to figure out how to bypass security parameters. It's best to go with a form from a reputable company that is continuously improving their offering.

For this reason, web forms are a vulnerability, so stay away from using free software to create forms for your landing pages. Go with a forms provider that has the revenue to keep their product current. Bad forms are a major vulnerability to list hygiene and web security. I use Gravity Forms, which is a WordPress plugin, but search "form builder" for a complete list of providers.

You can minimize bot registrations with captcha codes—a challenge-response test used in computing to determine whether or not a user is human—but those aren't perfect. There are also security plugins for WordPress sites that block bots by blocking countries where the worst offenders originate. On my site, the top five countries I'm blocking are India, Brazil, Turkey, Saudi Arabia, and Bosnia and Herzegovina. Those aren't big markets for me, so I'm okay losing out on those audiences. This is the first piece of the data hygiene puzzle to solve.

The second piece is making sure you don't pick up any spam traps on your list. A spam trap is an email address set up specifically to catch spammers. If your deliverability rate tanks overnight, chances are you've picked a spam trap. Unscrupulous competitors enter them into your email list to trip you up. A spam trap looks like a regular email address. When you send an email to a spam trap address, you get blacklisted, which means that your emails can get blocked by entire networks and internet service providers.

If you get blacklisted, it's not just your email marketing campaigns that get blocked. Every email coming from your domain, even the personal ones you send out yourself, can wind up getting diverted to spam folders or blocked entirely.

There are services like Webula and Blaze Verify that you can use to keep your lists clean. You upload your list, and they remove spam traps, poorly formatted addresses, habitual complainers, and even trolls who seek out and sue US-based email marketers for noncompliance with the CAN-SPAM Act. There are other requirements as well, but the CAN-SPAM Act is a law that says you need to give your recipients a way to remove their names from your list if they no longer want to receive email from you.

Another way email marketers maintain clean lists is by sending out a confirmation email with a link you have to click to confirm that you subscribed. This is called double opt-in registrations, and it's great in theory, because it prohibits competitors from adding spam traps to your list. But if you force a recipient to double confirm, roughly 30 percent of them don't do it. They forget or get busy with something else and move on. If you're a small or midsize business, losing nearly one in three sign ups is a steep price to pay for data hygiene.

List Segmentation

Email marketing list segmentation, at the most basic level, is about separating engaged from disengaged recipients. Put the names that have been opening and clicking on one list, and those that haven't on another. If somebody hasn't opened one of your emails in the last six months, they're probably just not that into you. Remove, rinse, and repeat. If they've lost interest in what you have to say, put them in another bucket and send them different messages, much less frequently. Don't just keep sending them your newsletter. They don't care. Plus, it drags your open rates down.

Send an email that says, "We miss you," "Where have you been?" or "We'd love to have you back." Give them a special offer or free shipping. Send them a more aggressive subject line. And if they open it, move them back into the engaged bucket. If you're a B2B, you should also segment by account, role, and industry. But at the end of the day, engaged versus disengaged are the most important market segments.

If you want to qualify leads, generate sales, and build your pipeline, email marketing remains the most effective conversion channel. At the time of this writing, the average email marketing open rate across all industries is 21 percent, according to research from Mailchimp.

CHAPTER 7

Content Marketing

R obert Rose, chief strategy advisor at the Content Marketing Institute and three-time best-selling author, rolled up his sleeves and got to work. A major pet supply retailer wanted to get into content marketing, so they brought him in to figure it out. Content marketing is the strategic use of helpful information to attract, retain, and convert a clearly defined audience online. Robert's point of contact was their chief marketing officer. To pivot from retail to e-commerce, she wanted a strategy to get their website ranking highly in Google for pet health-related search terms.

But there were two problems. First, they were retail merchants, not veterinarians, so they lacked the requisite subject matter expertise. And second, they paid minimum wage to temp employees to stock their shelves and had very heavy turnover. So the brand was trusted for value, but it wasn't the type of place you went to learn how to care for your pet.

There was a mismatch between the content marketing approach the CMO wanted to take, and the resources required to make that approach successful. So Rose convinced the CMO to pivot to value-oriented content, and their e-commerce business has been increasing steadily ever since.

Content marketing requires content that aligns with your brand. You have to start with a problem you can solve. If you're known for having great prices on dog food, a blog post written to get found when someone searches "dog is sick and throwing up" is not going to result in a sale, because low-priced dog food won't solve the problem.

A good content marketing strategy converts awareness to consideration through entertaining, educational, and informative online content that's easy to digest. You have a problem you need to solve. You search. And you find something online to buy that solves your problem. Content marketing materials should be created to get found against search terms aligned with the problems your customers are searching for answers to online. In addition to answering the searcher's question, content marketers also introduce prospective customers to the value of their products or services.

When a company comes up with a new product and hands it off to the marketing department hoping they can sell it, they're putting the solution before the problem. A more successful approach is to reverse engineer the process and thus create a product based on a proven customer need. You do that by getting to know your customers' problems. Sometimes, they may not even know what they are themselves. Content marketing that solves unperceived problems is worthless because no one is searching for answers to problems they don't know they have.

Perceived problems change as prospects move through a purchase funnel. Advertising fills the top of the funnel. Rather than market the science behind their drugs, pharmaceutical companies run ads about relieving you of certain symptoms so you can live a better life. If the perceived problem is urination frequency, and you message around prostate health you're not addressing a perceived problem for top funnel prospects because they don't know how it relates to their problem. But if you message around the freedom to go to a baseball ball game or a movie theater comfortably without having to side-step down the aisle to pee every thirty minutes, that solves a perceived problem.

Content Calibration

Content marketing materials should be attuned to the various stages of the conversion funnel. The perceived problem that a discount investment broker solves for top funnel prospects is lowering the cost of investing. Discount brokers promote zero-cost transaction fees and no minimum balance to get you in the door and make it up by selling you mutual funds that pay them commissions. You'd be better off paying a small fee per transaction and getting into a low- or no-cost index fund. But if you're hip to that, you're too sophisticated to be searching for a broker with unbranded keywords. You're already aware of Vanguard, Fidelity, and Schwab and you're searching their brand names and comparing their fees. Content around free transactions and no minimum balance solves the top funnel prospects' perceived problem. Content built around management fees appeals to bottom funnel prospects. Good content marketers create content to get found at every stage of the customer journey.

Once you've determined the perceived needs and funnel stages you want to target, create content that helps prospects solve their problem from every conceivable angle. Tell them what it is, how it works, how to use it, how long it takes to get, how long it lasts, how much they need, and anything else they might want to know before making a purchasing decision. In sales, this is called overcoming objections, which is a good way of thinking about how to change up your content marketing assets to win purchase consideration. A good salesperson is a master at overcoming objections. Buyers present them with problems, and they solve them. Content marketing does the same thing, but instead of a salesperson solving the problem, buyers do it themselves with Google.

At least they think they're doing it themselves, though the truth is they're consuming content created by marketers designed to get found against specific search terms and win purchase consideration. You're searching Google to get answers to questions so it feels like you're in control. But content marketers have anticipated the terms and phrases you're searching. They've researched seed and long tail keyword volume (which you read about in Chapter 4) for every possible term they can think of that might be indicative of a problem they can solve. So they already know what terms someone at your stage of the buying cycle searches. And they've created content to get found by you.

If you want to create content to get found when people search "dog food," write blog posts about the problems pet owners are trying to solve when they need dog food. Keyword research reveals the top questions they search:

- What is the best dog food?
- How much food to feed my dog?
- How long can a dog go without food?
- Is Iams a good dog food?
- How many cups in a pound of dog food?

We can even find out how many times these questions get searched. These are what we call "high commercial intent" content marketing topics for a pet food seller, because people make purchasing decisions based on the answer. If we want information about the health of our pet, we'd be more likely to trust a veterinarian than a warehouse store. Content marketing around solving pet health-related problems would be a better match for a company like National Veterinary Associates, which owns and operates pet hospitals nationwide.

Like a magazine, your content marketing choices should be topically thematic. If you're creating scattershot content marketing assets like blog posts or infographics that aren't cohesively connected to an overarching topic, you won't attract repeat visits due to content inconsistency; there's no reason to come back because there's no focus. If visitors can't count on you to deliver valuable, reliable, consistent content about a same topic, establishing your company as the go-to provider in a niche is impossible. Shot-gun-style content marketing is like publishing a magazine with no editorial focus. The best content marketing strategies are not necessarily campaign-focused; they are category-focused to connect with buyers over time.

You wouldn't take a race car driver seriously if he said, "I don't need a better race car, I just want to win the race," says Robert Rose of the Content Marketing Institute. It's the same with your web content. You can't pour some secret sauce on your website and get your content to rank number one. You have to have the best content for the keyword. When it comes to content marketing, think quality over quantity.

Your website should be constantly evolving. It's a digital media channel, and digital media is not static. There's no classic CNN channel, because old news has no value. There's the History Channel, but their content is always changing, too. When you align your content marketing efforts with a specific customer problem, each individual asset makes the overall collection of content more valuable. Like a great film that stitches together different camera angles to tell a story, the whole is greater than the sum of its parts.

Customers searching for answers to problems have already decided they need a solution. They've self-qualified. If you're marketing to business customers, write a white paper with step-by-step, practical information that are easy to apply. Tell customer success stories. Explain what they will have to change in their business, what the implications will be, and how your solution can help. Create digital content marketing assets in a variety of formats like articles, infographics, and video, to engage, entertain, educate, inform, nurture, and convert potential customers into qualified leads.

Buyers are much tougher to get in front of than they used to be. We use caller ID and spam filters to screen out unsolicited sales pitches. We evade cold pitches from brands we don't want to hear from. Since buyers use organic searches to find answers online, search optimized content marketing is how you get pulled through the filter.

Text is the basis of search optimization, so good content marketers are good writers. And good writers are avid readers. And if it's audio or video, it's the title, description, tags, and text transcript that gets indexed by Google. Content marketing is how you get discovered and considered online. If you don't have the right content, you can't get considered because you can't get found.

Content marketing is packaged in a variety of formats: white papers, templates, checklists, tutorials, webinars, blog posts, and service pages. In all these cases, the content is designed to get found and influence purchasing decisions. It's created by content marketers to nudge us in their direction.

Google calls the online research we do to get educated the Zero Moment of Truth because it's the first phase of the customer journey. Whether you're buying a refrigerator or a jet engine, you research products before you buy them. In fact, 71 percent of buyers use the internet on a daily basis to make business purchase decisions.[1]

---

1   https://www.thinkwithgoogle.com/marketing-strategies/micro-moments/zero-moment-truth/

B2B marketers create content to find, nurture, and qualify us for a discussion with a salesperson. So, content marketing automates the presales process.

Constructing Content

To estimate the resources required to create effective content marketing assets, search the keywords you want to rank for on Google and analyze the top-ranking results. Whatever resources you think you'll need to create better content than the top-ranking results for a keyword are the resources you're going to need to construct winning content marketing materials.

Search the phrase you want to rank for and audit the results. Is it mostly content published by known news media outlets, universities, and enterprise-class companies? If so, it's going to be pretty tough to rank for that term because you're competing against content-rich websites with a ton of backlinks that have high authority in the eyes of Google. Add niche-related or geo-specific keyword modifiers until you start seeing results you can compete against.

Now, how current are the top-ranking web pages? Are you seeing outdated content ranking on page one? Are they rife with typos and grammatical errors? What about the author? Have you ever heard of them? Are they well known? If the author lacks authority or expertise in the subject, that's a signal that you're onto something. If you're a bona fide subject matter expert yourself and you create useful content that's also search optimized, you've got a good chance of outranking them.

Content that reads like it was written by a non-native English speaker was probably outsourced to an offshore SEO firm. Maybe the writer knows more about SEO than the topic that's covered in the post. Read it. Is it any good, or just a bunch of fluff? Does it really say anything? "The internet is littered with three-sentence ideas pumped into 36-page ebooks," says Doug Kessler, co-founder and creative director of Velocity Partners, a B2B content marketing agency. If you see a lot of vapid content and me-too blog posts ranking on page one of search results for a keyword you want to rank for, that's another positive signal. When nothingness content ranks high, you've discovered an opportunity.

To assess the real value of top ranking posts, here are some things to look for:

- Is the post linear and easy to follow?
- Does it have diagrams?
- Are there videos?
- Is it as easy to follow as Google thinks it is?
- Do they talk about the tools?
- Is there an infographic?
- Do they have good data visualizations?

You outrank your competitors by finding and filling these kinds of gaps. Once you've found what's missing, your job is to fill those holes with better content. That's how you earn your position on page one. If Google ranks a poor-quality page highly, it could be because it's published on a content-rich website with high domain authority, in which case it's particularly vulnerable to being outranked. "Newbies need to understand that the ranking boost you get from backlinks doesn't usually come from the domain authority. It comes from the page authority. That means you can publish a guest post on *TechCrunch*. But if no one links to it, the page authority from that post would be very low, even though the domain authority of *TechCrunch* is high," says Tim Soulo, CMO of Ahrefs, a powerful SEO toolset for keyword research.

If the top ranking content is not as easy to digest as it appears to be in search results, you've found an opportunity. Ask yourself, "Do I have the people, processes, and technology to construct better content?" If you search a term like "sales operations," you would expect to find relevant information on managing a sales team. Analyze the top results for "sales operations" and look for what's missing. If there's nothing about strategy, that's a signal that you're on to something.

Content marketing to consumers isn't necessarily any easier than content marketing to business customers. Winning purchase consideration in consumer categories like hospitality, automotive, and retail is just as competitive as in B2B categories like human resources technology, CRM, and logistics. In both cases, you're competing against content quality and brand authority.

And this also is why it's a challenge for any company to expand their search presence outside their niche. It's very hard to rank for new terms unrelated to the ones you're already ranking for. Like a character actor who gets typecast and has a career as a bad guy in every movie, Google typecasts domains too. If a new CRM provider like Pipedrive wants to rank for terms that aren't related to customer relationship management software, it's going to be tough for them to break out of their mold. As a hypothetical, let's say a CRM provider like Pipedrive were to acquire an email marketing company like ConvertKit to expand their offering.

If Pipedrive wants to start ranking for email marketing terms on their own website, it's going to be as tough as it would for ConvertKit to rank for CRM-related search terms. That's why companies that get acquired often maintain their web domains, because they don't want to surrender their rankings. Topical websites are easier for Google to understand and categorize because they fit nicely into predetermined categories. Websites that try to rank too broadly are much more challenging to classify. Start by creating content about a single problem you solve and establish search rankings there first.

Organic B2B growth marketing is driving growth through unpaid digital media. It's easy to see how B2B growth marketing relates to B2B marketing and B2B lead generation. But in reality, organic B2B growth marketing is a broad discipline involves:

- Analytics
- Automation
- Web performance
- SEO
- Email marketing
- Content marketing
- Blogging
- Podcasting

- Digital PR
- Lead generation

If you wanted to rank for the term "B2B growth marketing," it's far too broad a list to create content marketing materials about all at once. Only the established players like Hubspot and Hootsuite with content rich websites built up over decades can pull that off. For someone just starting out, it's faster and easier to pick one thing to rank for and focus on that.

To decide which customer problem you're going to solve with original content first, consult your website usage data to see which pages have the most visits. Next, check your search visibility analytics to see which terms you're already ranking for that are relevant, but that fall outside the top ten results. Work on lifting the results that fall on page two of Google's search results to page one. Cover that base first. If there's nothing much to work with and you're starting from scratch, search for an opportunity where you can compete. Then, focus, land, and expand.

Road to Rankings

Gaetano DiNardi, director of demand generation at Nextiva who I wrote about in Chapter 4, is also a musician. Content marketing is a great gig for him because he's playing in a space that rewards him for his creativity. As I mentioned, Nextiva sells voice-over-IP telephon cloud communications solutions to business customers. So LinkedIn is a great channel for Nextiva to engage prospects. And DiNardi has spent a lot of time analyzing shares that get the most engagement in LinkedIn news feeds.

He also gets a ton of cold pitches on LinkedIn from software vendors. Often when he accepts an unsolicited connection request, it's immediately followed with a cold pitch from someone he's never met pitching something he doesn't need. To him, it seems ridiculous to cold pitch via direct message on LinkedIn. So he decided to make a pithy, funny video[2] of himself cold pitching shoppers at the mall.

He shared it on LinkedIn with a brief summary of his three top takeaways framed as lessons for sales reps. Instead of cold pitching on LinkedIn, his suggestions were to (1) make your pitches conversational (2) avoid generic pray and spray messages, and (3) borrow language from the pitches you receive that work.

That's a lot of effort for one LinkedIn post. But it got nearly 1,500 likes and 600 comments. On social news feeds, reach is a factor of engagement, so his post achieved enormous visibility as a result of all those likes and comments. While it was a heavy lift, the effort was commensurate with the results.

Here's how Herculean his content marketing project was: He produced and edited a video on location at a mall, shared it on LinkedIn, wrote a guest blog post about his experience, and pitched it to the HubSpot Blog, which accepted and published it. HubSpot rewarded him with a backlink to a product page on his website for the keyword "cloud communications."

2   https://www.LinkedIn.com/feed/update/urn:li:activity:6496452164855087104/

He did all that for a single link from Hubspot.com to his website. HubSpot has a very high authority website, and that link sent a message to Google to rank Nextiva's product page high when people search "cloud communications." That's content marketing from soup to nuts.

Another approach is simply outdoing what's already been done. Let's say you search "best sales tools" and the top result is a listicle post of the fifteen best sales tools. If you publish a list of the fifty best sales tools, you have a good chance of outranking it because your post is going to be more comprehensive.

If you're trying to rank for an informational "how to" query, consider these formats:

- **Step-by-step** - Written to help someone complete a specific job These posts are focused and include visual charts and video tutorials. An example might be "How To Apply For a Home Equity Line of Credit" or "How To Choose The Best Coach Seat on a Delta 747 flight."
- **Instructional** - Written to help someone make sense of a topic or category they're new to. This formula can be beginning, intermediate, or advanced. Unlike the step-by-step formula, instructional posts are broader. Examples include "How To Buy Directors & Officers Insurance" or "How To Install Outdoor Speakers."
- **Strategic** - Written to make a business case for why you should implement a system or technology. Strategic content targets senior business decision-makers at the very

beginning of the buying process, and is popular in B2B content marketing. The goal for this formula is thought leadership. Examples include "Why Artificial Intelligence is the Future of Digital Business," or "Parents' Guide to Saving for the Right College."

- **Opinion or commentary** - The easiest way to get noticed here is by arguing a controversial position or opinion. But be careful not to fake it. Don't put a controversial headline in front of a middle-of-the-road post. It will wind up hurting more than helping because the content won't deliver. The visitor will bounce, and you'll lose their trust. Examples for this are "Why Supermarkets are Dead" or "Reconstructive Surgery Industry Insider Tells All."

Sometimes, high-value content marketing assets are used to generate leads and build email lists. Instead of making these resources available publicly online, visitors to your website fill out a form and trade their email address for access. This is called gated content.

Gated Content

Before he joined Nextiva, DiNardi was the VP of marketing at SalesHacker. He noticed that they were ranking for the term "sales excel pipeline template." And they were getting a lot of traffic from that search phrase to a collection of different Excel templates on their site. The templates were searchable and downloadable. You could view and download them without having to give up your email address. But you had to download each one separately.

Because they were ungated, they got a lot of backlinks. If you can't link to something, it won't get backlinks, which is a major drawback of gating your content. So rather than gate the individual templates, DiNardi added a single click download option to save people the hassle of having to download each of the twenty templates one by one. He didn't force visitors to give an email address to check them out. But they were high-quality templates, so by adding the bundle option, SalesHacker got one in five visitors to trade their email address for an all-in-one download.

Content Injections

Once the bundle download option was in place, DiNardi inserted his own display ads in the body of his blog posts to promote his gated content. He created a display ad for his "20 Excel Sales Pipeline Templates " and inserted it between paragraphs of all his relevant blog posts. The display as was linked to his "sales excel pipeline template" bundle squeeze page, where visitors could sign and download them all.

Content injections promotions for gated content are an effective way to divert traffic from topically related content to your lead magnets. At Nextiva, DiNardi uses content injections in his "work from home" blog posts to promote his annual "State of Business Communication Report," which provides research, guidance, and insights for remote workers. He trades a useful report for permission to build a relationship with a prospective buyer. If someone is working from home and interested enough to download his report, they may also be interested in a cloud phone system. But instead of relying exclusively on pop-up promo windows with sign-up forms that cover the page, he prefers content injections for a less abrasive customer experience.

If you click on his "work from home" content injection promo, it takes you to the squeeze page for his report. There's a form to fill out with one field, and one field only. He asks only for your email address. It's as low friction a micro-conversion as possible.

At SalesHacker, DiNardi eventually added content injections for gated content offerings to all his relevant blog posts, matching the promo and editorial by topic. It's like slowly but surely climbing a mountain. When you get to the top, you start bringing in opt-in email addresses that grow your list. By pairing relevant, search optimized articles with gated content, you convert the right customer at the qualified awareness stage of the funnel to the purchase consideration stage.

Content Promotion

Content marketing is no field of dreams. Just because you built it doesn't mean they'll come. But a lot of companies make the mistake of thinking they're done after they publish content. "The best content doesn't win; the best promoted content wins," says Andy Crestodina, cofounder of Orbit Media and author of *Content Chemistry*. He says we need to be thinking of content promotion and digital PR *before* we sit down to create content marketing materials.

Prospects find your content marketing funnel through different channels like Google, social media, referral links, and email marketing campaigns. But once they get there, the customer journey can be broken into stages, which are awareness, consideration, evaluation, transaction, and utilization. To explain how someone moves through a content marketing funnel, Crestodina uses cleaning up your garage as an example.

When you realize the mess in your garage has gotten out of hand, you become aware that you have a problem that you need to solve. In marketing funnel speak, you've become "problem-aware." You're not sure if you can organize it yourself with the tools you have. And you're not even sure what tools you need.

You google "how to organize a garage." Once you've started researching and reading a few things online, you start to see some options. You're becoming solution-aware. The amount of time you spend researching and considering different solutions depends on how expensive the solution is, how fast you need it, and risk factors.

In the garage example, the buyer might want a shelving solution. But to consider it, they need more details. Will it fit? Do they need special tools? Do they need to hire a pro to install it? Is this a weekend project, or will it take a month? To get them through this stage of the funnel, content marketing materials must anticipate and answer all these questions.

If the prospect is confident enough that the solution meets their needs, they will convert and place an order. But if they can't get their questions answered easily, they're going to bounce to a competitor who answers their questions quicker. They may even be willing to pay more just to be sure they're getting what they need without the hassle of sending an email or picking up the phone to confirm some minor detail before they place the order. Online, the best content marketer gets the sale.

Now that you're armed with tactics for building your content marketing funnel, one final thought. Promoted content will fill the top of the funnel, but an incoherent conversion experience will lose customers before they buy—so stay on topic. It doesn't matter if you're a B2B or consumer marketer. If your product requires purchase consideration, content marketing is a good fit. The longer the prospect spends considering different solutions, the more important content marketing is. Conversely, impulse purchases don't rely on content marketing. Ads work just fine because they get you to consider a purchase that's impulse-based. So no research, and no content marketing is required.

CHAPTER 8

Blogging

The word blog is a portmanteau that fuses the words "web" and "log." A blog is an online diary. Like a bowl of instant soup that you just add water to and stir, a blog is an easy-to-use content management system that stores journal entries in reverse chronological order. Each entry is called a post and the blog is a collection of those posts, or journal entries. So blogs and blog entries are different things. You write blog posts that appear in your blog.

Before blogs, organizations communicated to the public through press releases drafted by committees and distributed via paid newswires, email, and snail mail to the news media. There was no way to talk to a large audience without going through a journalist. Blogs made it possible for organizations to bypass the news media gatekeepers and humanize big, faceless organizations with brand journalism. They also empowered journalists to start their own online outlets and compete directly against their employers. So blogs gave rise to a whole new category of media. There are political blogs, start-up blogs, fashion blogs, travel blogs, food blogs, fitness blogs, DIY blogs, sports blogs, and blogs about pretty much anything else you can think of. Blogs were the first iteration of social media, and the blog world is sometimes called the blogosphere.

Before social networks introduced algorithms to decide which posts to display at the top of the newsfeed updates, posts were listed in reverse chronological order, too. So blogs were the original social newsfeed, but they were article feeds, rather than post feeds. Social networks iterated the format by giving everyone their own microblog—essentially a social networking profile page—and bringing other people's posts into a newsfeed consumable in one place. Social networks transformed the blogosphere into an eternal, online cocktail party.

Most bloggers don't allow comments on their blogs anymore because they're spam magnets, but in the early days you could post a comment at the bottom of most blog posts. The comments also appeared in reverse chronological order and that's what made blogs the first social media format—because people could have conversations in the comment grist. And blogs became a popular way for CEOs, marketers, and subject matter experts to communicate publicly through their websites.

Just as applications are integrated into tech stacks, blog publishing software is part of a marketing stack. WordPress is the gold standard blogging platform. The reason I use the word "platform" to describe it is because third-party developers build all kinds of add-on software that you can use to add new features and capabilities to your blog site. At this time of writing, there were more than 58,000 extensions you could plug into WordPress to add e-commerce, enhance security, SEO content, and much more.

WordPress can also be used to publish a website of pages in any configuration you like. So the platform is no longer just for blogging. It has grown into a full-fledged content management system capable of hosting an entire website. Nearly 40 percent of the Alexa top 10 million sites run on WordPress, making it ten times more popular than the number two content management system, which is Shopify. WordPress software is open source, which means the code is in the public domain and anyone can develop applications for it.

Automattic, the company behind WordPress, makes money by selling premium upgrade plugins that minimize comment spam and provide e-commerce functionality, site security, and backups. The company's tagline is "We don't make software for free, we make it for freedom." The double "t" in the Automattic company name underscores the founder's name, Matt Mullenweg.

Automattic has always been staffed by a remote workforce, their employees distributed all over the globe. They are a very innovative organization even with no central offices. And they're constantly pushing the boundaries of web publishing. They publish three updates of their software each year with the help of professional developers and amateurs who contribute their time to keep WordPress ahead of the curve.

On a blog, you can easily bring together content from a variety of different sources. For example, you can display an Instagram post or YouTube video in the body of a blog entry without having to upload pictures and videos to your site. You don't have to host the image or video files, which means you can embed social media content, or any other third-party content for that matter, in your blog, marginalizing copyright concerns.

When I was a teenager, it was not uncommon to see a collage with images cut from magazines on the wall in a friend's room. You can do the same thing in a blog post. You can add images, galleries, videos, even audio clips to blog posts, transforming from a text article into a mixed media collage.

Adding rich media to a blog post is easy-peasy. In most cases, you just cut and paste the URL into a field, and the content appears on your site. If you embed a YouTube video or Instagram post into a blog journal entry, whenever someone comments or likes it on YouTube or Instagram, their likes and comments show up on your website as well. This method of displaying third-party content on your website without actually hosting it is called "embedding" content. It's a great way to convert website visitors into social media followers because the embeds often include "follow" buttons that visitors can click to follow you on a social network without leaving your website.

Blog posts are also a way to add search engine optimized content to your website. Based on the keywords you want to rank for, your blog is where you create the "if, but, then" problem–solution-oriented content I talked about in Chapter 5. This is where you write posts that answer the questions your prospective buyers have when they're problem solving online. For many marketers, blogs are also where they host the content that they share on social media. That way, they're using shared media to drive demand to their own website instead of someone else's. So blogs are a popular tool for search engine optimization and social media marketing.

Day in the Life of a Blogger

To help you appreciate what it takes to maintain a top-ranking blog that reaches, on average, 21,000 readers per post, meet Neil Patel. He's an entrepreneur who's bootstrapped a multimillion dollar empire. He produces a daily podcast and maintains a popular YouTube channel. But the core of his content marketing operation is his blog.

Patel blogs once a week about digital marketing problems his businesses solve, which dovetails nicely with Ubersuggest, a digital marketing SaaS (software as a service) toolset he owns. He also runs Neil Patel Digital, a marketing agency with seven offices worldwide.

You might think Patel has an army behind him churning out content. While he does have plenty of editorial and technical support, he's also surprisingly self-reliant. He authors all his own content and creates all his own images. And his process is very methodical.

For Patel, it all starts with a headline. He searches the phrase he wants to rank for and looks for headlines with the phrase that are most shared on social media. He uses keyword research tools to focus in on what search terms to target, and social media research to craft a clever headline likely to capture and keep someone's attention.

For each post, Patel writes four to five potential headlines. His objectives are to rank high in organic search and go viral on social media. By starting with a well-researched keyword in striking range and by analyzing most shared headlines, he gets a clear direction of how to create his article.

Rather than just sitting down and seeing which way the article goes, he maps it out in advance. That way, he doesn't waste time trying to shoehorn search terms into his post after it's written. And he doesn't have to reorganize to deliver against a compelling headline. Most people will never read the post, but they will read the headline. So it makes sense to start with the headline.

For Patel, content optimization is part of the content creation process, not a step that comes after the content is created. If you're writing a blog post designed to get found through search and then shared through social media, it's not just your headline that needs to be optimized. A good headline may capture someone's attention, but it's the post itself that keeps their attention. Which means that, just like the headline is created in advance, the post needs to be mapped out, too. The content of the post should be guided by research around what prospects are searching for. This is the key distinction between blogging for business and creative writing.

In creative writing, you sit down with a general idea, start writing, and see where it goes. In blogging you research where it needs to go and fill in blanks. You write your headlines and subheadings before you start, so you know what you need to cover. It's counterintuitive, because we often use the writing process to get clear about what we want to say. But that doesn't work if you're blogging to get found through search and shared through social media.

After he's got his headline, Patel writes his introductory paragraphs. But then he jumps straight to the end and writes a conclusion. This is a practice he's developed through years of experience. By analyzing heat maps and session recordings, he's learned that readers don't consume blog posts in a linear fashion. They scan the introductory paragraphs first. Then, they scroll to the end of the post. And after that, they often leave. To keep them from bouncing, Patel started adding a "'Conclusion" subheading at the bottom with a scannable summary of what you'll get if you read the post. And sure enough, it worked to get readers scrolling back to the top on the post to read more.

Patel's concluding paragraphs are written more as overview summaries that tease the key takeaways. He writes them to pique the reader's curiosity and get them to spend more time on the page. If the conclusion section of his post gets the visitor curious, time spent on the page increases, which means they're more likely to solve the problem they came to the blog for in the first place. And if they solve their problem, Google scores that page as delivering on the user's intent because they don't do a second search for that same term.

After his headline, opening paragraphs, and conclusion are in place, he inserts his subheadings, which typically contain supporting keywords that reinforce the one he's trying to rank for. Then, he fills in the body text under each of the sub-headlines. He creates his own images, usually screenshots, and that initial draft takes anywhere from two to five hours to produce.

Blogging for business is a serious commitment. As a point of comparison, a study by Orbit Media found that the most successful bloggers spend over six hours on each post, embed video in their posts, and publish multiple times per week. On average, their posts are over 2,000 words and have more than seven images. They test at least seven headlines, use multiple editors, and often collaborate on posts with other influencers in their sphere.

Images are key to keeping someone's attention. According to the Orbit Media study, you'd need an image for every 300 words of text to rank among the most successful bloggers. Images break up the text for someone scrolling through your post while dense copy blocks are a deterrent to holding someone's attention. Patel writes in one- and two-sentence paragraphs to make his posts as digestible as possible. He considers negative space to be his friend, and he keeps his posts light and airy.

Readability should be reflected in the design of your blog as well. If your font is too small, your line spacing too cramped, or your paragraphs too long, the message you're sending is that it's going to be a lot of work to read your content. And the popular acronym TL;DR—too long; didn't read—is a common response because many bloggers don't take the time to get the design of their blog right. Don't assume that a popular WordPress template is easy to read. If you want an example of a site that's very digestible, check out nytimes.com. They test everything so use them as a benchmark for design readability. Getting your blog template design right is a process with a lot of back-and-forth design tweaks.

To recap, here is Patel's blog post authoring formula

- Research the keyword or phrase you want to rank for.
- Write headlines based on what's trending on social media.
- Write your intro paragraphs.
- Write your conclusion.
- Write your subheadings.
- Explain the subheadings.

This formula has made Neil Patel's blog one of the top digital marketing blogs in the world. It's a methodical approach to create content optimized for search and social media. Once Patel had his standard operating procedures in place, he scaled his blog worldwide.

Because going international is the easiest way to grow traffic, Patel works with freelancers to translate his blog posts into Portuguese, German, and Italian. In addition to translating his posts into other languages, he modifies his content (more on this later) to better fit each market.

Ranking for Competitive Keywords

Even when he's working to get his clients ranking for ultra-competitive keywords like "online gambling," "credit cards," and "auto insurance," the blogging process is always the same.

Patel starts by googling to see who's ranking in the top ten for that keyword. Then, he goes out and creates better content. It's rarely easy, but he just goes into more depth. He includes more images and does a better job creating useful content that answers questions searchers might have using their search terms. He doesn't add images and videos for the sake of adding images or videos, but to genuinely answer the searcher's question.

If he wants to rank for "online poker," he creates the best content for online poker. He might create a detailed infographic that breaks down how to play poker. He'll produce video tutorials and whatever else is required to outperform the top ranking posts. If he were trying rank for "online gambling," he'd blog about:

- How to bluff.
- How not to bluff.
- When to double down.
- When to double up.
- How much to bet depending on your cards.
- And whatever else is getting search traffic.

He gets really specific. More so than the competition. And he makes his content practical. He calls it "newbie-proof" content, which means someone new to the subject can get an easy-to-scan breakdown, with step-by-step instructions. They can grasp comprehensive subject matter in a short period of time without getting confused.

Getting too deep into the weeds is tough if the reader doesn't know the basic lay of the land. So his blog posts assume nothing.

He starts from square one. Once he's got the content completed, he promotes it on the social web. Then, he emails it to his list and asks people to like, share, and link. In addition to sharing on social media, he asks bloggers to review and link to his content. That's his process. And while it isn't easy, it is simple. Allocate the resources, apply the formula, and you will achieve results. Not overnight, but over the long haul.

Blogging Worldwide

Anna Lebedeva, who heads growth marketing at Semrush, drives worldwide demand through the Semrush blog, which publishes posts in seven languages. Her company sells a tool to SEO consultants that helps with keyword research and competitive intelligence.

Lebedeva localizes her content for each market, which she learns by reviewing local blog posts to see what's already resonating there. By starting with a media audit in the local language, she figures out what topics are most popular and what type of content strikes a chord with each audience. Just as content marketing about the best bats for hitting a six in the game of cricket will only get found on Google in countries like the UK and India where the game is popular, Lebedeva matches the message to the market.

She uses Google Translate to get the general idea of what people are saying because she's only interested in seeing at a high level what works so she can tailor her editorial calendar to each market. Then, she tries to get a sense of how knowledgeable her audience is in each country about search engine optimization. That way, she knows if her content should be at a beginning, intermediate, or advanced level.

In Brazil, for example, digital marketers are advanced at content creation. They know how to develop rich buyer personas and generate engaging content that targets the needs of an ideal customer profile. But when it comes to the more technical aspects of SEO, that market is still evolving. To resonate with her audience, she entered the Brazilian market with blog posts focused on content marketing best practices, since that's what they audience is familiar with.

In Northern Europe, like Scandinavian countries and Germany, her audience responds to more technical info. They want quantitative insights; just repurposing posts written for English-speaking audiences is ineffective. Like the Brazilian market, English-speaking audiences respond best to qualitative content.

Unfortunately, she can't just translate content developed for the US and UK into Scandinavian languages or German because those audiences want numbers. So she focuses on developing more technical content for Northern Europe.

When Semrush creates content that specifically addresses the Australian market, they are rewarded with customer loyalty. Australian English uses British spelling and metric measurements, but grammar is closer to American style and usage. Americans say Mississippi River, while the Brits say the River Thames. But Australian vocabulary has entirely unique terms like outback, bush, and barbie. Most companies just rehash their English or British language content for the Australian and New Zealand markets. Australia is the most appreciative market she's developed, probably because they're so geographically isolated.

In many niche B2B categories, Australia is an underserved market. Whereas the US is developed and mature with respect to digital marketing and SEO, Australia is nascent. That's not to say the country doesn't have its share of digital marketing thought leaders like Jeff Bullas and Darren Rowse. And there are a number of top SEOs in Australia. But more broadly speaking, digital marketing is less evolved in Australia than it is in the US.

Lebedeva says the most advanced digital marketing audience is the US. As China assumes a leadership position in the development of artificial intelligence, we could see that lead dwindle. And Tim Soulo, Anna's competitor at Ahrefs, told me he's learning to speak Chinese, which makes me wonder whether or not the future of SEO is artificial intelligence-based keyword research. But purchasing decisions still happen faster and sales cycles are still shorter in the US than anywhere else in the world, which is why it's the leading economy, Lebedeva says.

Comparing the US to the Australian market for digital marketing services, she sees the US industry as mature and more competitive. If you're looking to start a digital marketing agency, she thinks Australia is a great market to develop because it's much less evolved. But from an overall global, audience content programming standpoint, Anna says basic introductory "101" and "how to" content about SEO is what performs best on the Semrush blog.

Guest Posts

Eighty percent of the posts that run on the Semrush blog are written by outside experts, most of whom are customers who submit expert opinion pieces. The other 20 percent are product-oriented articles by the Semrush content marketing team. Contributing authors don't get paid for those posts, but they do earn influence by having a byline on a very prestigious SEO blog. And they get a "nofollow" link from the Semrush blog back to their website.

The "nofollow" reference tells Google not to associate the link with the Semrush domain from an authority standpoint. Such links have less value from an SEO perspective, but they're still valuable because they send referral traffic to a destination of the author's choice. So even though guest contributors don't get any "reflected" link authority from Semrush.com, they still get the thought leadership association of being published by a prestigious blog, and they're able to drive qualified traffic to their website.

From the contributor's perspective, guest posting on a respected blog is an effective earned media tactic. The more prestigious the blog, the more credibility the contributor earns. Though it is not easy to get chosen, Harvard Business Review accepts guest posts on their blog. Imagine what that link would do for your personal brand. Semrush has built their blog into such a desirable destination that they enjoy a steady stream of guest contributor submissions.

The Semrush blog is the cornerstone of their owned media marketing strategy. And since they don't accept comments, digital marketers must share and discuss posts on social media. Once their blog became established, their social media community grew organically as people discovered and shared their posts organically. By sharing SEO insights with their followers on social media, those followers are positioning themselves as up-to-date and in-the-know about the latest search marketing strategies and tactics.

There is a caveat: unless you've got customers and traction, don't expect to stir up a lot of conversation on social media. People qualify you based on someone other than yourself. Just as reporters triangulate truth through third-party sources, social media engagement has become a measure of credibility as well. Blog posts that get shared and discussed establish your reputation—and build your authority—through owned and shared media in a way that ads and press releases cannot.

Blogging for Leads

You can lead a horse to water, but you can't make it drink. By answering questions your buyers have and optimizing them for search and social media, you lead the horse to water. But unless you can solve their problem with a product or service you sell, your content marketing strategy is misguided. If you're a commercial enterprise, what's the point of educating your market if you're not deriving some benefit? You can lure the herd, but if you can't convert that traffic transactionally, your efforts aren't commercially smart because your content is off topic. That's why SEO is foundational; if you can't conduct keyword research, you can't create content designed to be found when people search those terms. To make that horse (or in this case, our prospect) drink, you calibrate your content against your keywords to convert.

A blog post itself isn't a sales page. You're not selling. You're educating. You're guided by the principles of journalism rather than the rules of advertising. In my first book *Social Marketing to the Business Customer*, there's a case study about an unlikely B2B that is absolutely killing it through blogging. That company is Indium and they sell solder paste. That's the stuff used to attach electrical components to circuit boards.

Blogging is the backbone of their content marketing strategy. They've been so successful, they stopped advertising and attending trade shows long before the pandemic. They blog in Dutch, German, Spanish, French, and Chinese.

Indium leverages their knowledge of the electronic components manufacturing industry to connect with customers when a purchasing need arises. They're not writing search optimized blog posts to rank against the name of their company. Google gives them that one for free. And they're not writing to rank for top of the marketing funnel keywords like "solder" where the probability of conversion is low. They're writing to rank against low-volume search phrases that are indicative of an immediate purchasing need. Instead of going after high-volume terms, they focus on low-volume search phrases with a higher probability of conversion.

It's great to rank first for shoes if you're Zappos. But if you're Allbirds and only sell Merino wool shoes, it's much better to rank for Merino shoes even though search volume for that is lower.

B2B blogs that generate leads are focused on answering very specific questions. What is it you sell, how much does it cost, and where do I get it? The objective is to come up in organic search results when people search for answers to problems you solve.

The objective is to help customers make smart purchasing decisions by anticipating their needs and making sure they find answers when they search. Not by shilling or marketing or publicizing. But by sharing genuinely valuable content.

Here are some headlines from the Indium blog:

- Pareto Chart: Crucial in a Continuous Improvement Plan
- Selective Soldering: A Collection of Benefits
- Solder in Medical Devices

Most people aren't interested in this kind of information, but those that are "back up the truck," as my coauthor Paul Gillin put it in *Social Marketing to the Business Customer*.

Indium is catering to a small audience because it's a market with a small customer base. This is why in most industries, B2B content marketing is less competitive than it is in consumer markets. Not as many people are searching for solder paste as "Nike Air Max 1" or "Florida vacations," so it's easier to be successful.

Blogging for Economy of Scale

As I mentioned earlier, it's more cost effective to answer questions on a blog than it is to answer the same question over and over again on the phone or in emails. But good writers are harder to find than good customer service agents, so most companies still respond to problems customers have via phone or email. Since there's a real literacy glut in today's labor market, this is an enormous opportunity for digital marketers who are also good writers.

Blogs are a way to convert your customer service center into an automated lead generation engine. By analyzing the rich text comments that customer service agents store on your ticketing system with an analytics monitoring platform like Talkwalker, you can see which issues are trending with customers. If you use these insights to decide what to blog about, you're more likely to tap a popular nerve. If people are calling you about it, you can assume they're searching first and not finding anything useful.

A blog post that covers a topic well gets you in front of people who are searching that topic whether they're customers or not, whether it's during business hours or not, or whether they know about you or not.

Blogs are a way to give people access to the information they need to qualify your products on a self-service basis, which both generates leads and speeds up the customer journey. Blogging accelerates sales cycles since prospects don't have to wait for an email or a returned call.

But since it's easier to listen than it is to read, there's another form of blogging called podcasting that allows you to publish rich media content. In the next chapter, you're going to learn how to podcast.

CHAPTER 9

Podcasting

t had taken two years, but we were finally ready. Through sweat equity and hard work, I founded and bootstrapped iPressroom, an online newsroom service, and together with my team we built a bona fide software as a service provider and signed major clients. We were getting ready to exhibit at the Bulldog Reporter conference in San Francisco, which catered to the public relations trade, our ideal customer profile.

It was 2005, and we were launching a new feature called podcasting which would allow our clients to upload audio or video files to their newsroom and syndicate them on Apple iTunes. Few knew what podcasting was back then. We needed a way to demonstrate our new product feature. So I decided to record some podcasts that we could put on our website to demonstrate what they were and how our new feature worked.

Podcasting makes it possible for anyone to distribute electronic media to a global audience. Before that you needed a satellite or a broadcast tower. So podcasting brought rich media programming within the owned media marketing domain. Podcasting is a subscription format where the connection between the publisher and the audience is persistent. It's like a DVR, but for audio programming instead of cable TV. Radio turned a global audience of readers into a global audience of listeners. In some respects, podcasting did to radio what radio did to print.

Since our ideal customer profile at iPressroom was PR people, we needed a podcast that would appeal to that audience. At the same, we also needed a way to stand out and get noticed on the crowded floor of exhibitors at the trade show we were attending.

The textbook definition of public relations is managing the relationship between a company or famous person and the public. Before I launched iPressroom, I was director of promotions at a big PR firm. After that, I opened my own agency. And in all my years, clients always came to me for the same thing: news media coverage.

If you're in PR, you need relationships with reporters who will consider your pitch because they know you. Jim Sinkinson, the owner of Bulldog Reporter was well aware of this. So with the help of his conference organizer Fay Shapiro, his sessions were mostly meet-the-media panel discussions with journalists talking about what types of stories they liked to cover and how they liked to be pitched.

The year we launched our podcasting functionality, Jim and Faye had secured David Satterfield, the managing editor of the *San Jose Mercury News*, Nick Wingfield of the *Wall Street Journal*, Elizabeth Weise of *USA Today*, Chris Taylor of *Time* magazine, Brad Stone of *Newsweek*, and Jeffrey O'Brien of *Wired* magazine and others to speak at the conference.

If you've never spoken at a conference before, just know it's a lot of work. You have to think about what you want to say. You might have to put a PowerPoint presentation together or write a speech. You've got to get dressed up, go to a big hotel or conference center, go on stage, and give your schpiel. So the speakers are heavily invested, and they show up ready to go.

I contacted speakers on the agenda I was interested in interviewing prior to the conference and asked if they'd be willing to drop by our booth on the trade show floor for a podcast interview about their talk. At the time, podcasting was so novel many of them said yes because they wanted to know more about what podcasting was. And they also saw the value of recording a brain dump as a record of their appearance at the event.

With the help of Michael Butler of the *Rock 'n Roll Geek Show*, I recorded sixteen interviews live in our booth at the Bulldog Reporter Conference. We dressed it up to look like a local news set (see fig. 9.1). We even got one of those "On Air" signs to make it look official. Sure enough, the interviews were events that drew a crowd. Then we uploaded each interview to our website as it was completed.

Figure 9.1 Tech reporter Brad Stone appearing on my first batch of podcast recordings at Bulldog Reporter 2005 in San Francisco.

As a PR guy, I understood the difference between editorial coverage and advertising. I wrote press releases, which are written in a journalistic style. They're not supposed to be opinion pieces but rather an objective document of record that conveys the facts concisely. I figured if I could produce a podcast that effectively profiled the likes and dislikes of each of these journalists rather than talk about my company, it would attract PR people for years to come. I called the podcast *On the Record ... Online* because I was creating an on-demand dossier of each reporter. I was putting them on the record, online.

To preserve the shelf life of the podcast interviews, I intentionally steered away from news-of-the-day questions. It takes time for people to download and listen to them. Podcasting is an on-demand media format and I didn't want them to get stale too quickly. So I decided to produce a more feature-oriented, evergreen type of show that would be worth listening to for a very long time.

On the one hand, while I was producing a program with real value, rather like a house organ, I also needed to promote my company. So Michael inserted a prerecorded, pre-roll ad about iPressroom at the beginning of the program. We also made an intro with background music, and an outro as well. The process was simple: I'd interview the journalists live on the show floor, and when I was done, Michael would edit in the intro, the ad, the outro, and upload it to our blog with a photo of the guest.

While most people find podcasts through Apple Podcasts or Spotify, the technology behind podcasting is a blog. Podcasts have to have a home on the internet somewhere in order to feed any of the popular podcast listening platforms. Today, you can turn a WordPress blog into a podcast engine by installing a plugin like Blubrry PowerPress to get podcasting functionality. But at the time I got started, that wasn't the case, which made the feature very attractive to PR people who wanted to leverage rich media to promote their organizations.

We needed a text description of each podcast episode, too, because potential listeners on iTunes needed to be able to read what our podcast was about. So back at our offices in Los Angeles, each time a new episode was uploaded, my staff would listen to it, write up show notes, give the episode a title, and publish it.

I love learning new things. I love going to conferences and hearing smart people talk about what they do. The cool thing about podcasting was that I got to ask smart people tough questions. Since it was being recorded and would no doubt be heard by others, they gave me thoughtful answers. Sometimes I even went back and refined the show notes myself just to cement the knowledge they shared in their interviews.

After the conference was over, we pretty much forgot about the podcast and went on with our lives. A couple of months later, we saw we'd served tens of thousands of downloads and decided to continue producing the podcast as a way of making a market for our online newsroom service.

When it came to booking guests to interview on the show, my experience in public relations really helped. First, I knew many of the reporters who might come on the podcast, and second, I knew which media outlets were the most influential. It wasn't easy, but I convinced Walt Mossberg from the *Wall Street Journal*, David Carr from the *New York Times*, and Ken Auletta from *The New Yorker* to come on the podcast. After that, all I had to do was drop those three names, and any other journalist I asked said yes because they wanted to be in that august company. This is something to think about if you're planning to do an interview-style podcast. If you book the big names first, you're on easy street from there.

On the Record ... Online became so popular in the PR trade over the next five years, that Jim Sinkinson actually invited *us* to produce the podcast live from his Bulldog Reporter conferences. After that, Elizabeth Albrycht and Jen McClure invited us to podcast live from their New Communications Forum, which was the first conference on the use of technology for marketing and PR. We even became the official podcast of the Public Relations Society of America International Conference, recording interviews at their conference for almost a decade.

Over the years, I widened the show's focus and interviewed public relations gurus Harold Burson, Al Golin, and Larry Weber, the names behind the largest global PR firms. I spoke to communications professionals in the federal government and US military public affairs officers. And I had tech media personalities like Leo LaPorte and Doc Searls on the show. I won a slew of awards and was invited by Paul Gillin to coauthor my first book *Social Marketing to the Business Customer*.

Over the period, I used what I learned to benefit my clients as well. In 2006, I created the *Behind the Curtain at the LA Opera* podcast as a media channel to promote my client, Vincent Paterson, who was directing their production of *Manon*. The LA Opera became a client too, and that podcast continues on today.

I created and produced the *Hollywood Reporter/Billboard Film & TV Music Conference Podcast* sponsored by Associated Production Music for another client, Adam Taylor, featuring interviews with film, television, and game music composers. We recorded the episodes backstage in the greenroom at the event and used Hollywood Reporter and Billboard staff writers to host the interviews, but the podcasts themselves were hosted on the APM Music website, which meant we got inbound links from both publications, doing wonders for their search rankings.

It's a lot easier to produce podcast episodes in batches than one at a time, and professional conferences were a great place to find a bunch of high-profile guests in one location. While some people can wing it, for me, recording a good podcast interview requires advance preparation. I would research each guest prior to interviewing them and come up with a list of questions. I didn't always follow the questions verbatim, but at least I knew what bases to cover, which was particularly important when I was doing eight interviews on the same day at a conference. As a hallmark of the podcast, I never edited the interviews. I wanted them to be honest, unmanipulated digital recordings of our discussions. That meant I had to keep things moving, so I was substituting advance preparation for post-production.

There's a tactic in PR for generating broadcast news coverage called a video news release, which just as it sounds, is a video press release you produce and send out to news broadcasters. Five months before I launched *On the Record ... Online*, Shel Holtz and Neville Hobson had launched another public relations industry podcast called *For Immediate Release: The Hobson and Holtz Report*, which is the two of them discussing news developments of interest to the PR trade. FIR is a great podcast, and it's still around today.

FIR was a much harder podcast to produce then *On the Record ... Online*. Holtz and Hobson had to keep up with industry news of the day, decide collectively what they'd cover, and think about what they wanted to say. Plus, since the show covered the news of the day, past episodes had little archival value.

If you missed a few weeks, you didn't go back and listen to the old ones. You just listened to the current episode. Since my podcast was more feature-oriented, and since there were public relations people searching for information about reporters every day, I had a built-in audience for my past episodes, which increased my reach. In fact, thousands of episodes of *On the Record ... Online* are still being downloaded today.

To grow my audience moving forward, I decided to make podcast news releases of my episodes. I'd pull the three best quotes I could find from each of the episodes and package them up as a news segment with me as the correspondent. At the end of each segment, I'd tell listeners to subscribe to my podcast if they wanted to hear the full interview. I sent these segments to Holtz and Hobson who were appreciative and included them in their podcast. I became the *For Immediate Release* Hollywood correspondent and grew my audience to the point where, over the life of the podcast, which ran from April 11, 2005 through May 5, 2015, I delivered more than one million downloads.

Podcasting isn't for everyone. But if you're nurturing an audience, it is the most effective and efficient electronic media distribution format for building personal relationships with prospective buyers. Podcasting is a lot more competitive these days. But it is still a great way to reach buyers, particularly in underserved markets.

"There will always be something that hasn't been said yet or that needs to be said more. And the question is whether you can (a) get the audience for it and (b) do that in a way that you can pay your bills and maybe make a make a living off of it," says Nick Quah, who publishes a podcast trade newsletter called *HotPod* and hosts *Servant of Pod* on KPCC public radio.

Benefits of Podcasting

If you want to convince someone to take action, you have to be able to articulate why they should do it. In marketing and PR, persuasion is a vital skill. In the early days of podcasting, I found myself so frequently making the argument in favor of the nascent format that I decided to write out the top reasons why podcasting was a good idea.

I first wrote up these benefits of podcasting fifteen years ago, but they still hold true today:

- Podcasts allow listeners to time-shift and place-shift media consumption. It's an audio DVR in your pocket.
- Podcasts are more efficient because downloads are opt-in. You only download what you subscribe to.
- Unlike radio, podcasts are accessible to a global audience regardless of geographic boundaries.
- Research shows that podcasts draw a more educated, affluent, and influential audience than radio.
- Podcasts give you the ability to bypass the news media and get directly to your listeners.

- Podcasting is the most cost-effective way to distribute electronic owned media to a subscriber base.

Let's look at what you can do with podcasting as an owned media channel that you can't with social media.

Figure 9.2 With podcasting, content proximity impacts conversions and commerce. In this graph, you see the *Behind the Curtain at the LA Opera* podcast on their website, as well as what it looks like on Apple Podcasts on mobile and desktop devices. While the LA Opera can include an option to purchase tickets alongside their podcast on their own website, they cannot do so in Apple Podcasts.

The reason the LA Opera decided to continue producing *Behind the Curtain* was to develop a younger audience of patrons. You can't sell tickets on YouTube. And unless you want to pay out a hefty commission, it's always advantageous to transact e-commerce on your own website.

There's nothing wrong with distributing owned media through social media channels. But if the goal is e-commerce transactions, then proximity matters. Ideally, people should get your original content at the place where you prefer to transact e-commerce. If you're the LA Opera, you want to use your podcast to attract people to your website so you can sell tickets. Facebook is a great way to "socialize" your brand and build a community. And Apple Podcasts is a great channel through which to get found by a larger audience. But distributing content on a social network like Facebook or a podcast directory like Spotify benefits them more than you because it gives them a way to scale an audience they can sell ads against without having to pay you anything.

Granted, it's much more challenging to SEO your show notes, get podcast subscribers, and grow an email list that you can send your podcast to. If you have your listener's email addresses, you're in a better position to transact e-commerce against your content. If you're reliant on Apple, Amazon, Facebook, or Google for access to your customers, you're a digital sharecropper.

While Apple and Spotify distribute podcasts for free, the attention they aggregate allows them to profit in other ways. Originally, Apple profited by selling more hardware. Today, Apple and Spotify both sell subscriptions to their own, original content. Podcasts make their platforms stickier so they can nurture their own subscriber base.

If you have a subscriber's email address, you can maintain a direct relationship without relying on an intermediary. If someone subscribes through Apple or Spotify, you are reliant on those companies to reach your listeners. So strategically, the best subscriber is an email subscriber.

Proximity impacts credibility, conversions, and commerce. Having your own podcast on your website (1) raises your credibility as a content creator, and (2) allows you to present promotional content in close proximity to convert listeners into leads. Having a recurring, rich media program on your website lets you build relationships with listeners you can transact commerce with.

This is what makes owned media marketing so liberating. You're not dependent on a third-party media outlet or trade show organizer to reach your target audience. Podcasting is also a way to drive measurable transactions from editorial content. You can't draw a straight line between a mainstream news media placement and a sale. But if someone finds your podcast through organic search, subscribes via email, and buys something from you, that customer journey is 100 percent measurable.

Profitable Podcasts

Eric Siu runs a multi-million dollar digital marketing agency called Single Grain with clients like Amazon, Airbnb, and Uber. He also runs a SaaS SEO experimentation tool start-up called

ClickFlow and has a portfolio of online media properties that collectively draw millions of unique monthly visitors.

Owned media is Siu's sweet spot. He maintains two podcasts, a blog, and a YouTube channel. He invests the time to SEO his posts because 50 percent of his leads come through organic search, 35 percent from speaking at conferences and 15 percent from podcasting. But podcast leads are the best ones because listeners who have gotten to know him and developed an affinity for his approach close faster and spend more. The ability to build a sense of intimacy on a one-to-many basis is a huge advantage in podcasting, because for the listeners, it seems like the podcaster is just talking to them. There's a sense of intimacy.

I remember asking the folks at Disney why they were podcasting so early on when audiences were miniscule compared to mainstream media. I thought Mickey didn't get out of bed for less than a million people. Disney argued that they thought we were approaching an age where consumers would filter out messages from brands they didn't want to hear from. Podcasting was a way to whisper into the ears of their most loyal consumers and seed the marketplace through their self-appointed brand ambassadors.

Eric Siu produces a top-rated, short-form, daily marketing podcast with Neil Patel called *Marketing School* that generates $800,000 annually in sponsorship revenue. If you search the word "marketing" on Apple Podcasts, theirs is a top ten result, as is the perennial favorite *Marketing Over Coffee*, another popular ad-supported podcast featuring John Wall and Christopher S. Penn.

Marketing School is surprisingly unrehearsed and relaxed. Both Siu and Patel know digital marketing so well that all they really need is a headline and some bullets to share beginner-level, practical digital marketing insights, which appeal to a broad audience. To manage the workload, they leverage economies of scale and batch record a couple weeks of shows each time they get together. It took years for them to build their audience. That goes to show you that if you rely on hard data alone to allocate marketing resources, it's impossible to justify building something from nothing. In the case of podcasting, if you're launching a new show, you have to have faith in your own potential and grind out the first few years until your audience finds you. So there's definitely risk involved. But the big lesson from the *Marketing School* podcast is frequency increases audience size, and shorter formats tend to get more listeners, too. The other top marketing podcasts are also daily programs that are shorter than fifteen minutes per episode.

Repurposing Podcasts

When they produce new podcast episodes, Siu and Patel record in front of an audience on a webinar platform and stream live to their social media profiles as well. It makes sense because it only requires a little extra effort. Plus, if you livestream on a webinar platform, you can pull video excerpts and use them on YouTube to promote your audio podcast.

I pull juicy soundbites from my podcast interviews and post them to YouTube with a link to the full episode in the description field. I produce two podcasts. The first, *The Earned Media Podcast*, is about the people, processes and tools used to secure media coverage. And the second is the *B2B Lead Gen Podcast*, which is a weekly audio master class on how to generate, qualify and convert leads to revenue.

If the topic isn't something people are going to search, it's probably not worth blogging about. It doesn't necessarily need to be a 2,000-word blog post, but you still need some basic show notes to describe the episode to your listeners.

By the same measure, not all YouTube videos are going to work as blog posts. Some topics just don't make sense for an audio format. If it's a step-by-step process you're talking about that requires screenshots and back-up images, people are going to get lost. Sure, you can include images, URLs, and logos on screen in a YouTube video. But charts and graphics may not scale down or be readable at a smaller size. If it's an audio podcast, technical content may be too tough to follow without visual aids. So match the message to the media.

In my experience, interviews are the most pliable for repurposing in multiple formats. Even if you're recording a feature-oriented, evergreen interview, you can still pepper in one or two questions about current events at the end of the interview to get something timely to promote the episode with on social media. To make it easy to SEO your show notes, create your interview questions based on the keywords you want to rank for. That way, your guest will use those terms in their answers, and you can write about in your show notes. Go to Reddit and see what posts about the topic you're discussing are trending. By asking those questions, you're ensuring that they'll be covered in your show notes, which means your podcast will be easier to optimize for organic search.

Putting It All Together

As you've learned by now, publishing online content and search engine optimization go hand in hand. Remember, if what you're looking to do is generate leads, it's important to embrace popular language so that people can find you when they're using those terms to search for what you sell, even if they don't know who you are. Of course, doing that means taking the time to research keywords and phrases most likely to be searched by qualified prospects before sitting down to write or interview a guest for a podcast. This is why SEO is foundational to digital marketing, and why I covered it up front in this book. Even in the world of podcasting, SEO still guides content strategy.

CHAPTER 10

Digital PR

When you say good things about yourself, others take them with a grain of salt. But when a neutral, unbiased source like a journalist or a respected influencer says good things about you, it's considered to be more credible. Public relations is about building visibility and credibility through third-party endorsements. But in the case of digital PR, those endorsements also result in backlinks that lift your search rankings.

Not all endorsements are created equal. The more influential the news media outlet, influencer, or brand making the endorsement, the more credibility you earn in the eyes of your customers and the more valuable the backlink in the eyes of Google. News media coverage about you or your brand is an implied endorsement. If you're receiving news media attention, the takeaway is you're important. News media endorsements are more neutral and impartial than endorsements from online influencers or corporate blogs. As a rule of thumb, the harder it is to score a third-party endorsement, the more valuable it is to your organic search rank authority.

To appreciate what it takes to generate news media coverage, there's an old joke in broadcast journalism that goes like this. "You've got two minutes to cover the story. If it's the end of the world, I can give you two-and-a-half minutes." The joke is that TV time is more valuable than life itself. Incredibly cynical, yes, but journalists are cynical people because they're whistleblowers and tastemakers. If they're whistleblowers, they're exposing people for doing really nasty stuff, which would make anyone distrustful. If they're tastemakers, they're always telling people what's extraordinary. As tastemakers, they're smothered daily by people telling them how great they are, which would make anyone skeptical because extraordinary is, by definition, a rarity. Journalists and influencers get pitches by the armload, most of them barely newsworthy. So assume that your pitch will be considered boring until proven newsworthy.

According to the PBS NewsHour, journalists determine news-worthiness against these five values:

1   **Timeliness** - It's news if it's a "new" occurrence. Current events are newsworthy because they just happened or they are happening now.

2   **Proximity** - Things that happen close to home are news-worthy in a given geography. Local events are newsworthy to local news outlets because they affect the people in the vicinity, community, or region they cover.

3   **Conflict and Controversy** · Storytelling is conflict resolution. When people disagree over actions, events, ideas
or policies, that makes news. Conflict and controversy
attract our attention by highlighting problems or differ-
ences. The best stories profile different sides of an issue
and let us decide what's right and what's wrong.

4   **Human Interest** · We are interested in other people. We
like unusual stories about people who accomplish amazing feats or who find a way to survive a difficult life crisis
because we identify with them vicariously.

5   **Relevance** · We're attracted to information that helps us
make good decisions. If you like to cook, you find recipes
relevant. If you're looking for a job, business news is relevant. We use relevant information to make decisions.

These are the basic elements of hard news. If you're looking to
generate lifestyle or trade news media coverage, the list includes
these five soft news values:

1   **Click-worthiness** · Does your story lend itself to being
packaged in a way that can arouse curiosity, fear, or desire? If your client was a private investigator "Reasons
People Give For Cheating That Are Worse Than Actually
Cheating" is an example of a press release headline that
covers all three.

2   **Strange But True** · Far out and unusual things, situations,
or occurrences are newsworthy. Online tabloids like Daily
Mail and the Associated Press have "oddities" newsbeats

with examples of things that are newsworthy because they're so unlikely you almost can't believe they happened. If an artist gets arrested for trying to sneak one of his or her paintings into a museum, that's the type of media stunt that could garner oddity coverage.

3   **Something Useful** · How can your story save people time or money when it matters most? Stories about installing solar panels are more newsworthy during extreme weather events, since that's when heating and cooling costs increase and utility services are most likely to fail. Tax season, going back to school, and industry trade shows are perennial, cyclical opportunities for stories about something useful.

4   **Something Exclusive** · This is where celebrities come in handy, and where money often does change hands legally, but without public disclosure. Hiring celebrities to host product launch parties and limited beta software releases are examples of leveraging exclusivity to generate news coverage. Behind the scenes access at a special event or a view into any unique environment that is restricted to most people is another way of leveraging exclusivity to generate news. In entertainment PR, these are set visits. In restaurant PR, they're invitations to see a chef cook a signature dish. In B2B PR, it's an invitation to a special event with hospitability, entertainment, and a one-on-one with the founder.

5   **Something Hot** · This doesn't have to be visual, although editors like pictures of attractive men and women, as long as they're justified in conveying the story. Tips about how

to be more desirable is a theme that drives headlines ad infinitum.

If you're considering garnering attention with PR, you should know that a new product, sales promotion, or new hire is not necessarily newsworthy. If you're Apple or Amazon, it may be.

But if you're a relatively unknown start-up, you're one of the thousands seeking media coverage without a news hook. You need to differentiate yourself by figuring out what's newsworthy about your product or service and then package yourself to journalists from that perspective.

Two final truisms about what makes news:

- If a dog bites a man, that's not news. But if a man bites a dog, that news because it's the opposite of what you'd expect.
- If it bleeds, it leads because if people get hurt, we want to know about it so we can keep ourselves safe.

If you're looking for quick results, your best course of action is to buy people's attention with advertising. Like SEO, PR requires an up-front investment of time before you start seeing results. It's not uncommon for a go-to media strategy to start with a series of soft press releases sent out with no real hope of generating news coverage, but rather just to get reporters familiar with your brand or company. That way, when the real news drops, you're on their radar. In this case, it could take three months just to establish yourself with the targets you're looking to get in front of. News media coverage is never guaranteed, which is why it's better to get your sales and marketing in order before you invest in public relations.

How Much Does Public Relations Cost?

Edelman, the largest PR firm in the world, billed clients $892 million last year, with a staff of 5,700. That's revenue of $156,415 per employee, according to *The Holmes Report*.

If you're a global consumer brand that needs a presence in major markets worldwide, expect to pay a global agency millions of dollars or more for a coordinated, international campaign. If you're a venture-backed tech start-up prioritizing growth over efficiency in a winner-take-all market and you want a high level of service, expect to pay a high-tech Silicon Valley PR firm $20,000 to $50,000 per month, plus expenses.

If you're a B2B in a niche market or bootstrapping a start-up, you could easily spend $10,000 to $25,000 a month for competent representation. But regardless of who you are, established public relations agencies are going to want a monthly retainer of at least $10,000 and a minimum ninety-day advance termination clause for their rock-bottom level of service.

If you're relatively unknown and on a limited budget, large public relations agencies aren't a good fit. You'll get pitched by a senior executive then handed off to a junior employee to handle your account. You'll be paying at least $10,000 a month, but you'll be serviced by a shared resource who's learning on the job, and you're going to have to ride them hard to get much attention. Smaller PR agencies start at $2,000 per month with a thirty-day advance termination guarantee, but you'll still be handed off to a junior media relations person cutting their teeth. That's the agency model.

Independent PR practitioners—and there are some good ones out there who specialize in different industries—start at $2,500 per month, and they're usually looser about termination clauses and expenses. A three-month book PR campaign might cost $15,000 plus expenses. But hiring an independent practitioner is also risky, because if they overbook themselves or become unexpectedly unavailable, there's no backup. On the other hand, since sole PR practitioners are often former, senior public relations agency executives, at least you don't have to worry about being handed off to a novice.

PR pros who have been at it for a while have relationships with journalists. This doesn't mean they're going to pitch them your story unless it's genuinely newsworthy because they can't afford to alienate their contacts for one client by hitting them up too often. Remember, if the end of the world is only worth two-and-a-half minutes of news time, your story better be gripping or it'll never see the light of day. Whether you retain a PR agency or an independent practitioner, you want someone who:

- Has the skills to do the work.
- Has the relationships to do the work.
- Will actually do the work.

The thing to understand about all these options when you're hiring PR is that you're being represented nonexclusively, so you're sharing your PR representation with other clients. I've managed teams, accounts, and campaigns at large and small public relations agencies, so I know what goes into keeping a portfolio of clients happy. In my experience, it's the squeaky wheel that gets the grease.

Marquis name brand clients aside—because PR agencies are known to flaunt their bigger clients to sign new business, and may even charge those clients less as a result—that means you need to actively manage your PR agency in a way that demonstrates an understanding of the challenges they face pitching your story. You also need a high enough media IQ to make a realistic assessment of what's possible so you can motivate your PR reps appropriately.

It's about appropriate expectations. There are always exceptions, but if you're expecting the *New York Times* to review your self-published book, or the *Wall Street Journal* to cover a new product from an unknown company with few customers, you have a low media IQ. That, in turn, is going to discourage a public relations professional from taking you seriously and giving you their best effort because you're uneducated. Remember, you're paying them to get you news media coverage, not to bring you up to speed on media relations. If you're clueless about what makes news, you're a lousy client. You're also a prime candidate for getting over-promised and under-delivered. These are the clients that walk away thinking that PR doesn't work. In reality, they just don't know how to work it.

There are also performance-based PR specialists who offer per press release pricing. However, since public relations is a process, they have less incentive to perform over the long haul. They have limited skin in the game and can't really afford to be as thorough as a retained PR firm that's looking to sustain a monthly billing relationship. Similarly, hourly PR specialists are not incentivized to work efficiently. To the unsophisticated client, hiring by the hour may seem less expensive, but in the long run, you're paying more and getting less.

Composed PR Pros

Sarah Evans is highly skilled at the use of social and digital media to generate earned media coverage for her clients, who include PayPal, Cox Communications, MGM International, and Walmart. She's a digital PR strategist who knows how to leverage online tools to see what makes news on any given day—and she's one of the best.

Her Twitter lists[1] alone are proof of her ability to use technology in service of media relations. Check them out. She uses them to monitor what journalists in different categories are interested in by checking their tweets. Based on what's trending, she writes an informal, weekly email with a list of story ideas pegged to the news trends of the day. By sending a collection of pitches, rather than a single story idea, she gets more attention because her pitches have more potential.

When I first started at Rogers & Cowan, the largest entertainment public relations firm in the world, I was in a meeting with

1   https://twitter.com/prsarahevans/lists

the late Julie Nathanson, an executive and publicist whose clients included Raquel Welch and Terry Bradshaw, among others. We were putting together press materials for a new client before the internet became mainstream. At the time, we were still stuffing press releases, bios, fact sheets, and backgrounders into dual pocket presentation folders and snail mailing them out to reporters. I suggested we print a custom press kit folder with the client's name on it and do a mass mailing. Julie took a Post-it note, wrote the client's name on it, stuck it on a blank folder, and said, "Here, send this." She wanted the client to look undiscovered.

In journalism, a scoop is the first report of a story of exceptional importance. Scoops are what motivate reporters because they propel their careers to new heights. A scoop is a reporter's diamond in the rough. It's what they're always looking for. So the more exclusive a story is, the more desirable it is.

PR strategist Evans understands the law of exclusivity and incorporates it into her media outreach. She never blasts her story emails to her entire list. Instead, she customizes each email for each recipient, one by one. She starts with different templates for print, TV, and digital news media outlets, since TV reporters are more interested in the visuals and news publishers want more background information.

By personalizing the template, she's letting the recipient know that the email they're getting was written for them instead of blasted out to every one of their competitors. In terms of format, she keeps it short and sweet. Here's how she structures her story email pitches:

- Five to seven bulleted story ideas with brief descriptions.
- TV pitches include links to visual assets.
- Print pitches include links to background info.

Ready for Media

The digital pivot is sequential. Digital PR is Chapter 10 of this book and not Chapter 1 or 2 because, while it has the greatest potential to drive exponential growth, you have to set the table before you invite people over for dinner. That means your owned and shared media programs need to be in order first.

Your website and social followings must be ready to withstand the scrutiny of the news media before you start pitching for earned media coverage. Unless you're a name brand already, you need a good enough website and enough social media followers for reporters to qualify you. If you have a strong owned media presence and enough followers to prove you're legit but little to no media coverage, you're a potential diamond in the rough, showing half-hidden flashes of the glittering gem you will become when polished.

Getting press starts by building a website that journalists can use to qualify you for coverage. If you call a journalist and pitch them a story about a company they've never heard of, the first thing they're going to do is check out the company online. Both the usability and the content on your website impact your credibility. If your website has a bunch of broken links or there's a disconnect between what you're pitching and what they see, your credibility is at stake.

But if you've got a decent website and enough followers to prove you're not a ghost, you're ready to go after earned media. You don't need to have 100,000 followers on Twitter, like Evans has. You just need enough followers to prove you're real. It's labor intensive and risky for journalists to cover stories that can't be easily authenticated. If they can't substantiate your story to their editor or audience, they're risking their own reputation.

If it's difficult for a reporter to qualify you quickly as a candidate for news media coverage online, they'll move on. Why? Because they have to balance the amount of time they invest in each story against their quota. Stories that are too complex to cover adequately in 500 to 800 words are considered too thick and usually don't get covered at all.

PR professionals aren't magicians. They still have to deliver a newsworthy, credible pitch. So before you hire a seasoned PR person to hunt for earned media coverage, make sure you're ready for media first.

Earned Media Plus

Ryan Paugh is cofounder of The Community Company and the coauthor of *Superconnector*. In 2016, his company partnered with Forbes to launch the Forbes Councils, which are invitation-only communities that provide networking and publishing opportunities to vetted, paying members.

Forbes is one of the most influential business media brands in the world. As a result of their annual power lists, Forbes has enormous brand cachet. They are a symbol of success and wealth.

Forbes Councils make the associated credibility of the Forbes brand available to members for a fee, which includes the right to submit thought leadership articles for publication at Forbes.com. Based on a comprehensive set of guidelines, council members can submit articles that get published as "Council Posts" on Forbes.com. When you publish and share valuable, non-promotional content on a reputable, third-party website, it builds your credibility.

When it comes to building thought leadership by publishing on Forbes.com, you're not becoming a Forbes contributor. The *Forbes Council* editorial staff reviews all submissions, not the Forbes editorial staff. And the frequency with which a member can publish depends on the quality and credibility of their submissions. The value is that you can get a bylined article published on the site and use that placement to position yourself as a thought leader.

These paid placements also include a backlink. Online, there's a direct relationship between editorial oversight and the credibility of the news content. Generally speaking, the harder it is to get a backlink from a website, the more valuable it is in the eyes of Google.

Backlinks from social media and other websites that make it possible for anyone to publish content are discounted for authority by the Google algorithm because they are too easy to get, which means they can be used to try and game search results. On the other hand, a link from a credible news media outlet that exercises a high degree of scrutiny over what gets published carries more weight. Any site you can buy links on without advertising is going to be discounted in the eyes of Google.

So digital PR is about scoring coverage and backlinks from credible websites that exercise editorial judgment over what they publish. If you can sign up and publish, or someone else can publish on your behalf with no editorial oversight like so many people can and do on promiscuous news sites like Fortune.com and *Huffington Post*, it may build your profile as a thought leader and funnel referral traffic your way. However, the resulting backlink is not that valuable from an SEO perspective. On the other hand, getting published on *VentureBeat* or *Adweek* requires editorial approval.

Inside Outsourcing

If you're a niche B2B player, a solopreneur, an author, or a thought leader, there's another option. It's not for everyone, but if you're just getting started with PR and want to take a more resourceful approach, it's worth considering. If you're literate, informed, and have a high media IQ, with the right guidance you may be able to handle media relations yourself.

Some PR specialists may tell you journalists don't want to be pitched stories directly, but that's just a sales tactic. Journalists need good stories, regardless of where they come from. If you understand what makes news and can come up with a clever angle and news peg, it doesn't matter if you're a PR professional, CEO, or a junior company employee. If you can leave your ego out of it and package a story in a way that's mediagenic, that's what matters most, and that's really where an experienced PR professional provides the most value.

What if you could decouple strategic guidance from tactical execution? *Inside Out PR* is an alternate framework I developed for implementing PR in-house under the guidance of an external, senior public relations counselor. To understand how this approach utilizes human resources more efficiently, let's look at the traditional, out-sourced PR staffing model in figure 10.1.

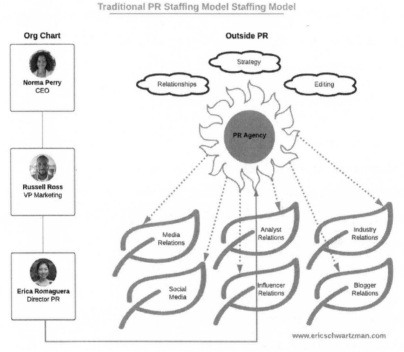

Figure 10.1 Organizational chart representing how clients typically interface with PR agencies. An employee on the client side serves as the agency liaison and outsources all aspect of public relations outreach, from strategy to execution, to an external PR agency.

Conventionally, an external PR agency is managed by an in-house PR director. From developing key messages to preparing media lists, from connecting with influencers to amplifying their coverage and measuring the outcomes, an external public relations firm does the heavy lifting while the PR director serves as the client's liaison. This staffing model makes sense for more mature companies, as long as the practical challenges of sustaining a long-term client–agency relationship are met.

Public relations agencies must find a way to maintain their own staffing levels in an environment where clients come and go. More than anything else, it is this stark reality that leads to PR agencies delivering shoddy work. To stay solvent, they're required to constantly drum up new business while satisfying their existing accounts with shared human resources. The more price-sensitive an agency's client base is, the greater the risk of underperformance. Price-sensitive public relations clients—whose need for publicity is usually short-term (real estate developers come to mind)—churn at a higher rate, so agencies serving them are in a more precarious position when it comes to making payroll.

The more flight risk clients a PR agency serves, the shoddier their work tends to be. Consider email outreach to reporters. If it's done well, email pitches are tailored and targeted to a select group of reporters. But that's not always what happens. And it's not because PR people don't know better. It's because firms are under tremendous pressure to deliver media coverage. If they're serving clients who are uncommitted to the long haul, shotgun pitching is a survival tactic.

Misguided media pitches don't get blasted out to reporters because PR firms don't know better, it's because they can't afford to invest the time to send custom pitches to reporters who may not be interested anyway. So they spray and pray because the client is paying for results rather than activity. The scattershot approach is less labor intensive. Never mind that the misguided pitches can damage the client's reputation. For the agency, it isn't pretty, but it requires less resources. Obnoxious as this approach may be, sometimes it works.

For decades, I produced "Meet the Media" panels for the Public Relations Society of America, and the message journalists shared was always the same. The best way to get their attention is to read their articles and pitch based on their prior coverage. But the truth is, that approach only marginally increases your likelihood of securing coverage since the number of pitches a journalist receives is always greater than what they can actually cover.

So PR specialists carpet bomb every "business reporter" with the same canned pitch, regardless of the types of businesses those reporters cover. Instead of building relationships with reporters, PR practitioners with a more fickle client base cast a wider net because short-term clients want immediate results. Agencies with long-term clients charge higher fees, which puts start-ups and companies that are new to PR and want to do it right in a pickle. Let's take a look at the inherent conflicts of interest in client–agency relationships.

Clients that are not consumer brands or enterprise players struggle with three distinct client–agency conflicts of interest. First, clients have different PR needs at different stages of their corporate evolution. When they're just getting started with PR, clients want growth, while the PR agency wants a long-term client relationship. Ironically, it's in the agency's best interest to keep you from getting too big too quickly, because if you do, you'll outgrow them.

Second, clients are experts in what they do, but PR professionals are generalists who specialize in media relations. So relying on those professionals to contact journalists who cover your industry is inefficient. While your PR representative may be well-respected by reporters covering your industry, they're not subject matter experts, so they're not always going to be able to engage at a high enough level to get journalists, who are also subject matter experts, interested. A more efficient approach is building direct relationships between your subject matter experts and journalists, and getting everyone else out of the way.

The third major conflict of interest is focus. Clients are 100 percent committed to their own goals. They show up every day and pursue the same objectives, but agencies are juggling a portfolio of clients, so their focus is split.

Under the *Inside Out PR* staffing model, an external PR counselor guides the client through a series of structured, one-on-one coaching sessions, providing the right tools at the right time. Through this approach, clients get up to speed on how to secure news media coverage themselves. Rather than rely on shared junior staffers at an outside agency for media relations, a senior consultant hires, trains, and manages an entry-level PR specialist who works directly for the client, under the organizational plan in figure 10.2.

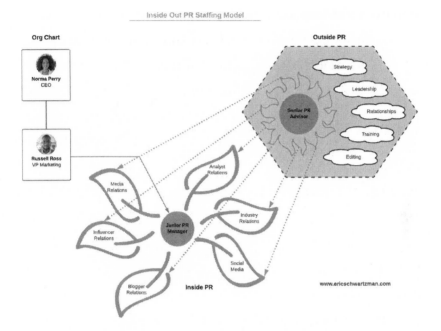

Figure 10.2 By decoupling the senior level, strategic counsel that a PR firm brings with tactical execution and moving that piece of the equation in-house, clients get a dedicated resource and more effective outreach apparatus.

By outsourcing the hiring and training of a full-time, in-house resource to a senior level counselor, the client gets what a PR agency would provide, but from a dedicated employee, resulting in a better value. But, they must be committed enough to the process to hire that internal resource or have the capacity to do the work themselves.

Inside Out PR is a well-suited approach for:

- Start-ups and companies searching for a product–market fit.

- Clients getting ready to retain their first PR firm.
- Clients in fundraising mode.
- Clients struggling with an existing PR agency relationship.
- Consultants and thought leaders.

As clients become more aware of the potential for driving organic traffic by securing backlinks through earned media, demand for digital PR skills will continue to grow, resulting in a seller's market for senior earned media consultants who understand digital PR and what makes news. This inside outsourcing model, as I call it, will gain momentum as clients look for better ways to handle earned media relations, and experienced consultants look for greater autonomy and earning potential.

Measuring Business Impact

Research shows that measuring business impact and lack of quantifiable metrics are the top challenges in public relations.[2] To effectively measure the business impact of PR, Jonny Bentwood, global head of data and analytics at the global PR firm Golin, says you need two things: quantifiable metrics, and you need to know how to present your metrics in language that the executive suite understands.

PR has always wanted a seat at the boardroom table. But PR agencies use obtuse metrics like *message pull through* and *share of voice* with CEOs who are focused on metrics like revenue and margins. Similarly, CFOs are interested in operating costs and making payroll, not inconsequential metrics like *impressions* or *click-throughs*. The problem is everyone speaks different languages. Bentwood solves the problem by changing the narrative. He uses the customer journey as the framework for measuring the impact of PR because the lead to revenue path drives bottom line value.

Brentwood recalls a retailer who came to him from another PR agency. The client had hired a performance-based agency whose compensation was tied to the client's brand awareness. Brand awareness skyrocketed but purchase consideration dropped. Without a customer journey map, they never would have known. By mapping out the path customers take as they move from awareness to consideration, Brentwood found that brand awareness was the wrong metric. He shifted the focus to increasing purchase consideration, because awareness was not a key indicator of future sales.

Brentwood demonstrates the business impact of PR by showing how he's plugging holes in the funnel and accelerating the lead to revenue conversion path. Real business metrics are connected to revenue. So the answer to solving the quantifiable metrics problem is monitoring and optimizing the lead to revenue path.

If you'd like to stay current on digital PR best practices, I produce a podcast called the Earned Media Podcast about building visibility and credibility through neutral, third-party endorsements that you can subscribe to here.

Now that you know the basics about how the public relations industry and the world of earned media outreach operates, you're ready to learn how to convert website traffic into sales and leads.

CHAPTER 11

Inbound Lead Generation

This is a book about using inbound digital marketing channels strategically to win purchase consideration or generate a sale, both of which are transactional. Up to now, we've talked about what it takes to attract website visitors and how to nurture them. But we haven't spoken much about what goes into converting a website visitor into a lead. In this chapter, you're going to find out how to generate leads online.

Content marketing, blogging, and podcasting are primarily channels for attracting visitors to your own website through Google. Social media is a channel for building community by sharing about a mission that resonates with like-minded people. And digital public relations is about earning visibility and credibility through implied, third-party endorsements. Even email, as long as people actually sign up themselves, is inbound because you built a list through attraction rather than promotion.

In businesses that were established before the internet, outbound lead generation is the more conventional approach of going out and finding prospects yourself through direct sales. As digital technology matured, door-to-door sales was replaced by telemarketing, unsolicited email (a.k.a. spam), and direct messaging to prospects on social networks.

With outbound lead generation, you find a way to distract prospects from what they're doing by cold calling, emailing, or messaging them directly on LinkedIn or Twitter to ask if they need what you're selling. With inbound lead generation, you attract prospects who are searching for what you sell to your website. While inbound leads convert at a higher rate because they're self-qualified, generating digital demand takes longer to get going than direct sales.

Inbound lead generation is the conversion of website visitors into potential customers, usually by getting them to subscribe to your email list, download gated content, or register for a webinar or event.

Not all leads that enter the top of the marketing funnel become customers at the bottom. Digital marketing funnels leak. If you split the funnel into stages, you can measure the number of leads that go from one stage to the next. Once you know your conversion rate, you can forecast sales based on the number of leads you attract into the funnel. It's a numbers game. More leads in, more sales out. Improving the rate of conversion is a skill known as conversion rate optimization (CRO) which is the continuous tweaking of your website design to get the highest possible percentage of visitors to complete a desired transaction, like filling out and submitting a lead form. At companies that have already pivoted to digital marketing, CRO is the chief revenue officer's key performance indicator, along with monthly recurring revenue and customer lifetime value.

Inbound lead generation is a cross-functional business process that brings together many parts of a company. It is the result of an end-to-end solution that allows marketing, sales, and service to collaborate in a digital environment in pursuit of revenue. Marketers create and manage the content on the website to attract visitors, convert them into leads, and nurture them. Leads flow into a customer relationship management system that sales uses to convert prospects into buyers. And service (or customer success, as software as a service businesses call it) uses a help desk application, knowledge base, and/or learning management system to make sure customers stick around.

Fine tuning an end-to-end solution that aligns marketing, sales, and service to collaborate cross-functionally and grow sales is called revenue operations or RevOps for short. Rather than hire different software developers or outside resources to support marketing, sales, and service at the departmental level, RevOps supports all three departments together. Instead of having different developers supporting the marketing tech stack and sales tech stack independently, RevOps supports the full revenue stack.

Lead generation is the part of the customer journey where you capture a potential customer's contact information so you can sell them something. With considered purchases, a sale is the result of a series of smaller micro conversions like signing up for a white paper, attending a webinar, and scheduling a discovery call with a sales development rep.

The length of time it takes for someone to move through the funnel from lead to revenue is based on the complexity of the purchase. If someone is aware of the brand, understands the product, and the price is low enough, it might be a simple, self-service sale that happens without talking to a salesperson. With a more complex purchase where the brand is unknown, the value not as well understood, and ongoing support is required, a salesperson talks to the prospect, diagnoses their problem, puts a proposal together, pitches, and closes the business.

Revenue stacks have the most upside for companies that sell complex products or services like real estate, financial services, software as a service, anything else subscription-oriented, and insurance. Getting an end-to-end solution up and running that can automate the lead conversion process is the overall objective. So lead generation is only one link in the revenue generation chain. Revenue is the real objective. That's why in this book, the chapter on stacks, automation, and funnels is toward the beginning. If you understand the entire system, you're better equipped to manage your digital pivot.

If you launch a static website that's basically just online brochureware without the ability to collect leads, nurture prospects, sell, and service customers, you're wasting time and money. Sooner or later, you're going to have to build a stack and get a digital business strategy, so why not do it right from the start?

To maximize the selling time of their top closers, sophisticated digital businesses like Cision (the earned media software company we learned about in Chapter 3) use a team of pre-sales reps to qualify inbound leads. Common lead qualification research tools include LinkedIn, ClearBit, Datanyze, or LeadGenius, which are used to qualify and enrich lead records. Pre-sale reps search for any info that can be used to confirm a need, interest, budget, timing, and purchase authority. If the lead matches their ideal customer profile (which we covered in Chapter 2), they get qualified and contacted by a sales development representative or SDR.

The digital pivot is a series of steps combined into one cohesive move. You build an effective digital demand generation and lead qualification engine in steps. In the opening, I likened it to a ballerina learning a pirouette. But now that your digital marketing vocabulary is more adept, you're ready for my mountain climbing analogy.

The Lead Gen Mountain

Nailing a lead generation sequence that works for your company is done by applying the different digital pivot skills you've been reading about up to now. To review:

- We started by getting our digital measurement platforms in place. (Owned media)

- We selected, integrated, and configured our end-to-end tech stack. (Owned media)
- We conducted keyword research to develop a content marketing program and used the art of rhetoric to share our content, build a following, and grow our email list. (Owned and shared or social media)
- We used digital PR to build influence and authority through implied third-party news media endorsements. (Earned media)
- And in this chapter, we're going to get into the specific methods for converting awareness into leads. (Owned media)

Now that you understand the steps, let's cement the knowledge you've acquired this far by climbing the lead generation mountain. The amount of time it will take us to reach the summit will depend on whether:

- You're marketing a simple or a complex sale.
- Your selling to individuals or committees.
- The value of your product is common knowledge.

If you're trying to grow RevOps in pursuit of a complex sales effort, and you're responsible for sales and marketing, you're also going to need to nail your outreach sequence. That means enabling your reps with the right ideal customer profiles, persona buckets, battlecards, email templates, case studies, and sales decks to open and close deals. If you're selling a simple product to consumers, you need to make it easy for customers to move seamlessly from marketing to sales, or customer service on a self-service basis. If your addressable market requires some education about the value of your product or service, you need an affordable, reliable way to acquire leads.

These are the factors that determine the tools you'll need to scale the lead generation mountain. If you already have search engine visibility, an email marketing platform, and a social media engagement dashboard in place, you're in the foothills. But without a funnel, stack, and automation, you're still not ready to climb. Until these platforms are integrated and configured, you're just beginning your ascent.

From a big picture standpoint, you need to get all your software settings and automation rules configured so marketing, sales, and service can collaborate on revenue generation. That means marketing can generate qualified leads for your salespeople to contact, sales can access those leads, and service can support customers in one, integrated, end-to-end stack. All companies operate a little differently. We may get there someday, but applications still can't configure themselves. They have to be configured up front to handle your business processes, which is why you learned about all that early on in Chapter 3.

As you discovered, this is where a lot of small businesses struggle because they skip this critical step. You have to figure out how everyone needs to use your stack to get their jobs done, write these needs down as business requirements, and configure your stack accordingly.

Until that's done, you're going to be operating at a deficiency. So the second stage of the climb is improving operational efficiency by making sure you've figured out how best to acquire, nurture, and convert the leads you're capturing. The end goal here is to be able to measure your lead capture, lead qualification, and lead conversion rates so you can benchmark them against your competitors and yourself.

Once your stack is configured, you're ready to ascend to the mid-elevation point. This where you start seeing returns. You're out of the forest now and can see the top of the tree line. Now is the time to lift your conversion rates. You know how many visitors it takes to generate a lead, how many leads it takes to get a meeting, how many meetings you need to generate a proposal, and how many proposals it takes to make a sale. And since you know how much revenue a customer generates, you can forecast sales based on traffic. Your digital revenue engine is up and running, with some latency. But let's continue up the mountain.

This next stage of the climb is where the importance of cross-functional collaboration comes into focus. Things are more dangerous the higher you ascend. Everyone has to pull together to map the final course to the summit. This is where things get start to get tense, where the air is thinner, and you need to outperform competitors spotting and plugging any leaks in the funnel. Sales might blame marketing for poor lead quality and marketing might blame sales for engaging prematurely. But don't worry. If that's what's happening, you're right where you should be. Start measuring your marketing against bottom-line revenue.

Marketing shouldn't be celebrating leads that aren't qualified, and sales shouldn't be pouncing on anyone who downloads a white paper. Improve lead quality by cross-training frontline sales reps with your marketing specialists so they can create content that truly addresses your customer's needs. And start scoring your leads based on how many times they open your email campaigns, click through, what pages they visit on your website, how long they stay, and whether or not they engage via social media. All of these metrics generate hard data that sales can use to rank and prioritize leads.

"You start by having joint meetings between sales and marketing to discuss what each function is seeing in their data and rename them revenue meetings," says Jeff Davis, author of *Create Togetherness*, a book about accelerating growth through strategic cross-functional alignment. When sales and marketing collaborate in service of revenue, you can decrease the latency or lag time between lead generation and qualification and advance upward.

You can see the peak. Qualified leads are coming in steadily at a rate that sales can handle. The air is getting even thinner and the temperature is dropping, so let's stop and build a warming fire. Before we close more *new* business than we can service, let's take a look at our existing accounts and our customer churn rate.

Are our customers happy? Are they sticking around? How many customers are we losing, and how can we better automate our stack to keep leads from slipping through the cracks? Before we set out for the peak, let's optimize our workflows to relieve marketing, sales, and service of as many menial, back-office tasks as possible. Before we make our final push to the alpine, let's first plug more holes in the funnel and maximize the lifetime value of our existing customer relationships.

Now it's time to drive our pitons firmly into the mountain face and link up our ropes with carabiners. We're on the ice cap. Our ascent is nearly complete. We've built an accelerated organization where leads become opportunities fast enough to generate a deal flow surplus. We grow the sales team, increase our delivery capacity, and reduce our customer acquisition costs.

We're ready to scale up, staff up, and grow up. We audit our customer acquisition channels, lower the cost per lead, and eliminate whatever isn't working. We've reached the mountain peak. And we've made a full digital pivot, landing as gently as a ballerina resolving a pirouette.

Solos and Silos

Jazz is often referred to as a democratic art form where band members jam, harmonize, and improvise collaboratively. Jazz musicians take turns performing solos in keeping with the melody. They have instrumental conversations, trading rhythms and riffs. It's not about winners or losers. They play a collective groove.

Tennis, on the other hand, is competitive. It's not enough to just win. College-bound players want to kill. They want to crush their opponent, because in competitive tennis, there's an algorithm called the Universal Tennis Rating that uses the game and set score of each match to handicap and rate high school players. College coaches use those ratings to make their recruiting short lists. Thus, tennis is a battle to the end for each and every point.

But jazz and tennis are also alike. They're both solitary pursuits mastered in isolation but enjoyed in the company of others. That mastery requires intense practice and conditioning, with much of it done alone. "Great creative minds think like artists but work like accountants," writes Cal Newport in his book *Deep Work*. It takes years for a musician to learn to sight-read sheet music, a tennis player to place their serve, and a salesperson to master the art of closing deals. Digital business is a series of solos performed in silos. And stacks orchestrate those individual performances into a single ensemble or team.

Tennis players who find their flow and stay in the present without fear are the ones who rise to the highest levels in match play. In jazz, as Miles Davis once told Herbie Hancock, "If you play something wrong, play it again."[1] That way it wasn't a mistake. There are no mistakes in jazz improvisation. Davis made it safe for Hancock to fail.

Like jazz, innovation is iterative, which means failure is a natural part of the process. If it's unsafe to fail, it's unsafe to innovate. Tennis players who play it too safe when it's time to close out a match all too frequently choke. Instead of playing to win, they choke and go from offense to defense, hoping their opponent will make the error. This is what happens when team members are afraid to fail. Instead of playing to win, they play to force errors. I've seen

1   Herbie Hancock Masterclass

people inside organizations who are vulnerable to being put out to pasture by innovative business processes try and sabotage digital pivots in just the same way. Make sure everyone feels safe because a digital pivot is a never-ending experiment. You're continuously tweaking your stack, content, nurturing, and engagement strategy to improve conversation rates.

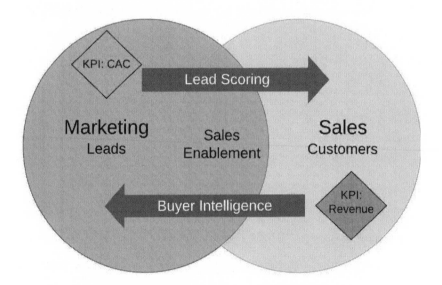

Figure 11.1 Marketing generates leads that sales converts into customers. The overlap of the two departments is an emerging discipline known as *sales engagement*, a collaborative effort to continuously improve lead quality and conversions. Marketing supports sales by scoring leads, so sales knows which ones are hot. Sales supports marketing by providing insights into what messages buyers respond to, so marketing can create content that addresses buyers' concerns. In this model, marketing uses customer acquisition costs as a key performance indicator, while sales uses revenue.

I created the alignment framework (see fig. 11.1) to show how to bring traditional sales and marketing silos and solos into harmony through the process of revenue alignment. Under this framework, both departments establish lead qualification criteria collaboratively, so marketing can't take credit for leads that won't close. Sales provides the buyer intelligence. Marketing uses those insights to steer problem–solution-oriented content marketing campaigns. That way, sales doesn't blame marketing for campaigns that fail to address customer pain points. Marketing implements scoring to rank and prioritize leads using the digital insights you read about in Chapter 2. This ensemble becomes a single digital business process we call sales enablement.

Since we know that buyers self-educate online, marketing "must have access to insights specifically relevant to the target buyer to give them information they didn't know before so as to educate the buyer on the business issues that challenge them," says *Create Togetherness* author Jeff Davis.

You can't play to win unless you can overcome the fear of failure, and that's impossible if you're worried about getting fired. Digital pivots bring cross-functional team members together to jam and solo, but not at the expense of weakening or overshadowing the domain expertise that sales, marketing, and service bring to the table.

The digital pivot is equal parts collaboration, competition, and—when it comes to developing mastery, as in jazz and tennis—performing in solitude is as important as playing together. It brings the mastery of sales, marketing, and service into a virtual ensemble performance where silos become solos, cacophonies become symphonies, and departmental competition becomes cross-functional collaboration.

B2B Lead Generation

Even if it leads to the occasional blackjack, hitting a 17 is always a bad decision because the odds are, in the long run, you'll lose. You aren't playing to win a deal or two. You're playing to lift conversion rates across the board. And as more companies mature from making impulsive decisions based on data in spreadsheets to making data-driven decisions based on statistics collected through automation and displayed on real-time dashboards, more marketers are minimizing risk and playing their cards by the numbers. In a finite market with a limited number of customers, building relationships with prospects early and often is the smartest approach to B2B lead generation.

In niche markets, it doesn't matter if the customer's not ready to buy. If they match your ideal customer profile, don't let budget, authority, need, or purchase time frame deter your effort to engage. If you wait until they have the budget to build a relationship, you're too late. Buyers are more than halfway through the purchasing decision process before they talk to a salesperson. Dig a well before you get thirsty.

Once the budget has been approved and the value is understood, chances are that whoever helped the buyer get up to speed has already earned the role of preferred provider. Now you have no other way to compete but on price, and who wants to play that game? Lead generation for B2Bs is about funnels and tunnels. Once you bring qualified leads into your funnel, you build tunnels to exchange information and educate. You can't always be selling if you want to build relationships. To engage early, you have to be seen as a valuable resource for information about your sector.

Marketers should be on the lookout for salespeople who present well. Get your salespeople involved in your webinars, podcasts, and other content marketing initiatives. Look for opportunities to tack content creation onto existing sales events. Record sales deck presentations and keynotes. Repurpose them as webinars and podcasts. Give salespeople a way to speak once and be heard everywhere. If you can position them as thought leaders, their opinions will be sought out from buyers in your sector and that's what you want.

Lead Acquisition Tools

Now, let's get into the fun stuff. The art and science of lead acquisition has spawned an entire category of amazing digital tools for collecting customer contact information. Discussed here are just some of the conversion rate optimization tools you have to choose from. There are tools for building web pages, embedding special offers, and widgets for feeding lead data right into your email list or CRM.

All you really need to nurture a prospect is their email address. The more contact information you try to acquire from each lead, the fewer leads you'll convert. If all you ask for is an email address, your conversion rate will be higher. But those leads will also be less qualified. By adding questions with lead qualification criteria to determine the willingness and readiness of a prospect to become a customer, your opt-in email conversion rates decline, but the quality of your leads improve.

The trustworthiness of your website impacts conversions. Website visitors assess trustworthiness based on transparency and security. "Our brains are wet wired to assess trust," says Daniel J.W. King, chief of cyber command at IBM. "And when we go into a trust relationship and that trust transaction is positive, we get a little squirt of endorphin that makes us want to do another trust transaction."

Having an "about" page and management bios with headshots both increase trust through transparency. These pages, in effect, attribute the content on the rest of the website to real people. Without this basic attribution, a website looks like it has something to hide. If the site is secure but untrustworthy, visitors may still fill out a form to download gated content, but they'll use their legacy email address, which they seldom check.

Web forms are used to transport contact information over the internet from a browser application to a web server. If a website is parked at an unsecure http:// address (rather than a secure https:// address) it won't convert as many leads because website visitors won't feel safe entering their personal information. They may even get a message that warns them that the site is not secure. or they'll see an open lock icon in their browser URL field. If you submit information from a form on an http:// website, that information can be intercepted by others as it travels over the internet. The "s" in https stands for security.

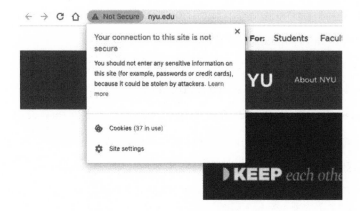

Figure 11.2 Screenshot of the website for NYU loaded in the Chrome browser. The website is located at an http:// address which is considered not secure by Google's browser.

To move a website to an https URL, you need to sign up for an SSL certificate, which verifies website ownership. Your "about" page and executive bios tell visitors who you are. But your SSL certificate verifies that you are who you say you are.

In conversion rate optimization, attribution is table stakes. If you aren't straightforward with visitors about who you are, they aren't going to trust you, certainly not to the point of sharing their primary email address. So before you implement any of the conversion tools I'm going to walk you through in the next part of this chapter, make sure your "about" page, bio pages, and SSL certificate are in place.

And as we discussed in Chapter 6, web forms are used by hackers to gain entry and disrupt sites by means of injection attacks. Hackers could vandalize your website, add content with backlinks, or worse yet, replace it with a blank page and charge you a ransom to restore it.

Hackers enter and submit commands instead of lead data into your form fields to try and break into your system. "Injection attacks are how hackers probe for application vulnerabilities," says King. "You use input validation to make sure that only things accepted in your lead gen form fields are alphanumeric characters. So you set up your forms to reject mathematical equations and commands."

Restricting bots registrations is one area where full stack providers may fall short. When it comes to web form builders, as I mentioned in Chapter 6, I augment my stack with Gravity Forms, a WordPress web form plugin that is interoperable with my CRM, which is Zoho. I bring my Tier 1 leads into Zoho CRM, and my Tier 2 leads into Zoho Campaigns, their integrated email marketing platform.

Once you have a website with search visibility that's bringing in traffic and converting leads, it is going to attract hackers. Even if they're not successful getting into your site, your email list is going to get filled up with spoofed email addresses, and that damages the quality of your list. You'll be sending out campaigns to nonexistent email addresses, which drives down your delivery rate.

Figure 11.3 Screenshot of a bot registration that found its way into my CRM. Bot registrations like this pollute email marketing lists.

In figure 11.3, you see a bot submitted a form that resulted in a bad lead entry. It's not uncommon for businesses new to digital marketing to get false registrations like these. If your web forms lack current security features, your only option is to replace the technology you're using to generate web forms. As long as you have an interoperable stack, you should be able to replace the web forms without having to migrate to a new content management platform. But if you're using an industry-specific solution that's not interoperable, you may have to migrate to a new stack. You need forms that can reject fake registrations. This is mission critical. Search "form builder" for a complete list.

Now that you're aware of the importance of conveying trust and managing the security risks, let's move into the different methods of receiving customer contact info. Without getting too deep in the weeds, here's an overview of the various tools you can use to acquire leads.

Landing Pages

As you know, not everyone starts at your homepage. They might enter through a service page or a blog post. In website usage analytics, a landing page is typically considered to be the page they land on when they first discover your website. But in the world of lead generation, landing pages are something else. They are the webpages you use to exchange customer contact information for some kind of offer like a free shipping coupon or a webinar registration. Landing pages have web forms on them for visitors to fill out and submit. B2Bs use their ideal customer profile to develop qualifying questions to score and segment leads. Figure 11.4 shows a landing page I use to trade content for contact info.

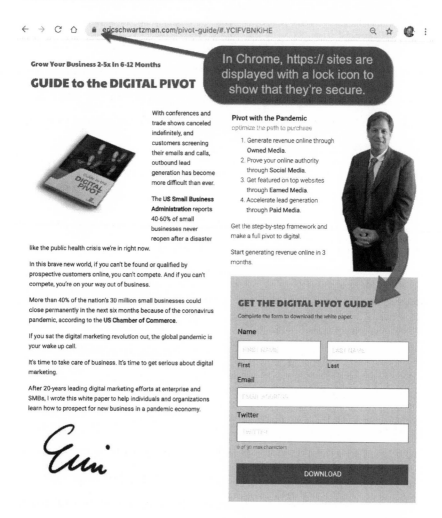

Figure 11.4 Example of a landing page for converting visitors into leads. Since I help clients pivot to digital, if someone downloads this gated guide, there is a good chance they may need my help.

The lock in the URL bar shows that this landing page is secure. As you can see, there are no header or footer links, and there's no site logo you can click on to go to my homepage. This is intentional. The only option is to convert.

Also note the landing page image. Smiling faces with eyes looking right down the barrel of the lens improve conversions, and the upper right-hand corner is where the eye goes first. The image is clearly not stock photography, and the arrow leads the eye to the conversion form.

The mock-up image of the *Guide to the Digital Pivot* (which was my first draft of Chapter 1 of this book) makes the value exchange more tangible. The signature is meant to add a touch of personalization and attribute the guide to a real person presenting unique, original content. If a visitor includes their Twitter ID, an automated workflow sends out a tweet thanking them with a link to the landing page and auto-follows their account. That way, other people who see it on Twitter may be enticed to download it as well.

Squeeze Pages

Squeeze pages are short landing pages used to acquire newsletter, blog, or podcast subscribers. Whereas a landing page can be long with lots of text and the same form repeated several times throughout, a squeeze page requires no scrolling and asks for nothing more than an email address.

Figure 11.5 Here's the landing page where listeners can subscribe to the *B2B Lead Gen Podcast*, which features the people, processes, and technology behind business-to-business lead generation, I ask for only an email address. Nothing more. If you want to stay current with the latest lead generation tools and tactics, you can check out past episodes at ericschwartzman.com/b2blg

Figure 11.5 shows an example of a podcast subscriber squeeze page, all the content is visible without having to scroll. It features a single field form in the top right position of the page, an aspirational image, a scannable, bulleted list with subscriber benefits, and a personal signature under that.

Pop-Ups

On-site messaging software is used to create and deploy conversion messages that appear in different places on the screen based on conditions you specify. Figure 11.6 shows common

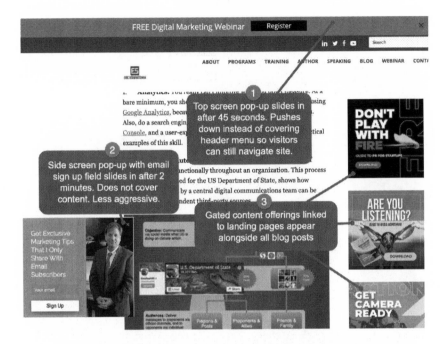

Figure 11.6 Items 1 and 2 are examples of pop-up windows that appear based user activity like session duration and mouse movement. Items indicated with the number 3 are permanent fixtures designed to entice readers to click to a conversion landing page. The click path users take is the path to purchase.

screen positions for pop-ups are the very top of the screen (item 1) and the side of the screen (item 2). While pop-ups appear based on conditions like length of session or specific pages visited, promotional images—which are display ads for your lead magnets or gated content—can also be situated in the sidebar of the page (item 3) in close proximity to the editorial content.

Instead of masking out the header menu, top screen pop-ups should push down the entire contents of the page. Center screen modal pop-ups block the contents of the page and are a more aggressive conversion tactic. If your offer or editorial content is desirable enough, center screen pop-ups can be effective, but these are more commonly triggered when a visitor attempts to leave your site. A modal pop-up is your last-ditch effort to strike a conversion before visitors bounce from your site.

Figure 11.7 When visitors move their mouse to the top of the browser window to leave my website, it triggers a center screen pop-up, which is number 1 in this chart. I also have a permanent email sign-up widget in my sidebar, which is number 2. I elect to give users the option to cancel the center screen pop-up and stick around if they like as well.

In figure 11.7, you can see an *Essential Digital Marketing Skills Guide* modal pop-up (item 1) appears center screen when a visitor starts to leave. Like the gated content promos in the previous image, the email newsletter sign-up widget in the sidebar (item 2) is always visible alongside editorial content.

If you're not careful, it's easy to overwhelm visitors with pop-ups. So don't be too aggressive or you'll bounce visitors. Think about not just how much time delays before you load pop-ups, but which pages they display on, too. Ideally, your pop-up should be directly related to the editorial content it is presented alongside. Always give visitors the option to close your pop-ups (item 3). And never display pop-ups on landing pages or squeeze pages because it could have the opposite effect and distract them from converting.

Page-Specific Forms

You can also put opt-in forms in the body of your blog posts and on web pages. I already showed you an example of an email newsletter sign-up form that is displayed permanently in the sidebar. But you can also create gated content offers for blog posts that align with the problem that the post addresses.

So in addition to running conversion pop-ups and sidebar widgets, you can also put a white paper download right in the body of a blog post too. But the topic of the paper should align with the topic of the blog post.

Page-specific forms can also be targeted to the media channel from which the visitor came to your site. A visitor who arrives from Facebook could see a different form than visitors who arrive from Google organic search, even though they're looking at the same webpage. You can even target forms that appear on mobile phones by location. This is great when you have multiple retail locations and want to use geodata to make mobile forms location-specific.

Chat Bots

A chat bot is a tool that uses artificial intelligence to answer frequently asked questions that your website visitors may have. But bots can also be used to collect lead information. Chat bot software creates a floating icon, usually in the lower right-hand corner of a website, that appears on every page. You can see an example of an unexpanded, floating bot icon in figure 11.9.

Figure 11.9 Expandable, floating chat bot icon shown in the lower right-hand corner of the screen.

If you click the bot icon, it opens up. You can set up bots to ask questions to your site visitors, like "How can I help?" or "What would you like to know?" During business hours, your reps can answer their questions live. During off hours, you can use bots to ask for customer contact info. Figure 11.10 shows what an expanded bot looks like on mobile and desktop.

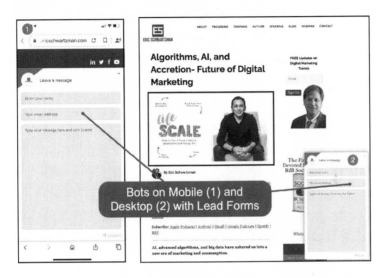

Figure 11.10 Example of an expanded chat bot on both mobile and desktop.

Bot software should be integrated into your stack so new leads flow directly into your CRM. You can also configure those new lead entries in your CRM to trigger notifications and workflows to alert market development reps to qualify these inbound leads before they're shared with sales.

Social Widgets

If you can't capture a visitor's email address, the next best thing is to convert them to a social media follower. That way, you can grow a social following to prove yourself to cold traffic. There are three ways to integrate your social media presence into your website and figure 11.11 illustrates these options. You can do so by linking social network logos to your profile page (item 1). You can put buttons (item 2) on your pages that make it easy for visitors to share your content on their social media profiles. When sharing buttons are clicked, a new window pops up with a preview of the page, ready to be shared on the visitor's social media profile. And finally, you can embed social networking widgets (item 3) to grow your community.

Figure 11.11 Three examples for how to integrate social media into owned media to convert visitors into followers. If you can't get visitors to fill out a form and give you their email addresses, getting them to join your community of followers is the next best thing.

In the right-hand column of the webpage in Figure 11.11, you can see different social networking widgets embedded in the sidebar. This area is highlighted in yellow. At the top of the right-hand column is a Twitter button that displays my follower counts. Under that is a Facebook page plugin, where visitors can like and share my Facebook page. And at the bottom is a LinkedIn profile badge to give cold visitors who are checking me out direct access to my professional profile, so third-party attribution is just a click away. People have a higher degree of trust for background information on LinkedIn than they do for background information Facebook or Twitter profiles. Each social networking widget embedded in the sidebar serves a unique purpose.

By integrating social media into my owned media presence, I'm leveraging my online content to grow my follower base. For a cold visitor who doesn't know me, my followers are social proof that a community cares enough about what I have to say to have subscribed to my point of view. Just as you use conversion web forms to collect leads, you use social networking links, buttons, and embeds to grow your follower base.

Digital Media Outreach

If every company is a media company, then every company must be able to generate leads through owned, shared, and earned media. Just as television networks produce content to drive ratings, digital businesses need to learn how to produce compelling content to drive search. Whereas ratings measure audience attention that can be sold to advertisers, rankings are Google's measure of brand preference. Audiences trust Google to help them find what they're looking for. So becoming Google's preferred brand in search results drives traffic. If visitors click to consume your content, and you've got landing pages, pop-ups, and widgets in place to convert them into leads and followers, that's demand generation.

Major brands invest heavily in this activity. Small and mid-size businesses, however, are falling behind because they haven't read this book and aren't aware of what you now know. You need more than just a website. A digital pivot is comprised of analytics, stacks, funnels, automation, SEO, virality, email marketing, content marketing, blogging, podcasting, digital PR, and demand and lead generation. Some combination of these activities is required to drive traffic and revenue. Lead generation is the culmination of digital marketing.

A modern-looking website without a strategy for driving demand, generating leads, or transacting commerce is bound to fail. But if you follow the steps laid out in this book, chapter by chapter a take this sequential approach to owned, shared, and earned media outreach, you can pivot your business and career from analog to digital.

In the final chapter, we'll look at what it takes to accelerate a digital pivot from a staffing perspective, and what comes after that.

CHAPTER 12

What's Next?

"Companies rarely die from moving too fast, and they frequently die from moving too slowly," wrote Netflix CEO Reed Hastings.[1] But that's easy for him to say. He has access to top-notch digital leadership and plenty of money to spend. If you're a consultant or a small or midsize company getting beat up by digital start-ups, chances are you lack those same resources. Without seasoned digital leadership and cold, hard cash, that's a very real challenge.

If you do it yourself, you run the risk of picking the wrong stack, hiring specialists out of sequence, and losing sight of the big picture. Even with guidance and money, digital pivot failure rates are high. "A whopping 73 percent of enterprises failed to provide any business value whatsoever from their digital transformation

---

1   https://www.mckinsey.com/business-functions/strategy-and-corporate-finance/our-insights/an-incumbents-guide-to-digital-disruption#

efforts, according to an Everest Group study" and 78 percent fail to meet their business objectives.[2]

Like the shell of a building on the backlot of a movie studio, a website is just a digital facade. To film exterior scenes in a controlled environment, studios build fake streets of buildings without interiors. If they need to get a shot of a performer at an upper floor window, they use a ladder. Imagine how frustrated you'd be if you showed up at a store to buy something and it was just a facade.

But a website that's just an online brochure is like the hollow shell of a backlot facade. It looks nice from the outside with its fancy fonts and pretty graphics, but it's not functional. Visitors can't configure and price your products or services themselves. Like a backlot facade, there's nothing there. It's a fake out, so visitors can't find what they need, enter a marketing funnel, and submit a lead form. What's the use?

A website is just the presentation layer of your tech stack. It needs a back end constructed from the concepts in each of the chapters in this book. If you're not aware that your website is just one piece of a larger puzzle, you've got an analog business with a digital facade. For those who are new to the process of pivoting to digital marketing, this is understandably what they miss. They invest too much time and energy in the window dressing, only to realize six months later that all they have is a digital facade with street appeal. Sadly, it's just a hollow, nonfunctional shell.

2   https://enterprisersproject.com/article/2019/8/why-digital-transformations-fail-3-reasons

We are living in a period of transition. Demand for digital transformation leadership and know-how has never been higher. There are more companies that need digital expertise to guide their pivot than there are digital marketing experts out there to hire.

At the same time, there are fewer experienced demand and lead generation generalists than specialists. The best of them work full time at an enterprise or open their own agency and maximize their earning potential by hiring, developing, and marking up the work efforts of their junior staffers. That way, they can provide strategic guidance and tactical client services at scale. If you're a business owner or leader, getting someone to supervise the process and doing the grunt work yourself is tough; most seasoned generalists don't want to decouple strategy from tactics because they end up earning less on those accounts.

Like the different building trades on a construction project, business analysts, web developers, web designers, and SEOs are specialists, too. They lack broad experience with customer journey mapping, advanced analytics and reporting, or tech stack audits. To manage specialists, you have to know who does what in what order, like the general contractor on a construction project job site. Plasterers don't make structural repairs; sometimes they won't even tell you there's a gaping hole in the wall. If you hire a front-end web designer to figure out what business processes your site needs to automate on the back end, you're in for an equally rude awakening. Much as you need a general contractor to supervise the trades on a construction project, hiring a digital marketing consultant to oversee your pivot is a prudent move, because you'll avoid headaches, surprises, and streamline the process.

If you tap a social media marketer to oversee your pivot, as many without the benefit of experience building and maintaining stacks do, you'll have followers but no revenue. Like your website, social media is just one piece of the digital marketing puzzle. By the same measure, relying on a search engine optimization specialist to do your email marketing is like hiring a carpenter to lay your asphalt. To a hammer, everything looks like a nail. But it takes more than carpenters to build a building.

To execute the architect's plans, the general contractor schedules trades to perform tasks in sequence. You can't frame a structure without a foundation, and you can't pour a slab before your drain pipes are in place. You can't build a functional website without business process maps, and you can't automate cross-functionally without a full stack, as we learned in Chapter 3.

A digital marketing consultant—by definition a generalist—is the equivalent of a general contractor. They coordinate specialists to deliver the cross-functional process automation that your analyst scopes. The more detailed and thought out your specifications, the greater your likelihood of success. Measure twice and cut once. And don't expect a website designer to handle SEO.

In Los Angeles County, you need a contractor's license to get a permit to build a structure. But there is one exception. Owners may need a licensed trade to assume responsibility for the plumbing or electrical, but they can otherwise pull their own permits without a GC license because they have a vested interest in doing a good job. After all, they own the property. So while strategic, big picture thinking is critical to your pivot, if you can't afford to hire a qualified digital marketing consultant, your only option is to lead your own charge.

Each chapter of this book was written to give you the baseline fluency you need to lead a digital pivot and be your own general contractor. Again, you start by documenting what you need your stack to do and stay focused on developing and optimizing minimum viable functionality with plenty of room for growth. Once you've documented your business requirements, you choose software that you can grow into and bring in specialists as needed along the way. You plan it out so you don't paint yourself into a corner.

Competitive digital businesses attract the right customers, answer their questions, convert leads to customers and transact commerce online. You do that by thinking through each step of the digital customer journey and building it out in reverse chronological order. You start by creating business process maps that illustrate how customers get what they need from you, and how you deliver on their needs. After that, you go to the bottom of your funnel, analyze your web stats, configure your marketing automation tools, and optimize the performance of your website. Then comes social media marketing, digital PR, and advertising. Too many first-timers start at the top of the funnel by hiring a social media or digital advertising guru, only to realize that they're driving traffic to a digital facade that can't convert visitors into customers.

It's not the companies with the best products or services that win online. It's the ones with the cross-functional tech stacks and the best digital marketing. Without a tech stack you can't convert leads to revenue, which means you don't have a website worth driving traffic to. And without digital marketing, you don't have a way to drive demand. Until you've got the right tools and processes in place, you can't compete. If you can't compete, you can't generate revenue. And if you can't generate revenue, you don't have a business. You just have a really expensive hobby.

The Digital Posse

Now that you're familiar with the structure of a digital business, let's talk about how to either find good people to help you configure a tech stack, drive demand, and generate leads, or how to do it yourself.

Digital marketing is a broad discipline. You need business analysts, software vendors, and people who configure software to deploy and manage your tech stack. And you need search engine optimization specialists, email marketers, copywriters, campaign managers, content marketers, bloggers, podcasters, lead generation specialists, and pre-sales reps to drive demand, generate, and qualify leads. If this seems overwhelming, that's because it is. The digital pivot is a journey from the old to the new way of doing business. Seven of the ten largest companies in the world today are digital brands. Given the trajectory of commerce we've witnessed over the last twenty years, the only real alternative to pivoting is obsolescence.

You can learn to do any of these things yourself, as long as you're willing to invest the time, energy, and money. You can also leverage the same disruptive technology your competitors are using against you to outperform in your sector. Freelancer online marketplace sites like Upwork, Fiverr, and Guru make it possible for you to hire specialists all over the world, including countries where the cost of living is low, to help execute your pivot. I have assembled and managed remote teams to develop stacks, handle content marketing, social media, and email nurturing campaigns for dozens of small businesses with less than $2 million in annual revenue. The key is understanding who does what, retaining specialists in the right sequence, and using remote workforce management best practices.

Smart remote workforce outsourcing involves breaking tasks down and coordinating individual specialists, rather than outsourcing to an agency to quarterback complex projects. If you're outsourcing podcast post-production, hire an audio engineer to edit your show, and a writer to create your show notes. It's when you hire an audio engineer to get your show notes done, or a writer to edit your audio that you get into trouble. Or if you outsource to a full-service podcast agency, things get pricey.

There is a large community of worthy and well-qualified digital nomads based in countries where the cost of living is low. These specialists can do everything you need done to pivot to digital. There's even an online community at www.nomadlist. com where they network among themselves. If you're a small business owner or a midsize business on a tight budget, gig economy freelancer marketplaces are a way for you to retain talent nonexclusively without breaking the bank.

Even with ample budget, if you want to outsource an entire pivot, there's still a shortage in the marketplace when it comes to agencies that have the following capabilities under one roof:

- Business Requirements Gathering
- Tech Stack System Integration
- Marketing Ops Development
- Landing Page Optimization
- Conversion Optimization
- Social Media Marketing
- Earned Media Outreach
- Lead Scoring
- Lead Nurturing
- Sales Enablement

There are very few firms out there that do owned, shared, and earned media well. Most specialize in either leading horses to water or making them drink.

Neil Patel, who runs one of the few digital agencies that can handle both sides of the equation, says he sees very few firms focused on helping affordable, software as a service solution providers grow recurring revenue. At most digital marketing agencies, monthly recurring revenue (MMR) and customer lifetime value (CLTV) are foreign concepts. As more and more companies transition to subscription billing models, demand for digital marketing consultants who know how to grow MMR and CLTV is on the rise. Patel also says local businesses are an underserved by digital marketers.

Smart Outsourcing

When my company built the online media center for Target stores, I wondered why they didn't build it themselves. It's not like they couldn't afford it. But their strategy was to focus their internal IT resources on developing proprietary technology to support their core competency, which is retailing profitably on razor-thin margins. At the time, digital marketing and e-commerce were not considered core competencies. Why should they invest their limited IT resources in learning to search optimize their website and set up funnels if they could outsource those capabilities?

At the time, e-commerce was less than 5 percent of all retail sales worldwide. If Target were building that website today, I wonder if they'd still decide to outsource. According to research from eMarketer, brick and mortar retail sales dropped 24 percent during the pandemic lockdown. But during that same period, e-commerce transactions rose by almost exactly the same percentage.[3] So the contagion accelerated digital transformation. And commerce, no doubt, will only continue its pivot from analog to digital.

The more revenue you get from digital channels, the riskier outsourcing that activity is. When it comes to pivoting to digital

---

3   https://www.emarketer.com/content/us-ecommerce-will-rise-18-2020-amid-pandemic

marketing, these are early days. If you're reliant on a big company like Amazon or Alibaba to get your products to market, you're at a huge disadvantage. In some sectors like book publishing and travel, this may be inescapable truth. But even boutique hotels can build their own stack and sell direct to consumers and forego paying a commission to Travelocity, Tripadvisor, or Kayak. If you want to control your destiny, you need to be able to sell direct without relying on a digital middle man.

Now that teleconferencing and e-commerce are mainstream, we've learned that our physical presence is not required to do business; we don't have to be in the same room with people anymore. Virtual meetings save time, money, and leave no carbon footprint. Comments and star ratings are even replacing personal recommendations when we search for professional services. Digital technology continues to gain in adoption in the practice of marketing, sales, and customer service regardless of industry or provider. It's only a matter of time until all information transactions start and end online.

"Technology investors recall the legend of Instagram securing 100 million monthly active users in two years and Fortnite snagging 100 million monthly active users in eighteen months, but we have never seen a business-focused app rise from 10 million to 200 million daily meeting participants in three months as Zoom's video collaboration platform just did," wrote legendary industry analyst Mary Meeker.

Even for businesses with a bias for sales over marketing, it has become increasingly risky to ignore the stark advantages of online channels for new business development. Although sales-oriented organizations may refer to inbound marketing as "online positioning" or "sales enablement," it's still digital marketing.

Digital Marketing Explainer Cheat Sheet

Now that you have a better understanding of the pieces of the digital marketing puzzle, you're going to want to share what you've learned with friends, family, and coworkers on your own. It's hard to explain what digital marketing is to someone who knows nothing about it and hasn't read this book. Don't sweat it.

I'm including a cheat sheet to help you explain digital marketing to someone who knows zero about everything you just learned. Use any or all of these answers when someone asks "What is digital marketing, and how do you do it?"

- I figure out which people visiting my website are most likely to buy from me, and focus my sales efforts on them. (Chapter 2 - Data-Driven Marketing)
- I make sure it's easy for my customers to get information about what I sell on my website so they can buy more stuff from me. (Chapter 3 - Stacks, Automation, and Funnels)
- If my website goes down or loads too slowly on people's phones, they leave and I lose money. So I monitor my website's performance, and if there are problems, I get them fixed quickly. (Chapter 3 - Stacks, Automation, and Funnels)

- I research the words people search when they're looking for things I sell and make sure to use those same words on my website so I can get found through Google. (Chapter 4 - Search Engine Optimization)
- I write persuasive web copy that uses rhymes, repetition, stories, and metaphors to capture and keep people's attention online. (Chapter 5 - Laws of Virality)
- I write emails that get sent to thousands of people who have signed up to receive updates from my company. (Chapter 6 - Email Marketing)
- I write articles about unique ideas for my website so my brand is seen as a thought leader, instead of a thought repeater. (Chapter 7 - Content Marketing)
- I write articles, produce webinars, record podcasts, and make videos for people searching for answers to problems that my company solves. (Chapters 8 and 9 - Blogging and Podcasting)
- I build visibility and credibility for my company by getting reporters and online influencers to say good things about us and recommend our products. (Chapter 10 - Digital PR)
- I get people to follow my company on social media so, when people check us out, they see a community that endorses our point of view. (Chapter 11 - Inbound Lead Generation)

Now you can tell your friends, potential clients, and even

your grandma what digital marketing is in language they can understand.

Hiring Digital Marketing Consultants

Here's what to look for if you're planning to recruit a digital marketing consultant to oversee your pivot. From a big picture standpoint, the three cross-functional bases you're going to need to cover are sales, marketing, and service. Digital marketing is one spear in a three-pronged revenue engine.

If you already have a CRM you're using to manage a sales pipeline, you need someone with experience in digital marketing development operations and tactical growth marketing. If you're already acquiring inbound leads but struggling with conversions, you need someone with experience in digital sales development operations and sales enablement. If you're selling a subscription service or anything that requires on-boarding or support and you're struggling with customer retention, you also need someone with digital customer service operations and customer success experience. If you need all three, you want someone experienced in revenue operations development, demand, and lead generation.

But if you're an individual or a small or midsize business and you need the works, start with a software agnostic business analyst—someone who doesn't have a vested interest in selling you a certain type of software—to gather and document your requirements and use that as the basis of a request for proposal to solicit bids from full stack developers. Since a website is only your facade, a web designer is not a full stack developer. Full stack developers use HTML, CSS, JavaScript, programming languages, databases, version control, deployment, hosting, and APIs to get best-of-breed applications talking to each other so they can stand up end-to-end solutions.

As your solution starts to take shape, that's when you're ready to hire someone to generate demand and leads. If the focus is lead acquisition, look for someone with experience driving growth in multiple industries on best-of-breed platforms. If you're migrating to a vertically integrated stack, look for someone with experience with that platform. But unless you're an enterprise, you're better off hiring someone who's pieced together solutions from multiple providers than you are going with someone who's a Salesforce, NetSuite, or Oracle expert. Experience in your industry is also valuable, but unless you're poaching from the market leader, growth marketing experience is also relevant.

If you're considering off-shoring your pivot by using one of the freelance marketplaces like Upwork or Fiverr, you're still going to need a strategist to guide your project. Execution can be out-sourced for pennies on the dollar as long as you have very detailed specifications of what you need done, know which type of special-ist to hire, and understand the sequencing.

If you're hiring a social media marketing specialist, qualify them by looking at their own social media accounts, because you can be 100 percent sure that they alone established it. If you use a client's account they say they worked on to assess their capabilities, there's no way to know exactly what their role was in attracting those followers. Check the social networks they link to from their website to determine whether or not their content gets any engagement. If it doesn't draw engagement, they're not getting seen.

With the exception of YouTube, beware of social media marketers with fewer than 1,000 followers on any social network they link to from their website. The skills required to spark engagement on Facebook and Twitter are not transferable to YouTube. So if YouTube is important, you want someone with a minimum of 1,000 subscribers there, because each social network is a little different. To qualify a social media consultant as legit, I'd want to see a minimum of 10,000 followers across all their social networking accounts.

Welcome to the Club

If you read this book from cover to cover, you are now among the 0.10 percent of people in the world who understand how to pivot a business from analog to digital marketing. You know everything you need to know to get started.

I intentionally stayed away from telling you what products to use and how to configure them because those details are in flux; I'd rather you have a compass and map. This is not a technical manual. The important things to understand are the people, processes, and technology required to build your digital vision. All you need now is experience.

Ballet dancers train hard to learn to spin elegantly. Like digital marketing leaders, they make it look easy. But they begin by learning the basics. Before they spin, they learn their pliés, relevés, and arabesques. And the same is true of what it takes to pivot from analog to digital marketing. Businesses that do growth marketing, sales enablement, and customer success well make it look easy. But it is the result of business requirements gathering, technical specifications, configuration, and optimization.

Now, it's time for you to pivot. The chapters of this book are your choreography. You know the steps well enough now to get started. Remember the logical sequence—owned, shared, and earned—and stay focused on the big picture. You can't pivot elegantly without the proper set-up.

If you want to stay current on the latest developments in digital marketing, in addition to facilitating, mentoring, and leading clients through my Digital Pivot Programs, I produce podcasts, useful how-to guides, and a blog featuring my latest insights on pivoting to digital. You can subscribe to my content feed at www.ericschwartzman.com/blog. And if you found it useful and would like to support this book, please consider leaving a review on Amazon.

If you want help pivoting from analog to digital marketing, I have a program for facilitating owned, shared, earned, and paid media pivots. I cover each of these media formats with clients over a twelve-week period, and you can get detailed information about how it works at **ericschwartzman.com/pivot**. You can also reach me on Twitter **@ericschwartzman** or on my website.

Author Bio

Eric Schwartzman is a digital marketing consultant, entrepreneur, and bestselling author of *Social Marketing to the Business Customer*. He has led digital marketing initiatives for Boeing, Britney Spears, Cirque du Soleil, the Environmental Defense Fund, Johnson & Johnson, North American Aerospace Defense Command (NORAD), the Olympics Games, and dozens of small and midsize companies.

Over the course of his career, Eric ran promotions at a global PR agency, founded a content management platform with clients such as Dunkin' Donuts, LinkedIn, NVIDIA, and Verizon, and oversaw the center for digital innovation at a $1B company where he led pivots from homegrown to enterprise software, and developed an online marketplace.

Eric is an award-winning podcast producer and host of *The Earned Media Podcast* at ericschwartzman.com/prtw and the *B2B*

Lead Gen Podcast at ericschwartzman.com/b2blg. His library of on-demand digital media compliance and literacy training courses are used by more than 420,000 enrollees. Eric has been featured in *Adweek, Business Insider, Forbes, Hollywood Reporter, PR Week, Variety,* and *VentureBeat.* Eric lives in Santa Monica, California, with his wife, Celia, son, William, and dog, Ace. Eric enjoys tennis, performing arts, gallery exhibitions, and BBQ.

Connect with him at:

- **Twitter** at twitter.com/ericschwartzman.
- **LinkedIn** at linkedin.com/in/ericschwartzman.
- **Facebook** at facebook.com/ericschwartzmaninc.
- **YouTube** at youtube.com/ericschwartzman.
- **Pinterest** at pinterest.com/ericschwartzman.
- Subscribe to his blog at ericshwartzman.com/blog

Index